What Readers Say About *Swimming Against tl*

Chris Blake's imaginative wordsmithing has made him one of this generation's favorite writers of religious nonfiction. "Nonfiction" because truth is stranger (as you're about to discover), and "religious" because Chris wittingly joins the heart of a believer with the mind of a skeptic. Which, for a generation still looking for God, may be the best surprise of all. And which, for a generation that's already found Him, will make *Swimming Against the Current* a fresh new manual for living boldly on the edge.

—Dwight K. Nelson
Senior pastor, Pioneer Memorial Church

Chris Blake is one of the most perceptive thinkers in the Adventist Church today. And his latest book, *Swimming Against the Current*, is an outstanding example of how to translate biblical principles into contemporary settings. This book is quintessentially Blake—serious issues communicated skillfully, sensitively, thoughtfully, and entertainingly. There's enough here for a second or third read.

—Stephen Chavez
Managing editor, *Adventist Review/Adventist World*

With *Swimming Against the Current*, Chris Blake presents fresh perspectives on what it means to be a Christian and an Adventist today. However different his perspective and experiences often are from mine, I love his writing, his creativity, and the very personal way in which he shares himself in these stories.

—Clifford Goldstein
Editor, *Adult Bible Study Guide*
Author, *God, Gödel, and Grace*

Chris Blake is an engaging storyteller. He hooks us with humor and situations we can relate to and then reels us in with a powerful, thought-provoking point. I love how he tackles real issues in fresh, significant ways with courage and passion. Warning! Reading this will heighten your spiritual sensitivities, jolt your commitment level, challenge your old ideas, and stir up new questions. I can't wait to shake up my small group with it!

—Erin Miller
Associate pastor, Foster Seventh-day Adventist Church

Chris Blake's *Swimming Against the Current* is a delightfully written, in-your-face collection of spiritually meaningful and memorable stories. There is no mistaking his passion for Jesus and his courage for calling oblivious Christians to take their rightful places in being salt to a world desperately in need of savor. Blake delivers prose in a way that leaves us wanting more despite feeling grabbed by the collar in his attempt to wake us up from a world of complacency and irrelevance. This is a must-read for every thinking third-millennium Christian.

—Willie Oliver
Director, Family Ministries,
Seventh-day Adventist Church in North America

Principle. Faith. Daring. In *The Great Controversy*, I read that these are the qualities that powered history's great reform movements and that are needed to carry forward the work of reform in our time. The stories and reflections in *Swimming Against the Current* make principle, faith, and daring about as vivid as words can. If you're not interested in a megadose of all three for the onward cause, don't read this book.

—Douglas Morgan
Professor of history and political studies, Columbia Union College,
Director, Adventist Peace Fellowship

With penetrating insight, Chris presents to his readers the vital issues of our time: doing justly, loving mercy, and walking humbly. Sitting in the waiting room of my car dealership's service department, I laughed out loud and then, with the same enthusiasm (though inaudibly this time), said, "Lord, help me be a Christian." My hope is that every Adventist will read this book.

—Ryan J. Bell,
Senior pastor, Hollywood Adventist Church

Reading Chris Blake is like reading Philip Yancey or C. S. Lewis. You find the depth of a philosopher, the relevance of a journalist, and the practical, everyday spirituality of Jesus that has both challenged and changed hearts for nearly two thousand years. From the very first paragraph, Blake takes readers on a thrilling and often humorous journey of discovering God and life as you never saw them before.

—Sam McKee
Senior pastor, Sunnyvale Seventh-day Adventist Church

Through stories that make us laugh and think, Chris Blake articulates what we as Christians should already know but too often ignore: We are not to be isolationists. The theology in this book is intelligent, compassionate, and honest. This is the direction in which Adventism must move if it is to be relevant and alive. I came away from the book feeling that there's hope for the future of Adventism.

—Sharon Fujimoto-Johnson
Translator, *Rainbow Over Hell*
Freelance writer

SWIMMING
—against the—
CURRENT

Also by Chris Blake

A Reason to Believe

Insight's Most Unforgettable Stories

Reinvent Your Sabbath School

Searching for a God to Love

CHRIS BLAKE

SWIMMING
—— against the ——
CURRENT

Pacific Press® Publishing Association
Nampa, Idaho
Oshawa, Ontario, Canada
www.pacificpress.com

Copyright 2007 by Pacific Press® Publishing Association
Printed in the United States of America
All rights reserved

Cover design by Mark Bond
Cover design resources from iStockphoto.com
Back cover photo of the author by Erik Stenbakken
Inside design by Steve Lanto

Except where the author has quoted from the King James Version or where indicated
otherwise, all Bible quotations are from the Revised Standard Version of the Bible, copyright
© 1946, 1952, 1971, by the Division of Christian Education of the National Council of the
Churches of Christ in the U.S.A. Used by permission.
Scriptures quoted from NKJV are from The New King James Version, copyright © 1979,
1980, 1982 by Thomas Nelson, Inc. Used by permission.
Scripture quotations marked NIV are from the HOLY BIBLE, NEW INTERNATIONAL
VERSION, copyright © 1973, 1978, 1984 by the International Bible Society. Used by
permission of Zondervan Bible Publishers.
Scripture quotations marked Phillips are from J. B. Phillips: *The New Testament in Modern
English,* Revised Edition, copyright © J. B. Phillips 1958, 1960, 1972. Used by permission
of Macmillan Publishing Co., Inc.
Scripture quotations marked *The Message* are copyright © by Eugene H. Peterson 1993,
1994, 1995. Used by permission of NavPress Publishing Group.
Scriptures quoted from Jerusalem are from The Jerusalem Bible, copyright © 1966 by
Darton, Longman & Todd, Ltd., and Doubleday & Company, Inc. Used by permission of
the publisher.

Library of Congress Cataloging-in-Publication Data

Blake, Chris, 1951-
Swimming against the current : living for the God you love / Chris Blake.
p. cm.
Includes bibliographical references.
ISBN 13: 978-0-8163-2141-4
ISBN 10: 0–8163–2141–8
1. Christian life—Seventh-day Adventist authors. I. Title

BV4501.33B3702007
248.4'86732—dc22   2006053289

Additional copies of this book are available by calling toll-free 1-800-765-6955 or
by visiting http://www.adventistbookcenter.com.

07 08 09 10 11 • 5 4 3 2 1

To Yolanda,

who swims by my side

Acknowledgments

My heartfelt thanks to

Mark Robison, who remains a true friend and a perceptive evaluator, even when he wrote "bloated" by a paragraph.

Gary Krause, confidant and adroit reviewer, who continues to travel faithfully for Global Mission while he thinks about his baby daughter, Bethany.

Andy Nash, former colleague and fellow dreamer, who carries a fine ear for language and a passion for Zinsserian simplicity.

Nathan Blake, the lawyer, who dispenses thoughtful, incisive, and encouraging critiques on short notice.

Geoffrey Blake, the pastor, who knows instinctively what works in our post-postmodern context and breaks my occasional anachronism to me with grace and good humor.

Yolanda Blake, my best friend, who reads with a warm, feminine style and an unerring eye for excellent writing.

Bonnie Dwyer, who honed three pieces and who shares with me a longing for more healthy dialogue and openness within our church.

Ashley Barber, who in her typical pleasant and competent manner aided with inputting.

Keil Wilson, who retrieved material from deep within the murky caverns of my computer and resuscitated my heart.

James Cavil, copyeditor extraordinaire, who for eight years edified, battled, and sharpened me.

Lori Peckham, who worked cheerfully next to me as a colleague and helped tighten and focus a few articles.

Editors at the *Adventist Review*, who ran articles in my column Leaving the Comfort Zone.

Insight, Adventist Review, and *Spectrum* magazines, which first published many of these pieces.

Tim Lale, who desires his church to communicate truthfully, and who helped jumpstart this manuscript.

David Jarnes, who edited carefully and wisely, and who patiently handled my odd requests.

Also, to readers of *Searching for a God to Love* who contacted me in creative, rewarding ways; to the worker at Camp MiVoden who told me one night that the book had transformed the direction of her life; to Myrna Baldwin, who requested that a copy be provided to every person who attended her funeral; to the bookstore manager at Maplewood Academy, who reads passages to her customers; to Mic Henton, who read it twice while stationed in Iraq and decided to attend Union College; to Joe Collini, who called me after picking up a copy in a sidewalk bin in Baltimore; to my former student, who decided after reading it with his wife to come back to his church; to scores of others who communicated renewed hope and freedom—you provided additional unction for finishing this sequel.

Thank you.

Contents

PART III: WALK HUMBLY WITH YOUR GOD

What does the Lord require of you but to do justly, and to love mercy, and to walk humbly with your God?—Micah, chapter 6

Preface

San Francisco's famous Bay to Breakers race covers 7.46 miles (12 kilometers), from the San Francisco Bay through Golden Gate Park to the Pacific Ocean, winding along downtown hilly streets from water to water. The race, which in 2006 hosted 62,000 entries, is renowned for its colorful, exotic, and bizarre atmosphere. At the start, contestants toss thousands of corn tortillas into the air, creating a tortilla shower and a slick surface to skate across.

Runners dress in outlandish personal costumes, or don't—some run without any costumes, others run without anything but shoes. Teams of people called "centipedes" run connected to each other via ropes. Onlookers cheer on Smurfs, a woolly mammoth, storm troopers from *Star Wars*, and a snaking Chinese dragon. But to me, the most fascinating runners aren't seen where the race starts.

They call themselves Spawning Salmon. Wearing hoods like bishops' miters with fish eyes painted on, they begin at the finish line and race toward the starting line. For a few miles they run unimpeded. Then the elite runners blaze by them, and gradually the course fills with dozens, hundreds, and tens of thousands of runners. The Salmon fight against the current, surging and wriggling through the streaming mass of humanity. After penetrating and moving through the great crush, they confront hundreds, dozens, the stragglers, and finish the final stretch free and clear.

These runners emulate one of nature's marvelous spectacles. Salmon swim upstream—scaling waterfalls!—against the current. Impelled by a drive beyond memory, mature fish struggle to return to their origin. In doing so, they mirror human existence. All of life is a struggle to get to the source, the breeding ground for everything that is real and hopeful and creative and deep. The God source.

≈

The following pages contain offerings of stories, poems, questions, and observations. You will likely find something in them you don't agree with, which is fine, of course. In the true Lord's Prayer in John 17, Jesus prays not for simple uniformity but for complex unity. What a predictable, boring, blah world we would be in if we all thought the same. Ax sharpens against stone because they are different. Differences are God's design.

In addition, you will likely find something in this collection that you agree with. *Hip, hip, hooray! Yowzaflotzam! Razzle-dazzle!* It may affirm or freshen your flagging faith. You may muse, *I thought I was the only one who thought that.* You might even photocopy it and stick it on the refrigerator or share it with a close friend who will later say, "Now, what was I supposed to get from that?"

It's also possible you'll encounter a thought that challenges a predisposition. Aristotle maintained, "It is the mark of an educated mind to be able to entertain an idea without accepting it." At some point I may be writing to (brace yourself) another reader. When Jesus says, as He does often, "He who has ears, let him hear," He means *hear what you should.* God exhorts the lazy to "work harder" and the workaholic to "take it easy," so the sluggard relaxes as the frenzied worker increases effort. The question is not, What do I agree with? The question is, What do I need to hear?

Most of what's here is meant for everybody. The primary target audience, however, is narrower than that of *Searching for a God to Love,* which was written for "believing unbelievers"—people who believe in God but who don't believe what they hear about God. *Swimming Against the Current* is for those who searched for and found a God to love and, lives brimming and eyes shining, asked, "What's next?"

Portions of *Swimming* target Adventists simply because I need to talk to my church family. However, even if you're not a Christian or an Adventist, feel free to peek over our shoulders. On occasion I glance through women's magazines ("How Not to Look Fat in a Bathing Suit," "Is Hugh Jackman the Nicest Hunk on Earth?" "Oprah's Aha! Moment") though, obviously, I'm not their primary audience. Observation can prove to be revealing, intriguing, and endearing.*

While my hope is that this book will prompt a laugh, a tear, a deepening comprehension, a life change, I'm cognizant of the process. As Annie Dillard noted in *The Writing Life,* "This writing that you do, that so thrills you, that so rocks and exhilarates you, as if you were dancing next to the band, is barely audible to anyone else."

Once we have reached out and touched the face of God, what does He expect of us? Micah gives the clearest, most succinct directive I know: "What does the Lord require of you . . . ?" He answers his question with another question. His implied answer: Nothing more than this.

"Do Justly" is the most countercultural of the three sections. To begin with this requirement may be off-putting, but old Micah wrote it this way, so we follow suit. Maybe its prominence is meant to startle and offend, to make us raise our eyebrows, sit bolt upright and pay attention, to serve as a springboard for our swimming.

---

*Yes! Hugh Jackman *is!*

"Love Mercy" is for lovers—all of us. While love and mercy make up the first and last names of God's signature, they are phenomenally misinterpreted. Love is not an abracadabra experience. Amid life's screaming tedium, we become unmoored. Tumbling deep into dark water, we wait until we see bubbles rise toward the light and we again know which way is up. Love quiets our fear as we wait.

"Walk Humbly With Our God" aligns us with a reality that exists apart from what anyone believes. As Mother Teresa confessed, "Humility is nothing but the truth." What an enormous relief to holster our pride, to loosen and unload the dripping weight of insufferable hubris. In a culture where image dominates and self-promotion prevails, Micah's remarks hatch a humble revolution and a cause for ridicule. "In a world of fugitives," T. S. Eliot observed, "the person taking the opposite direction will appear to run away."

The pieces in *Swimming* are variously whimsical, serious, short, long.* Some have been published previously, some are altered, some appear fresh-baked here. At times the chronology hops, skips, and backpedals—our sons appear as teenagers, infants, adults, children. The tone may be a squawking goose, an orchid blooming in the desert, green air dancing around a tornado, or a mug of hot chocolate on a shivering afternoon.

I believe I could have written a more wildly popular general book,† but I tend to aim at specific, pragmatic shifts and growth. In another millennium, I saw bumper stickers that urged "Visualize World Peace," but I preferred the sticker "Visualize Using Your Turn Signal." When I was baptized, wide open were my eyes.

As always, the ultimate goal is to continue falling in love with God and His creation. The current is ever-changing; we cannot plunge our hand in the same river twice. Yet each stroke brings us closer to the source.

Enjoy the swim.　　　　　　　　　　　　　　　　　　　　　　　　❏

---

*"Redeeming Our Sad Gay Situation," for example, is more than one thousand times longer than "What's Greater Than God's Love?"

†*Harry Potter's Purpose-Driven Da Vinci Code's Chicken Soup for Jabez's Sudoku Soul.*

Do Justly

Justice without mercy is tyranny,
and mercy without justice is weakness.
Justice without love is pure socialism,
and love without justice is baloney.

—Jaime Cardinal Sin

How are we changed for better? Let the journey begin . . .

Traveling Necessities

The airplane was stuffed like a jumbo burrito with the works. Unfamiliar exclamations swirled around my aisle seat. I clutched my precious Spanish-English pocket dictionary and extracted recognizable words from nearby conversations.

"*. . . más tarde . . . puede . . .*"

"*Entonces . . . ayudar . . . bien . . .*"

"*. . . escuela . . .*"

Apparently, three years of high school Spanish had not given me total fluency.

Of course, I knew that before. That was why I was flying from Los Angeles to Guatemala, to learn Spanish. For one month I would live with a Guatemalan family in the beautiful city of Antigua and be privately tutored in Spanish for eight hours a day. *Sí.*

Glancing around, I noted a singular aspect to the passengers. Only one person in the plane did not have black hair. I felt a strong urge to purchase a hat.

Suddenly, the man in the adjacent window seat nudged me. He looked deadly serious. This was my first test. Summoning my vast arsenal of thirty-eight words, I peered intently into his dark eyes and waited. I shall never forget what he said.

"Canpas?"

My arsenal did not contain that word. I held up one hand—the universal gesture of "wait"—and fumbled with the dictionary. "*Un momento, por favor,*" I said, somewhat proudly.

But he couldn't wait. "Canpas?" he insisted.

Desperately I raced through the C's. Nothing.

The man stood and glared down at me menacingly. My heart pounded. I was apparently about to be punched out for committing some heinous, politically incorrect insult. *If only I had studied high school Spanish more devoutly. I'm sorry, Mrs. Currie.* He bumped my leg with his knee and demanded, "Canpas!"

At that instant, like a blind man receiving sight, like a caged bird granted release, I understood. "Oh, sure, you *can pass!*" I exulted, and stepped quickly into the aisle while he rushed to the restroom.

≈

It was March 1976, one month after the earthquake that killed twenty-three thousand Guatemalans. The country was crushed, literally. When the quake struck at 3:02 A.M., adobe walls crumbled and heavy tile roofs crashed on sleeping inhabitants. Entire villages had been bulldozed. The air smelled of death. I saw clumps of villagers slumped in grief and shock, unsure what to do next, while vultures stood like choirs in the trees.

The family I stayed with—Luis, Angelica, and their daughter, Pati—had survived: Their house was wooden. While staying with them and attending classes, I met Steve Bloch, a Jewish student from Los Angeles who had been in the house when the ground shook. He recalled the scene at 3:02 that black morning. After racing out of the house, he looked down the street. *Everyone*, he said, was kneeling and praying.

I remember other incidents from my month in Guatemala. My first tangle with a slippery, sweet mango. Climbing Volcán de Agua after a breakfast of *pan dulce** and raw egg pooling in a saucer. Energetically humming "On Wisconsin!" during icy showers. Villagers streaming out of their homes to stare at my shirtless torso and short pants. The flutter and cluck of chickens. The it's-still-dark crowing of a mad rooster. *Semana Santa*—a festival of processions and floats and streets decorated with intricately colored sawdust. Black sand and warm ocean water. When I readied to swim, I learned that the deserted beach towers weren't lifeguard stations. They were shark lookouts. *Gracias, no.*

One weekend, Steve and I decided to fly to Tikal, renowned site of ancient Mayan ruins. As we hovered over Tikal's landing strip, however, my driveway back home seemed bigger. I asked Steve for a piece of paper and solemnly scribbled, "Give my baseball mitt to my brother." We giggled through our terror.

Two restaurants graced Tikal—one we couldn't afford, and one we could. The latter stood at the back of a thatched hut where a handwritten menu boasted three choices.

No. 1: Eggs, rice, and beans
No. 2: Beans, eggs, and rice
No. 3: Rice, beans, and eggs
I usually opted for No. 2.

During those four weeks I learned *mucho Español* and gained so much more. A broader perspective. An appreciation for humanity's common concerns. An awareness of life's inequities. A commitment to justice for all people.

When I returned home, I was a different person. I discovered life's true luxuries are hot showers, clean sheets, and drinkable water. I found I could survive just fine on a bus with two children (not mine) on each knee and a goat beside me. Simply being understood became a treasured gift.

There is no education like travel, whether flying, pedaling, walking, riding, rafting—or listening to, reading, and thinking about fresh ideas. People who refuse to travel remain stunted in their prickly nest of provincial perspectives.

---

*Sweet bread

Christians are created for travel. Jesus blazed the trail when He left heaven's brilliant splendor and trekked to our poor, bewildering planet.

In addition, there is no nobler experience than that of serving others. I know parents who want their children to graduate from college or earn an M.D. or an M.B.A. or a Ph.D., and those accomplishments are laudable. But my highest ambition for my children's education was for them to travel and serve—to be student missionaries.

Because there's a world of difference out there.   ❏

No matter their circumstances, these 120 did what they knew to be right.

Free Indeed

It was New Year's Eve, and I was in prison. This wasn't the first time. Over the past two years, I had grown accustomed to the gray massive walls, clanging gates, and barbed wire that make up California Men's Colony at San Luis Obispo.

Why was I there? I was guilty of volunteering for the prison ministry outreach of my church. Before I became a sponsor (as workers in prison ministry are called), I had to go through an orientation along with sponsors from other faiths. The most memorable part of the orientation was our viewing a training film prepared for prison staff workers.

To put you in the mood generated by that film, imagine yourself sitting in a dark room. You're relaxed. The surroundings are as you expect them to be. Then a man approaches you. Smiling, he leans over to speak into your ear and emits the following phrase, screamed at 135 decibels: *"WATCH OUT!"*

Get the idea? After watching this film, you don't need to ask for a spiked haircut.

The film highlighted prisoners in various threatening situations. Their acting impressed me with its . . . um . . . realism. I remember vividly one scene in which a convict with arms the size of my thighs was about to assault another convict. As his locomotive fist descended, the picture froze with the fist two inches from the other man's face and a calm voice-over advised, "Often the best way to stop a fight is to note the warning signals before they develop."

Right.

When the lights came on and we stopped wincing (not from the lights), we were herded into a room that served as a museum. Displayed under glass were dozens of artifacts the guards had confiscated from prisoners. Funny little toys such as sixteen-inch knives and zip guns and forks welded into barbed claws. About that time I was certain I heard something. Yes, of course. It was my mother calling me to come home right now. But before I could notify the guard, the orientation had ended.

My first Bible study began the next Sabbath afternoon in a prison classroom. Our pastor had told me a little about the prisoners who had been attending, but I was unprepared when I met them.

After my experience at the orientation, I expected Thigh-arms to saunter into the classroom escorted by a posse of utensil-clanking henchmen. Then, of course, they would wonder aloud during the study how I knew so much about the state of the dead without firsthand experience, and offer to help me with the "research."

Instead, what amazed me about the prisoners who entered the classroom, and what continued to intrigue me over the next two years, was how much these men were like people on the outside. I couldn't distinguish a difference. There were accountant types, factory types, friendly types, quiet types, brash types, grim types. They joked and questioned and bragged as we all do. The only trait that seemed to distinguish these men from "regular" people was their keenly felt sense of need.

I grew to be comfortable in their presence, yet I was wary each time I entered the prison. I couldn't wear blue shirts or pants because in case of a "disturbance," I had to be quickly identifiable in a crowd. Some weeks I couldn't get in because of a lockdown—someone had been attacked or had escaped.

Each time I parked in front of the prison, I prayed fervently before entering. I prayed for God's protection. I acknowledged that I was here on His business, that I was His servant, that my life was in His hands. From that point on I felt peace, and I walked confidently, with my head up. And I never regretted going.

≈

I had been called three days earlier and asked to be the sponsor for the New Year's Eve get-together, to be held from nine to eleven at night in the interfaith chapel. I accepted, though I was curious how the celebration would be handled.

When I arrived, the men were placing hymnbooks on the chairs. For the next two hours, we enjoyed what "back in the day" was called a testimony meeting. The 120 men sang robustly, pausing between songs to listen to each other thank God. Then they sang some more.

Their final song made an immense impact on me. They sang:

Would you be free from the burden of sin?
There's power in the blood,
Power in the blood;
Would you o'er evil a victory win?
There's wonderful power in the blood.
Then,

There is power, power,
wonder-working power . . .

Now, when I tell you that never before had the word *power* meant that much to me, I trust you'll understand. When those 120 men shouted it—those miserable convicts; those lowly, lonely prisoners—it was *powerful.* Like the blast from fifty thousand sports fans when the home team rallies from way behind, the chapel reverberated with sound and energy. If those men were convicted of anything, they were convicted of these words.

The power they sang of was the power to transform the most caged, worthless, hopeless life into a free, vital, caring person. These men admitted absolutely their need of a Savior, and their response was to do justly from now on through the forgiving, accepting, enabling power of the Lamb. With this admission, they opened and entered the very door of heaven.

Then came the prayer, arm-in-arm in a circle, and afterward we hugged each other and thanked each other. And then it was eleven o'clock, so they left to go to their cells and I walked past the *clang-clang-clang* clanging gates to my car.

I drove home thinking about what I had witnessed.

As I passed through town, my headlights caught a figure hurrying across the street. He was a college student in this college town, and he seemed nervous and excited. He held in one hand a paper sack in the shape of a bottle, the way I've seen homeless alcoholics carry their "meals."

Something about the student struck me. His posture, perhaps. He seemed to scurry like a trapped animal, his head low, his eyes darting right and left. Seeing this student in the open night air made me think about the joyful men locked behind bars at the prison. I thought, *Who is more free?* ❏

Nine symbols challenge our concepts of duty, truth, and justice.

Adventists in Freedom Park

Most people have never heard of it, much less visited it. When asked about its location, even Washington, D.C., area residents scrunch their noses and wag their heads. "Sorry," they say, "can't help you."

One sweltering July day (even the trees seemed to be sweating), our family boards the Metro blue/orange line in D.C. for the Rosslyn exit in Arlington, Virginia. Directions to our final destination appeared obscure; I vaguely recall wandering through a parking garage and down a long fluorescent-lit hallway. Definitely no tourist buses here. Passing the former Newseum, we pause at the Journalists Memorial.

And then, suddenly, we are there: Freedom Park.

Much like freedom herself, it isn't easily found, but the payoff is well worth the trip. The park follows a grassy swath tucked behind skyscrapers. As we walk, we encounter eloquent symbols of liberation in the form of replicas and actual relics:

- The Statue of Freedom, which stands atop the Capitol dome.
- Women's suffrage banners—carried before women's voting rights were granted in 1920 through the nineteenth amendment to the U.S. Constitution.*
- Martin Luther King Jr.'s jail cell door. It stands on a concrete pad approximating the area in which he wrote the magnificent "Letter from a Birmingham Jail."
- A small homemade boat used by Cuban refugees, found on the Florida Keys in 1966.
- A ballot box from the election of Nelson Mandela in post-apartheid South Africa.
- Cobblestones removed from the Warsaw Jewish ghetto.
- A toppled, headless stone statue of Vladimir Lenin.
- The Goddess of Democracy from Beijing's Tiananmen Square.
- Nine sections of the original Berlin Wall beside an East German guard tower. A backdrop mural depicts celebrations when the Wall fell.

I find myself marveling at the risky courage of the people who breathed meaning into these icons. And I wonder, *How many Seventh-day Adventists were at those historic events? How many Adventists publicly championed voting rights for women? Marched for civil rights at Birmingham, Selma, and Montgomery? Faced tanks in Tiananmen Square?*

"Oh, no," someone says. "Is this another liberal rant on social activism? Let's just stick to spreading the gospel."

Precisely my thoughts.

I'm willing to let other people stand up for freedom and justice. I can't see myself ever chanting slogans on the Capitol steps, and frankly (perhaps because I missed out on Pathfinders), I don't like marching. I prefer to make a more practical impact than "raising awareness." While I may be willing to die for a cause, I'm not willing to be misled and embarrassed for one. And causes these days are often complicated.

But then, once again, I am caught up short, stumbling over my excuses, by the

---

*Two placards read, "Objection: Women are too pure for the dirty pool of politics." "Answer: If the pool is dirty, the time has come to clean it. Women have had long experience cleaning up after men."

one Person who loves me too much to let me shuck and duck and rationalize my life away.

Jesus.

≈

I see Him clearly, announcing His public ministry by standing up in the place where He had worshiped all His life, and reading in a strong voice from Isaiah: " 'The Spirit of the Lord is upon me, because he has anointed me to preach good news to the poor. He has sent me to proclaim release to the captives and recovering of sight to the blind, to set at liberty those who are oppressed, to proclaim the acceptable year of the Lord.' "*

He rolls up Isaiah, hands it to an attendant, and sits down. As the congregation stares at Him, He concludes, "Today this scripture has been fulfilled in your hearing." And everyone murmurs, "That was nice."

But Jesus never leaves it at *nice*. He always seems to "agitate, agitate, agitate," in the urgent words of Ellen White. I can imagine His mother, who had "kept all these things in her heart" for eighteen years, about then thinking, *Uh-oh, here it comes.* By the time Jesus is finished instructing and admonishing the very people with whom He used to play games and cut wood, they are so "filled with wrath" that they want to kill Him.

They will have to wait.

The more I study Jesus' words from Isaiah, the more troubled I become. *Surely He's speaking metaphorically—setting captives, like the poor, free in a* spiritual *sense. Or liberating the oppressed* medically. *We have doctors for that. (Go, Loma Linda!) Anyway, this is the Lord talking. He can do anything.*

Looking through the Bible, however, I find other troubling words. Jesus explains the final judgment with a tale of sheep and goats, but the speech isn't really about separating livestock. It's about hunger, drinkable water, homelessness, health care, and prison ministry. Apparently, God insists that we must respond personally to these social issues.†

Jesus goes out of His way to bring healing on Sabbath, explaining, " 'If you had known what this means, "I desire mercy, and not sacrifice," you would not have condemned the guiltless.' "‡ Sabbath observance restores human dignity.

Encountering systemic corruption, the peacemaking activist Jesus brings out a new condiment, the Miracle Whip, and drives from the temple courtyard all the corporate business "thieves." When He returns years later and finds the same oppressive conditions, He clears the crooks out again!§

---

*See Luke, chapter 4.
†See Matthew, chapter 25.
‡See Matthew, chapter 12.
§See John, chapter 2; Matthew, chapter 21.

When asked, "Who is my neighbor?" Jesus replies that our neighbor is anyone in need—even if they don't look, sound, or think as we do.*

I turn to Isaiah, where my Master turned. The opening chapter informs me that God *will not listen* to my prayers until I "seek justice, correct oppression, defend the fatherless, plead for the widow."†

Later, in exquisite chapter 58, God comments on fasting, " 'Is not this the fast that I have chosen? To loose the bands of wickedness, to undo the heavy burdens, and to let the oppressed go free, and that ye break every yoke?' "

After studying Scripture, I reach an inescapable conclusion: Working for justice, peace, and dignity (by fighting oppression, poverty, and corruption) is just as certainly a spiritual discipline as are prayer and fasting. Perhaps more.

In 1998, on the fiftieth anniversary of the Universal Declaration of Human Rights (UDHR), the Seventh-day Adventist Church released an official statement: "Coming from the best and highest part of the human heart, the Universal Declaration is a fundamental document standing firmly for human dignity, liberty, equality, and non-discrimination of minorities. Article 18, which upholds unconditionally religious liberty in belief and practice, is of special importance. . . . Politicians, trade union leaders, teachers, employers, media representatives, and all opinion leaders should give strong support to human rights."

Do Adventist teachers, administrators, media specialists, and opinion leaders (such as pastors) give "strong support to human rights"? It's true that when we see Article 18 violated, we head for it faster than a greased bobsled down a glacier. It could also be argued that a tinge of self-preservation triggers our rush. What of all the other fundamental rights of God's children? Are we—as our official church statement suggests—*strongly* supporting these from Adventist pulpits and in Adventist classrooms, TV programs, and magazines?

> **Article 5:** No one shall be subject to torture or to cruel, inhuman, or degrading treatment or punishment
>
> **Article 14 (1):** Everyone has the right to seek and to enjoy in other countries asylum from persecution.
>
> **Article 19:** Everyone has the right to freedom of opinion and expression; this right includes freedom to hold opinions without interference and to seek, receive and impart information through any media and regardless of frontiers.

---

*See Luke, chapter 10.

†See Isaiah's astounding chapter 1.

Article 23 (2): Everyone, without discrimination, has the right to equal pay for equal work.

Article 25 (1): Everyone has the right to a standard of living adequate for the health and well-being of himself and of his family, including food, clothing, housing and medical care and necessary social services . . .

Article 26 (1): Everyone has the right to education.*

Ellen White declares to pastors, "Ye will not give your voice or influence to any policy to enrich a few, to bring oppression and suffering to the poorer classes of humanity."†

Though early Adventist pioneers were far from silent on social issues, in the past century the Adventist voice—in pulpits, classrooms, programs, and papers—on social ethics and human rights has largely been muted. We may well ask, "Why?"

≈

Let's admit that Seventh-day Adventists have tended to elude, ignore, and distrust human rights issues. I have been as guilty of this neglect as the next person. How could we become so content with the existence of large-scale evils? Four chief reasons emerge—the sins of I.

1. Isolation. The dominant mind-set of North America, where the Adventist Church began, is individualism. By contrast, today we live in a world community. Global issues have morphed to personal issues. How a pharmaceutical factory is treated in Muslim Sudan affects how a Christian mother is treated as she flies in a plane over Pennsylvania.

Adventists want to help people on an individual basis—medically, educationally, evangelistically. Yet shouldn't we help to fix the economic and social structures that cause poverty, disease, ignorance, and hopelessness? The principalities and powers that work to lead one person to lose eternal life are the very ones that lead a community, a nation, and a culture down the path of darkness. Their dividends pay off in millions.

We also recognize that political solutions are not final. Our noble stance on separation of church and state has bred an isolationist posture—we back *way* off sociopolitical issues. Unfortunately, we have failed to see that these are often ethical issues.

Moreover, as peculiar members of the remnant, we may believe that the world's concerns do not apply to us. "Not of this world" mistranslates to indifference. Environmental ravaging? Child prostitution? Pandemic poverty? Discriminatory practices? *Don't bother me; I'm on God's business.*

---

*You can access the full text of the thirty articles by searching on the Internet for "Universal Declaration of Human Rights."

†See Ellen White, *Testimonies to Ministers and Gospel Workers,* p. 333.

Communities, nations, and cultures are God's business, too. All of us are connected—our umbilical cords wind back to God.

2. Inevitability. Whom can we believe? Politics breeds deceit and money favors. Corporations sell their souls for profits. News networks are slanted.

I once asked a group of Adventist college students, "Why don't you get involved more?"

"Because we don't trust anybody," a young woman explained. "We really can't do anything anyway."

Inevitability results in a diminution of compassion, a dearth of hope, a death of promise. Jesus' words, "The poor you shall have with you always," can come to mean, "Don't be too concerned about them—they probably deserve it."

As Thucydides observed, "Fatalism tends to produce what it dreads."

3. Industry. Seventh-day Adventists are generally hard workers, but there is an industry that is intemperate and imbalanced.*

We become too busy to care. Too tired to get involved. Too overwhelmed to add one . . . more . . . thing. We're just trying to survive, after all, and this added guilt about human rights doesn't help one bit.

If we are sacrificing and working too hard to get involved in the freedom of others, to care about justice and equality and peacemaking, God says, "You are working too hard."

4. Imminence. "Jesus is coming soon." Good news! Liberating news! And potentially disempowering news. In peering continually through the telescope, we become carelessly farsighted. If we focus only on the "Bridge Out Ahead" sign, we never stop to rotate the tires or bother to check the oil. We remain on constant, breathless, emergency alert.

So we take emergency shortcuts. We concentrate on counting decisions at the expense of creating disciples. We erect poorly constructed buildings ("We won't need them long.") and sell acreage at dirt-cheap prices. Raising educational endowments is viewed as faithlessness, though had we begun them early enough, every Adventist young person today and thousands more could afford a well-equipped Adventist education.

On the world's stage, we let people's rights erode and their poisoned environment collapse. We ignore materialism's dreadful grip. Anticipating a future time of trouble, we overlook times of opportunity. The danger of living in the future is brought out powerfully in *The Screwtape Letters* by C. S. Lewis. The demon Screwtape admits that God wants us to live in the present, for that is the point where time touches eternity. "Love [looks] to the Present; fear, avarice, lust and ambition look ahead. . . . [Demons] want a whole race perpetually in pursuit of the rainbow's end, never honest, nor kind, nor happy now." Adventists particularly need to live by this precept: Be here now.

---

*SDA can also stand for Sleep-Deprived Adults.

The sinful side of imminence focuses purely on escape. *Get . . . us . . . out.* It's a selfish, petulant child's approach to planetary discomfort. In *The Advent Hope for Human Helplessness*, Samuele Bacchiocchi describes some Christians: "They regard any attempt to improve social conditions as futile and unnecessary, since Christ at His Coming will destroy the present sinful world-order." When we flee from the world's woes, we lose our witness.

Jesus wrestled with imminence in an olive grove called Gethsemane. He felt isolated. Betrayal and loss were inevitable; all of His industry had come to naught that night. God's Son wanted *out*, and He wanted it deeply and sincerely and passionately enough to ask for it three times.

You and I were saved by one word: *nevertheless*.

Jesus will return for us. Nevertheless, we will live in the present, for the present is the only time we can serve God.

≈

Thomas Kelley rightly observes, "We cannot die on every cross." Even with the best intentions, it's easy to become paralyzed by the countless needs of humanity. The Adventist Church provides a wonderful selection of ministries. In addition, the following is a sample list of pro-life human rights issues and groups we can all support. Choose two you truly care about. Get involved.

The arms industry. From 1998 through 2001, the United States, France, and the United Kingdom earned more income from selling weapons to developing countries than they gave in aid. Former U.S. President Jimmy Carter said, "We can't have it both ways. We can't be both the world's leading champion of peace and the world's leading supplier of arms" (see http://www.controlarms.org).

Sex trafficking and child prostitution. An estimated two million women and children are held in sexual servitude around the world. I can think of no more hideous existence for a child (see http://www.captivedaughters.org).

Asylum for refugees. Jesus was a refugee. Fortunately, He and His parents were granted asylum in Egypt. Today, millions of people are seeking a safe place for their families to escape persecution and butchery (see http://www.refugee-action.org).

Tobacco. "Tobacco use is one of the largest preventable causes of disease and premature death in the world. . . . Halving tobacco consumption now would save 150 million lives by 2050" (see http://www.internationalcancerfoundation.com).

HIV/AIDS. In Africa and Asia, the pandemic HIV/AIDS is undoing decades of development. Globally, about forty million people are infected—two million are children. Education in this area is an amazingly effective change agent (see various "AIDS in Africa" Web sites, http://www.adra.org, and search for "AIDS").

Other worthy causes include literacy, violence against women, universal health care for children, ending extreme poverty through the ONE Campaign, Doctors Without Borders, eradicating land mines, and the Invisible Children of Northern Uganda.

Suppose we chose to exhibit Adventist symbols of social justice and freedom. What historical images might we place in an Adventist Freedom Park? A few come immediately to mind—every one strongly swimming against the current.

- The steering wheel (helm) from Edson White's steamboat *Morning Star,* for opening the work to Black people in the segregated South.
- Desmond Doss's medical kit and Medal of Honor, symbolizing commitment to mending relationships through noncombatancy. Around the kit are copies of *Peace Messenger* from the recently established Adventist Peace Fellowship (visit http://www.adventistpeace.org).
- Photos of Ana and Fernando Stahl, wearing their *altiplano* hats while riding burros, for their visionary and revolutionary missionary work among the peoples of the Andes and the Amazon.*
- An Underground Railroad station, run by Adventists and activists such as John Byington (later the first General Conference president).
- A mosaic of *Liberty* magazine covers, proclaiming the wisdom of church and state separation.
- A tablet of Ten Commandments highlighting the Sabbath, which makes all people equal before God and liberates the planet in rejuvenating and jubilee ways. God's genius is evident: Time is universal, so no person stands in a place of advantage.
- A Maranatha Ultimate Workout church door, along with the Golden Cords sculpture from Union College, signifying the work of student missionaries around the world.
- An ADRA-dug well. Next to it, a large container filled with The Original Really Useful Gift Catalogs (http://www.adra.org).
- A bullet-riddled Jeep, symbolizing the martyrdom of Adventists who bravely worked and died for others.

What a park! Wouldn't you proudly bring your family and friends here? But something is missing. The ultimate symbol of freedom:

- The cross of Jesus. Through the Cross, the grace of the Son, the love of the Father, and the fellowship of the Holy Spirit† create an antidote to the sins of I. Through the Cross, we experience freedom from sin's guilt, freedom from sin's power, and eventual freedom from sin's presence. The

---

*See The Stahl Center Museum of Culture at La Sierra University.
†As listed in 2 Corinthians, chapter 13.

Cross exposes our violent world for what it is, extends God's love to the violated, and opens a hopeful future of creative reconciliation.*

Most people have never heard of Adventists, much less visited an Adventist church. They can, however, locate us by our love. We can be discerning and courageous enough to seek ways to protect and uphold all human rights, and in doing so, fulfill our Master's mandate—the same one He announced long ago in a Nazareth synagogue. This is historic Adventism at its best.

And it's well worth the trip. ❏

Don't rub your eyes. If you do, you'll never stop rubbing them.

Dangerous Intersection

One summer I spoke for young adult Adventists at Camp Junaluska, an idyllic setting nestled in the wooded hills of North Carolina. Above magnificent Lake Junaluska (owned by the Methodist church) towers a twenty-five-foot cross.

Taking a ride around the lake, my friend Erin Miller and I came upon a remarkable juxtaposition. A blind merging of streets loomed, and in front of that cross appeared a yellow warning sign: DANGEROUS INTERSECTION. From our perspective, the sign described the cross.

This is not a sign of the times. Today's "Christian music" often portrays our friendship with God solely as a yearning for protection. He is our hiding place, our sanctuary, our comfort, our shield.

Safe. Safe in the ironic arms of Jesus—the greatest risk taker in history. Yes, if we follow Him—taking godly risks, as He did—we too will be as safe as He was. You can bet your life on it.

After searching for a God to love and finding Him, we must move beyond a self-absorbed preoccupation with salvation's safety, both behaviorally and doctrinally. The current here is strong against us. Soul salvation is indeed the basic milk, yet "everyone who lives on milk is unskilled in the word of righteousness, for he is a child. But solid food is for the mature, for those who have their faculties trained by practice to distinguish good from evil. Therefore let us leave the elementary doctrine of Christ and go on to maturity" (Hebrews, chapters 5 and 6).

We shouldn't forsake the "elementary doctrine of Christ"—it is the foundation to build upon, the harbor to launch from. However, while mother's milk is generally

---

*See Daniel L. Migliore's *Faith Seeking Understanding*.

the perfect food for babies, who would want to live on it for the rest of their life?

Sometimes I think of the perfection of Earth's moon—without flaws or disturbances before we fired missiles into her skin, then stepped, golfed, plucked, shoveled, and drove over her. Moonscapes are hauntingly appealing, arid and austere. Compared to Earth's passions and tears and nuisances and yelping discord, the moon seems so . . . peaceful.

On second thought, though, the moon was flawed and disturbed long before we invaded her. Giant craters pock her surface, the result of immense rocks slamming into her again and again. The moon in reality is defenseless. And no erosion from wind or water wears away the craters, so they remain unchanged—until the next impact. While Earth's atmosphere provides fertile soil for life's imperfections, it also protects us from nearly all the frozen death balls flying through our solar system.

The moon is dead. If holiness means only the absence of sin, Earth's moon is holy ground. But holiness is so much more, as light is more than the absence of darkness. Holiness is proactive. Dag Hammarskjold observed, "In our world the road to holiness necessarily runs through the world of action." That's why sleeping away Sabbath doesn't keep us holy, nor does avoiding hazardous amusements, "rejuvenating" beverages, or illicit drugs. We are called to bear fruit, not to avoid leaf fungus. Trying merely to abstain from everything unclean makes us susceptible to austere death, the condition of too many churches.

In *Your God Is Too Safe*, Mark Buchanan wrote, "The safe god has no power to console us in our grief or shake us from complacency or rescue us from the pit. He just putters in His garden, smiles benignly, waves now and then, and mostly spends a lot of time in His room doing puzzles. . . .

"The safe god is actually your worst enemy. . . . He breeds cowardice. . . . He keeps you stuck, complacent, bored, angry."

The twenty-eight fundamental beliefs of the Seventh-day Adventist Church are much like multiplication tables. They are fundamentally valuable for aid in real-life situations. We don't walk around repeating, "Eight times six is forty-eight, eight times seven is fifty-six . . . ," but when we need to balance a checkbook, we can do it. Similarly, we are spiritually sound when we use foundational beliefs to balance real thoughts, desires, and actions.

"Doctrine is a wonderful servant and a horrible master," wrote Rob Bell in *Velvet Elvis*. The litmus test of doctrine is our application. Stopping with a downcast colleague, listening, and offering to pray. Making friends with those who don't believe or look as we do. Forgiving someone who hurt us deeply. Volunteering to lead Sabbath School in a room filled with hormone-crazed early teens. "*Do this*," Jesus says, "and you will live."*

---

*See Luke's magnificent chapter 10.

Adventist News Network reported the Eastern Africa Division's plans to send out one hundred thousand Global Mission pioneers.* These were to be added to the thirty thousand pioneers currently working around the world, who in the previous eight years established more than eleven thousand Adventist congregations. Lately, I'm contributing more of my church offerings to Adventist Global Mission, believing as Jesus obviously believed that the best investment is risk-taking *people*.

My friend Buell Fogg described his visit to an onion-ring factory. As you might imagine, the air inside the factory was redolent with onions, tens of thousands of them assaulting his streaming eyes with stinging fumes. Amazed, through his tears he looked around and noticed that workers there appeared unaffected.

"Don't rub your eyes," his guide advised. "If you do, you'll never stop rubbing them." Sure enough, within minutes, Buell's eyes adjusted and he could see clearly.

Jesus announced, " 'I came into this world, that those who do not see may see, and those who see may become blind' " (John, chapter 9). As Christians, we enter a dangerous world clear-eyed and unblinking. God will not support an antiseptic approach.

The orbit of the Son intersected the orbit of our blue planet to create an enormous explosion. A blinding flash of God enveloped us in a mushrooming cloud of peace and hope. Now we are all contaminated.

Father, lead me not into sleepy temptation. Lead me out of my comfort zone to intersect with this dangerous world You love. ❑

Now war arose in heaven, Michael and his angels fighting against the dragon; and the dragon and his angels fought, but they were defeated and there was no longer any place for them in heaven. And the great dragon was thrown down, that ancient serpent, who is called the Devil and Satan, the deceiver of the whole world—he was thrown down to the earth, and his angels were thrown down with him.—Revelation, chapter 12

The Dialogue That Didn't Happen

Gabriel: God, as You know, many of the angels are expressing second thoughts about Your rule in their lives. They're starting to follow Lucifer's wiles. It seems all of creation is listening to him. What are You going to do about it?

God: Believe Me, I have a plan of action, Gabriel.

Gabriel: Could I hear it, please?

---

*Global Mission pioneers are native to the country they serve. They already know the language and culture and possess a well-developed network of relationships.

God: Certainly. Just don't spread it around yet—keep it under your halo. It's a two-part thrust, actually. I'm calling the full campaign "Winging Back Home."

Gabriel: Nice touch, Lord. How will You counter Lucifer and his lies? He's cutting deeply into the ranks—and the morale.

God: Yes, it's about time to fight fire with fire. So, let it begin: He tells a lie about Me, I cut *him* down, spread a few stories about him. Let him know he's not dealing with an Infinite Pushover.

Gabriel: What type of stories? You mean nasty stuff?

God: Nothing really bad. Just enough to make the angels distrust him. Innuendos about his motives, that sort of thing.

Gabriel: All true, of course.

God: Not necessarily. Variations on the truth. Who can prove it, anyway? Listen, a *lot* is at stake here. This is *evangelism*. Believe Me, we can afford to fudge a little. If they think Lucifer's slick, they haven't seen anything yet. We'll entice them back to the table by employing a sprinkling of glittering generalities, a slice of character assassination, a garnish of illogical but potent appeals to emotion.

Gabriel: So our overall approach is . . .

God: Whatever *works*—that's our approach. The end will justify the means. The second part of our campaign is an appeal to fear. We tell the fence sitters about the hideous events that are just ahead, frighten them senseless, and they'll turn to Me faster than a fleeting thought.

Gabriel: You *scare* them into the kingdom?

God: Right! We circulate an image of evil Lucifer sucking them into a swirling black hole. Surround it with exploding stars, hideous beasts, angels dying.

Gabriel: What's "dying"?

God: I'll explain later.

Gabriel: Sounds fearful, for sure. But even if this approach reaches some, won't it turn others away forever?

God: Some, maybe, but more will listen to us if we hit them where they're vulnerable. They will *flock* to our doorstep. Believe Me, the most effective recruiting tools will always be fear and deception.

Gabriel: What about truth and love?

God: Truth and love just don't draw enough attention—we're talking about their eternal destiny! You don't understand the seriousness of this threat. We could lose one-third of the angels. This way we lose 10 percent, max.

Gabriel: It just doesn't sound . . . right.

God: Look, Gabriel, the bottom line is this: *How many can we win to Me?* That's all that ultimately matters. *How* we win them isn't really a factor. A little lie here, a shortcut there . . . Anyway, afterward they'll thank us.

Gabriel: I suppose so, Lord.

God: As I said, believe Me. ❑

In the heat of the game, what really matters?

"Breathe, Justin, Breathe!"

One of the longest basketball games ever played—sixty-nine days from the opening tip to final buzzer—didn't even run into overtime. The game began on December 2, 1993, and ended February 9, 1994, with a finish that moved fans on both sides to tears of joy.

On a cold Thursday night in December, the College View Academy (CVA) basketball team headed out for their first game of the season. This Lincoln, Nebraska, team, formed three years before by Coach Larry Aldred, had produced a winning record the previous year. This year I was helping coach the junior varsity and varsity teams.

Our group arrived in Palmyra, twenty-three miles from Lincoln, on schedule. After the usual player introductions and national anthem, the game began. It soon became a seesaw affair. If Palmyra ran off six points, CVA reeled off six of their own. The packed gym pulsated with energy. Palmyra High School's pep band and nearly nonstop cheering made normal conversation impossible.

With less than five minutes left in the game and Palmyra ahead 46–42, Justin Schober, a six-foot-two CVA junior, intercepted a pass and sprinted for the opposite goal. Behind him and closing fast came Palmyra's Josh Vollertsen, a six-foot-five center who looked like an NFL linebacker—weighing 240 pounds.

Josh reached Justin at the basket. From my angle on the bench, I could see that Justin had slightly misjudged his takeoff and had drifted under the backboard so that he had to lean back, off-balance, to make the lay-up.

That's when Josh Vollertsen reached him. Josh leaped and swatted at the ball, hitting Justin's arm and head instead.

A hard foul. Not a dirty foul, but one intended to prevent an easy basket. The referee blew his whistle instantly. But Josh's momentum carried him into Justin's legs, spinning him like a pinwheel. Already off-balance, Justin didn't break the fall with his arms, and his left temple smacked unprotected onto the floor.

I've watched thousands of games, seen millions of drives to the hoop, but I've never seen anything like what followed.

As the whoops from the Palmyra side subsided, Justin lay inert under the basket. The referee approached him lying there, then pivoted toward the stands and started yelling, "EMT! EMT!"

For an agonizing moment, nobody moved. Then six people clambered down the wooden stands and ran across the court. Blood pooled around Justin's head. His eyes rolled back. Anxious teammates pressed toward him and then turned away, their faces masks of revulsion. Justin's father joined the group kneeling under the basket.

One of the first to reach Justin was Rich Carlson, chaplain at Union College and a trained emergency medical technician. He and the others attempted to open an airway, for Justin had ceased breathing. Though they spoke to him repeatedly, he didn't respond. Eventually, Carlson had to thrust his finger down Justin's throat to hold open the airway. He would keep his finger extended there, first aching and then numb, for the next twenty-five minutes.

The six people kneeling around Justin obscured everything from the watching crowd except his giant white basketball shoes. They couldn't see the helpers checking his vital signs and stemming the bleeding. Then one horrific, chilling plea from an EMT reverberated throughout the silent gymnasium: "Breathe, Justin, *breathe!*"

As long as I live, I won't forget that plea.

People prayed. Shocked fans silently cried and hugged each other. Nobody left. The gym was eerily quiet.

Josh Vollertsen wept. We later learned that his father had died in his arms a few months earlier. One look at Justin had brought back the terror and sadness of his dad's death.

The scoreboard still read 46–42. Time—4:21.

While Justin lay under the basket, the CVA team huddled and prayed. After the ambulance attendants wheeled Justin away, our team met in the locker room. Coach Aldred asked whether they wanted to continue the game.

"I sure don't feel like it," one player admitted.

"No way I'm going to play now," another declared.

The team emerged from the room. Coach Aldred informed the public-address announcer that CVA had decided not to continue.

And then an incredibly classy thing happened. Each member of the CVA team walked to the other end of the court, where Josh Vollertsen sat on the bench, head in his hands. Every player shook Josh's hand, telling him there were no hard feelings and that it was just an accident. The crowd watched in stunned amazement.

As the final player shook hands, the crowd rose to their feet to give the CVA team a standing ovation. Days later, a letter to the editor of the *Lincoln Journal* nominated the entire CVA team for sportsmen of the year.

A somber caravan made its way from Palmyra to Lincoln General Hospital, where Justin had been admitted. Consoling one another, longing for some hint of good prognosis, seventy people filled a waiting area next to the emergency entrance. Justin's mother, attending a nursing instructors' convention in Indianapolis, had been notified of the accident and would fly back to Lincoln in the morning.

In time, the gathering received sobering news: Justin was in a coma. He had suffered a brain-stem bruise, with some bleeding in the ventricles and several small bruises in his brain. At about one o'clock in the morning, the supporters, some of them from Palmyra, went home.

Justin's condition made the city newspaper and the TV news. College View Academy received scores of calls from residents of Palmyra and Lincoln, inquiring about Justin's progress and always adding, "We're praying for him." One caller said that she offered a prayer for Justin at every stoplight. Another person related that all of Palmyra was praying.

While the doctors found Justin progressing more rapidly than anticipated, he was still unconscious. Various churches, cutting across denominational lines, held prayer vigils for him. Television news reports updated his progress. A TV reporter interviewed three of the CVA players to hear how they had been affected. Senior Brian Carlson remarked, "We'll all sleep a lot better when Justin wakes up."

Justin was moved to Madonna Rehabilitation Hospital and remained in a coma for five days.

And then, he woke up.

It was a gradual awakening. At first, he could only open his eyes. He couldn't track a figure crossing the room. He didn't recognize people, not even his girlfriend. He couldn't speak. He couldn't feed himself. He couldn't walk.

Every day he made amazing progress. One day he spoke three words. The next day he said three sentences. He smiled at someone. He sat up. He stood without help. Jeff Sparks, a student at Union College who had himself recovered from a traumatic brain injury, spent time with Justin and his family.

Get-well cards and letters poured in, including a banner signed by scores of students at Palmyra High School. Justin was told he would need at least three months of therapy, perhaps a year. Justin later related, "Three months seemed an eternity. I was driven by the need to get out of there and back to school."

Five weeks after being admitted to Madonna, Justin was released. His family and friends maintain that his remarkably speedy progress was the direct result of prayer.

The final 4:21 of the game was rescheduled for February 9. Although Justin wouldn't run the court, he was slated to shoot his two free throws.

However, the conditions of the December 2 game could not all be duplicated. The clock did still read 4:21, and the same players and referees stood on the court, but Justin wasn't wearing his original uniform, which had been cut away in the ambulance. He looked paler, and his reflexes weren't nearly as quick. Another difference was that in the crowd sat newspaper and television reporters from Lincoln and Omaha.

Justin stepped to the free-throw line, drew a deep breath, focused, and lofted his shot. He sank it. Players from both teams gave him five, while the crowd on both sides roared with delight—standing up, whistling, stomping, and applauding. Justin shot the next one and missed. Time-out was called. Amid thunderous applause he walked steadily to the bench, where he watched the rest of the game.*

Justin later quipped to the *Lincoln Journal*, "At least I canned one. I said a prayer before I shot. I should have said two prayers."

To this day, Justin remembers nothing of his collision with Josh Vollertsen, nor any part of that December game when time stood still. Though Justin expects a near-complete recovery, he and all of us who saw the accident know we will never be the same.

"It's made me a changed person," Palmyra Coach Mark Oltman told the *Journal*. "I think of kids more as people, and not just my athletes."

The value of competitive sports will continue to be debated, and so it should be. For once, at least, God transcended the game. Those of us who witnessed all sixty-nine days know the truth behind the scripture, "Even though I walk through the valley of the shadow of death, I fear no evil; for thou art with me" (Psalm 23).

When we look at the stat book of Justin Schober's life, we credit God with the biggest rebound of all. ❑

The wind howled in my helmet. I stopped moving. What was happening?

All the Way Out

My legs dangle out the door. The roaring wind whips them at 110 miles per hour.

"Right now?" I ask plaintively. Clearly, I'm stalling.

---

*Palmyra won, 58–52.

Dave Schwartz, our licensed jumpmaster, again commands, "Get all the way out."

The "landing" over the plane's right tire that I'm supposed to step on looks to be the size of a Barney sticker. Three thousand feet beneath my basketball shoes extends a golden grid of Nebraska's harvested fields.

I move out grudgingly, cautiously, gingerly, like a 103-year-old stepping off a curb. I grasp the wing strut, and my legs blow behind me as my gloved hands slide along until my chute pack jams under the belly of the wing. The wind howls in my helmet. I stop moving.

"Get all the way out!" yells Dave.

From this height, I should land in about three minutes. If neither parachute deploys, I land in twenty seconds, flat. I know the best way to ensure a safe static-line jump is to "get all the way out." So I do.

After I've let go, arched, and—*whap jolt wheee*—succumbed to sensory overload, I find myself floating to earth. A voice (my *bestest* friend in the whole world, whoever he is) talks me down through a radio tucked into my left shoulder sleeve. "Turn left." "Flare now." "Turn right." I steer for the grassy airstrip of Weeping Water, which seems an unfortunate name for a skydiving destination.

For the past twenty-five years I had longed to skydive, but Yolanda wouldn't consent. "I need you around here," she observed bluntly. Thus, I interpreted her decision to grant permission as both good news and bad news.

Actually, I'm not endeared to heights. Ladders and roofs raise concerns. I get nervous watching children climb tall trees. Fellow hikers stride confidently to peer over cliffs, while I've been known to crawl to the edge. Perhaps I desired this experience not in spite of my unease but because of it.

My two skydiving companions and I were superbly trained. On Thursday night, we watched two hours of videos and asked every conceivable question. "What if," I asked improbably, "the static line doesn't release me and I'm being dragged behind the plane like those messages that used to fly around stadiums?"

"Then," Dave said with a smile, "we cut you loose."*

Sunday morning we practiced PLFs (parachute landing falls) from a picnic bench seat. (Elevation: eighteen inches.) We entered a hangar and hung from a harness, made an X-arch, and counted "*One* one thousand, *two* one thousand . . ." to five. We peered up at photos of possible chute malfunctions.

"What are you going to do?" Dave asked, jerking, twisting, and bouncing my harness. "You don't have much time!"

"Uh . . . look, pull, and release." Or, "Pump the toggles."

---

*Of course, I still would have my two parachutes, along with my "Enroll at Union College" banner.

Repeatedly, we reviewed each possible problem and practiced our reactions until Dave was satisfied. We climbed into the plane to simulate what would happen in the air. I actually gripped the wing strut and, walking on solid ground, slid "all the way out." We completed a written test and discussed every answer. Throughout the process, Dave remained honest, accessible, and helpful. At the end of my training, I had faith that I knew what I needed to know.

Faith is trust. Period.

So when we talk of building or growing faith, let's affirm that *training breeds faith*. My faith grew as I learned and practiced what should happen in a real-life situation.

The same is true for church life. Wouldn't it be helpful if we were *trained* to respond justly to church malfunctions? Suppose a special class was created where a spiritual trainer held up pictures and asked, "What are you going to do now?" Our brainstorming and problem solving could ensure the best possible outcomes. We could even substitute parachuting terms for church malfunctions members may encounter:

Bag lock—church offices perennially locked up

Horseshoe—attendance down, tensions up, morale dropping fast

Slider up snivel—judgmental lip curling and finger pointing

End cell closure—unwillingness to deal with reality and necessary change

Streamer—ethical compromise by church leader

When these malfunctions hit, how do young people, new converts, and even older members handle them? Do we know how to react? Have we considered the options? Far too often we take believers up without training, throw open the door, and say, "God bless!"

That's not good enough. It's no wonder people won't go all the way out in faith. If I hadn't benefited from Dave's superb training, I don't know that I could have gotten out of the plane even though I'd paid my money. For the actual skydive, Dave strapped a video camera to his helmet to record the "precious moments." Look closely at the video. Uncertainty and terror spark in my eyes when the door is thrown open to the roaring. *I hadn't anticipated the force of the wind.*

Of course, reality is surprisingly powerful. No amount of training fully prepares us. There comes a time when you must battle your howling fears and step out on your own. *You can do it.*

Fortunately, God is with you, directing the way. Isaiah, chapter 30, promises, "Your ears shall hear a word behind you, saying, 'This is the way, walk in it,' when you turn to the right or when you turn to the left."

Letting go is not only leaving. It's arriving. It's listening to the good, true voice of the Holy Spirit—our bestest Friend in the whole world—who guides us home. ❏

You see, your life is an ongoing thing. Work at the important things—selflessness without timidity, honesty without shame, love without greed—and you will recognize how much better off you are the next time you pause to check the score.— James H. Blake

The Important Things

I didn't really know who my father was until the summer after my sophomore year in college.

Dad and I were walking between the desks of the district administration office on our way to sign me up for a summer job of working in the Chaffey High School gymnasium. The day was warm, and the offices were air conditioned. The remarks that workers made to my father as we passed were cordial, but there was a chill in the air.

"Missed you last night, Jim."

"Sorry you couldn't make it, Jim."

I saw my father's jaw tighten. Then he said, "A man has to do what he has to do." And on he walked.

My father was highly respected in the community. He'd taught history to high school students for more than thirty years. He was a successful varsity basketball coach. A superb artist. A captivating public speaker. Colleagues, parents, and players liked him. So why did this tension hang heavy in the air?

After filling out a few forms, I walked outside and asked my dad about it. He offered me a brief explanation. The previous night he was to have been honored. The district had selected him as one of three educators out of thousands to receive awards for outstanding service.

My father, however, did not attend. His chair at the main table remained empty that night. Why? Because the presentation took place in a building owned by a men's organization that bore an animal name—and that organization discriminated. On the basis of race. And religion. And wealth. And so, Dad didn't attend. He had written a note of explanation, and his chair was empty that night. Because of the *place* where the presentation was held!

I remember nodding vaguely as I listened to his explanation. After that, I began recognizing a pattern of commitment in his life. In his first year of teaching, he had stunned his supervisor and principal by refusing to participate in racially denigrating humor. At coaching clinics, he spoke up consistently for the unpopular view of treating athletes as growing students rather than as mindless slabs of talent. He once benched me for a crucial basketball game because I hadn't finished a term paper.

His history classroom was a forum for denouncing war, intolerance, dishonesty, laziness, and other evils. Students came to understand the noble possibilities of the present by considering the "impossibilities" of the past. Determination, fortitude, and integrity were always uplifted.

My father once said, "I like people who walk up escalators." I think I know what he meant. Some people aren't satisfied simply to be carried along with the current. They do more than what's expected. More than what's convenient.

God calls this type of people *His* people, because they dare to be different. God's followers stand up (or leave a chair empty) for those on the fringes—the stepped on, the unlovely, the ignored.* Jesus Himself stood up for them—and stood up and stood up until He stood up on the cross.

My father was a telegraph operator, a World War II veteran, a journalist. He read widely—from Abelard to Zwingli—yet he couldn't tell a carburetor from a camshaft. He daily completed the *Los Angeles Times* crossword puzzle with his pen. He was compassionate and combative. He was rigorous in his thinking and casual in his approach to diet, dress, and deadlines. He was a loving, faithful husband.

I could tell you other stories, but even more revealing is a piece of correspondence I came across after Dad died. A fellow history teacher and friend named Ulla Bauers wrote the following:

> Jim Blake was first and last a teacher—in the classroom, on the basketball court, and by example whenever people learned to know him. Sometimes they didn't realize they were being taught, such as when he sat daily with fellow social studies teachers, a leader in the banter and warm discussions about sports, politics, education, and things in general.
>
> He never waffled, nor did he cling stubbornly to one side. He cut it where he thought the knife ought to be placed, using a sharp wit, a logic, and an intellectual integrity that put to shame some of our biased opinions—if we had the courage to admit them.
>
> Certainly, he had his favorite points of view, but he didn't shrink from criticizing the home team or coaches or praising the opposition. Usually he criticized not because of mistakes or poor performance, but because the sport had been elevated above what he thought should be its level of importance or because violence had been done to some important principle.
>
> That's what he taught when he made his top players sit out crucial games because they had broken important rules. That's what he taught when he had them suit up for practice but spend the session in the bleach-

---

*Michael Quoist says, "The road to Jericho today, the road of the Good Samaritan, runs through every underdeveloped country."

ers doing homework. They were there because they had thought that throwing a ball through a peach basket was more important than learning how to prevent wars or how to keep children the world over from starvation while overfed Americans played games.

When I learned a while back that Jim had cancer, I thought to keep his mind off possible doom, so I asked him to write some "think pieces." He had taught so many people how to live, I reasoned, why not give him the opportunity to tell us all how to approach the valley of the shadow? Or if you want a sports analogy, how to contemplate the end of the season?

With those words, Mr. Bauers prefaced my father's response, which I enclose here.

A few people may have noticed that I wasn't at school recently when nobody made dumb wisecracks at the last department meeting. I was in the hospital taking tests. I remember thinking, *Uh-oh, this is serious, and you might die.* Last week the doctors agreed with my own diagnosis—except for the uh-oh.

That four-week experience gave me something to say that goes way past a wisecrack, and I want to get it down in case someone can use it.

Let's skip over the question of "Why me?" or better, "How do I feel about this calamity?" While it's the natural first question, I'm saving the answer for last.

The second one is, "Has my life been worthwhile (and by implication, of course, has anyone's)?" Is it possible to feel a sense of achievement after rejection by so many of our students upon whom our best efforts seem to be wasted—even after having become the object of ridicule? To be passed aside by an incredible number of taxpayers who have clearly testified that what we are doing in the classroom and on the playing field doesn't matter to them?

Well, if your reason for being a teacher, or a coach, or whatever you are depends upon continuous approval by everyone—you have my deep sympathy. If your sense of worth over 10 or 20 years can be obliterated by one day's (or week's or year's) idiocy, you either don't recognize your own worth or you aren't worth much.

My reason and my measurement are based on the boy who says, after the semester is over or the season has ended: "You really changed things for me." Or the girl who writes: "I love you and want to be like you." Or the children (maybe not many) who show I made a difference by an act, a gesture, or perhaps a smile.

Whatever road you are traveling, if your only reward is financial or material, you are in for a bumpier trip than I have had. Maybe it's a cliché, but if you teach or coach or do anything entirely for money, you sell yourself too cheap. But if you do those things because you want to improve the lives of those around you, and through them this struggling society, you are in short, dearly needed supply.

I may be giving a pedantic lecture on the simple verities of life, but you won't get an apology here. I suggest you imagine how my truths hold up when you—sooner or later—have to walk in the moccasins I am wearing.

Which brings me to the delayed answer of question one—"Why me?"

I don't know or care why it's me. I'm not even sure it *is* me. My life has been made to seem worthwhile so often and so fully by those people I love (and that group of loved ones is so large) that my only regret in leaving this life is in not continuing to have what I have had for so long. Of course I'd like to watch my children grow to further maturity and see what they'll become, but I already know the outlines. What more delightful sight on which to close your eyes than a posterity like mine?

The greatest part of me remains here—my advice and jokes, my children, the impressions I made on students and athletes, the love for my wife. Those things will be as real in the future when I'm gone as they are now.

I can live with those thoughts. If necessary, I can die with them. ❏

What do heroism and steadfastness look like in today's church?

A New Courage

When I was editor of *Insight* magazine, in the course of producing four hundred issues and more than two thousand articles, we printed one article on wearing makeup. The article was scripturally based, sensitively written, and proposed a moderate stance established on simplicity. Soon we received a letter from a church informing us that their board had decided, based on their disapproval of that article, to cancel all subscriptions to *Insight*. They had cut their youth off from a voice—a consistently Christ-centered voice—that prayerfully delivered hundreds of other articles each year on themes as varied as temptation, evangelism, and how to avoid divorce.

I thought of that church board's decision when I read letters in the June 1998 *Adventist Review*, in which Dan Lopez declared, "We make [our youth] very uncomfortable to the point of leaving the church." Robert Oster maintained further, "We need people who are understanding and caring, and who show it by their actions. We need people who are not afraid to stand up and be counted, and are willing to take the flak that inevitably will darken their skies."

The plain fact is that too many people are bullied out of church. Spiritual bullies impose their tastes on others, insisting that only one type of music or appearance demonstrates reverence, and demanding that everything in the church be acceptable to them. Bullies often employ the two marks of the beast—coercion and deception.* Spiritual bullies are selective in their approach to Scripture, ignoring some of God's obvious commands. In pursuit of purity and power, they sacrifice love, tact, balance, and vision.

We cannot allow the elbows in Christ's body to determine our direction. When they do we become sharp, hard, and reactive. We also cannot afford to indulge all the whims of demanding older children, however "influential" they are. Such indulgence, frankly, keeps small churches small and large churches sterile.

In addition, we must recognize spiritual bullying in ourselves, and in humility pull back. In *Toxic Faith: Understanding and Overcoming Religious Addiction*, Steve Arterburn and Jack Felton list ten rules for a toxic faith system: control, blame, perfectionism, delusion, perpetual cheerfulness, blind loyalty, conformity, mistrust, avarice, and spotless image. Could I be projecting these poisons myself?†

Standing up against spiritual bullying requires discernment and gracious tenacity. "Speaking the truth in love" (Ephesians, chapter 4) is living the tough love of Jesus. This also means standing *for* something—especially for risky, fun, sacred involvement, which is how wonderful short-term mission projects, student missionaries, the Giraffe Society, church plantings, Youth for Youth, prayer conferences, and soup-kitchen ministries began, even when "friendly fire" darkened their skies.

One more story: In the late 1980s, the Review and Herald Publishing Association began a Resurrection memorial enactment. Using props from the art department, dozens of "actors" wore authentic costumes. My friend Stuart Tyner wrote a script that included a scene from the chaotic, heartbreaking Sabbath without Jesus. It was creative, moving, musical, passionate—a highlight of my worship experience. The city of Hagerstown, Maryland, discovered that Seventh-day Adventists believe in revering the Resurrection, that the risen Christ is indeed at the heart of our message, and in the memorial's second year, more than five hundred people gathered at the base of a grassy hill to worship the Son.

Not so fast! Two local Adventist pastors didn't approve of our proceedings. You see, Jesus had the bad timing to be resurrected around sunrise on Sunday, so in commemorating the event at that approximate time, we were manifestly worshiping

---

*The mark on the hand represents coercion; the mark on the forehead represents deception.

†Hannah Arendt coined the phrase "the banality of evil" after witnessing the trial of Nazi leader Adolf Eichmann. She contended that Eichmann was an innocuous man who operated unthinkingly, following orders and routines with little consideration of the effects of his actions on individuals. In essence, he was involved in evil because he failed to exercise thinking and self-reflection.

"the sun." The pastors and a few members voiced their complaints, and the memorial was halted. It has not been seen again.

I'm still bothered by this (obviously). I regret not protesting more when that plug was pulled, as well as when the church canceled their *Insight* subscriptions. I fervently believe I let God down, and after those incidents I vowed no longer to allow spiritual bullies to have their unopposed way. I also wish those in decision-making positions had shown more backbone—had with calmness and courage said, "Yes, we will receive criticism. But this is the right thing to do, the godly path, and based on our prayers, our best thinking, our love for God and people, and on His Word, we will go forward."

That's the type of revival God needs to see in Adventist churches. ❑

Approved for posting.

(In Case of Fire)

How to Stop a Fire

A circuit shorts. The wild spark leaps. Smoke curls, rises, and presses against serene stained glass. Fires *do* break out, even in the church.

What can church members do? Be watchful, be vigilant. Look closely for these warning signs:

- Incendiary anger is stacked against the world's explosive suffering.
- Sparks of enthusiasm leap from the cold flint of formality.
- Fervor flares and spreads.
- Church heats up dramatically.

The following three simple steps can extinguish any developing fire.

1. Locate a blanket. A most effective blanket is woven from an insecure blend of 60 percent comfort, 25 percent fear, and 15 percent jealousy.

2. Wet the blanket. For best results, douse generously with good intentions. Be aware that any cloth, including Sabbath clothing, may be employed as a blanket in an emergency, and that even holy water can be employed conscientiously.

3. Smother the fire. Suffocate the blaze with phrases such as "We've tried that." "We've always done it this way." "That's never worked before." "Sounds like another dumb idea." "You're wasting your time." All are effective smothering agents.

Scatter, disunify. Pick at small, insignificant items. Isolate the burning parts. Work to stifle and choke the flames. Whatever you do, cut off the fire from its air supply. (*Never* open doors to the outside!)

CAUTION: You may need to apply the above procedure repeatedly. There's really no telling when a blaze will grow beyond human control. " 'The wind blows wherever it pleases. You hear its sound, but you cannot tell where it comes from or where it is going' " (John, chapter 3, NIV).

How to Start a Fire

The church reposes. A congregation slumbers. Serene stained glass prevents any stray whiffs of fresh air. But fires *can* break out, even in the church.

What should church members do? Be hopeful, be vigilant. Look closely for these opportunities:

- A dry, juiceless environment cries out, thirsty for the searing Spirit.
- Flames lick up old wounds and crack hardened hearts.
- True sanctuary emerges, providing a safe place for glowing warmth.
- Religion becomes applicable to real life, generating spontaneous combustion.

The following three simple steps can stimulate any fire.

1. Believe deeply that this kindling really does matter. In doing so, you will treasure the life of every piece of fuel.

2. Guard your fire. Don't allow suffocating forces to choke the fire. Be aware that the true enemies—the powers of darkness—will exploit their extinguishing arsenal of overwork, criticism, and hopelessness. *Keep your eyes on the flame.* That's how you know the fire's true condition. This faithful battle calls for watchfulness, prayer, and persistence.

3. Continue adding fresh fuel and air. New material equals new life. Fan the flickering with phrases such as "I'm so glad you have different ideas— we need diversity." "Could you use some help?" "Let's involve as many people as possible in this." "I'm sorry, I was wrong. Will you forgive me?" "That sounds great. We haven't done it that way before."

Stack as many parts as possible together. Whatever you do, keep the air supply fresh and strong. (*Always* open doors to the outside!)

CAUTION: You may need to apply the above procedure repeatedly. There's really no telling when a blaze will grow beyond human control. " "The wind blows wherever it pleases. You hear its sound, but you cannot tell where it comes from or where it is going. *So it is with everyone born of the Spirit'* " (John, chapter 3, NIV; emphasis added). ❑

If you look closely at your life, you may see some prejudices. Then again, you may not—you may simply be seeing dislikes. Can you distinguish the two?

Now You See It

Our friends and our enemies help to define who we are. Upon my office wall hang a rock and a letter—one from a friend, one from an enemy.

The rock is, in fact, a chunk of concrete splashed with multicolored paint as thick as German strudel. It's suspended in a frame on black velvet background above the word *FREEDOM*. My friend Hans Steinmuss surprised me with the rock. He told me after he returned from a trip to Berlin that he brought it to me because he knew I'd appreciate it. He had picked it up from a wall that once stood there.

The letter is dated January 9, 1988. Howling at the top, next to a drawing of a soldier brandishing a Confederate flag, are the words "WAR White American Resistance." Here's a portion of the letter's text:

Editor,

Your October 31st issue of *Insight* is the most brazen piece of race-mixing propaganda I have seen from any church. . . .

Racial treason is an attack on nature itself. Hopefully politicians and preachers alike will sooner or later be brought to trial for their ignorant crimes.

Sincerely,

Tom Metzger

Shortly after writing this fan letter, white supremacist Tom Metzger was out of the WAR business. Morris Dees, co-founder and chief trial counsel for Southern Poverty Law Center, brought a $12.5 million judgment against Metzger for inciting the bludgeoning death of an Ethiopian student in Portland, Oregon, in November 1988. Metzger lost the case. Bankrupted and isolated, his prejudiced, racist influence virtually vanished.*

---

*Hooray for lawyers! Dees chronicles the case in *Hate on Trial: The Case Against America's Most Dangerous Neo-Nazi* (New York: Villard Books, 1993).

I guess I keep that letter because—well, it isn't often that a real celebrity gives me such a compliment.

Lots of people confuse prejudices and dislikes, which is unfortunate. It isn't unjust to dislike many things, and for you, those things may include smelly feet and runny noses. You just don't like them. That's you.

I dislike many things myself. For examples, just scroll down my M column of dislikes.

I don't like Meanness.
I don't like Most of what I see on TV.
I don't like Misplaced apostrophes on mailboxes that read "The Miller's."
I don't like Mocha-flavored anything.
I don't like Mptying mousetraps.
I don't like Mosquitoes.
I don't like Mushroom-shaped clouds.

That's me. But would you say that I'm *prejudiced* toward these? I hope not.

"Oh, but you are," you might say. "Suppose from now on all the mousetraps you emptied held only containers of luscious chocolate mousse. Would you still cling to your prejudgment against emptying mousetraps?"

"Well," I'd say, "then they would be *mousse traps*. That's different. You shouldn't make those sorts of snap judgments."

Ahem. This brings us to prejudices.

Prejudices are indeed prejudgments, as the word implies. But prejudgments aren't necessarily wrong—we should make them often in our lives. For instance, when the traffic light changes to green, we make a prejudgment that—based on experience—we may now proceed safely.*

The crucial question is, When do prejudgments become wrongful prejudices?

Basically, we are being prejudiced when we do any of the following:

1. Draw unwarranted conclusions about groups *from our limited experience with* individuals. Janie is walking down a crowded high school hallway with her senior friend when a freshman boy bursts around a corner and crashes into them.

"Er, ah, sorry!" he mumbles. He's carrying *The Hitchhiker's Guide to the Universe*† and is wearing taped glasses, a shirt buttoned to his chin, and pants suitable for wading.

Janie rolls her eyes and mutters, "Freshmen are such nerds!"

---

*Perhaps after quickly checking side traffic, based on experience.
†The book, not the DVD.

Let's analyze Janie's conclusion. From this one freshman (or a few more) she has determined that *all freshmen in creation* inhabit the mythical country of Nerddom. She's wrong.

You've heard people use similar "reasoning" to draw unwarranted conclusions about females, males, teachers, politicians, blondes, Arabs, Jews, California, the Midwest, truckers, environmentalists, urban rappers, and senior citizens. They're wrong, too.

William James mused, "A great many people think they are thinking when they are merely rearranging their prejudices." This rearrangement inevitably results in strange mixes. The same person who says, "Mexicans are lazy," complains that "they're taking all our jobs." Once, as we conversed across our backyards, a neighbor of mine began demeaning Mexicans.

"I know," I replied scornfully, "they're everywhere! Why, I woke up this morning and there were three of them in my house."*

He looked at me with shock. "Oh, I didn't mean . . ."

"No, no," I said. "Of course not."

The further we are from people, the more certain we are of their motives. This makes it so much easier to hate Iranians or North Koreans or *them*—whoever is the enemy *du jour*.

2. Depict people entirely by one trait. This is trickier. As I mentioned earlier, I don't like meanness. But if I say I don't like mean people, I'm exhibiting prejudice, because that statement implies (a) certain people are mean *always,* and (b) meanness is the only quality in them that deserves attention. Both are unwarranted prejudgments.

We see this form of prejudice clearly when talking about a person who carries a handicap. "A person who is deaf" is not the same as "a deaf person." How would you like to be referred to by your handicap? (And we all have at least one.)

Philip Yancey wrote, "I sometimes threaten to produce my own line of get-well cards. I already have an idea for the first one. The cover would read in huge letters, perhaps with fireworks in the background, 'CONGRATULATIONS!!!' Then, inside, the message: '. . . to the 98 trillion cells in your body that are still working smoothly and efficiently.' I would look for ways to get across the message that a sick person is not a *sick person,* but rather a person of worth and value who happens to have some body parts that are not functioning well."

Moving away from prejudice means we stop judging groups by individuals, and we stop classifying people by one trait. Instead of using the group statement "Rich girls are snobs," we could say, "Lisa acts like a snob sometimes." The expression "I hate lazy people" could be "I hate laziness," or "I hate it when Carl won't help Mom with the dishes."

---

*My wife and sons.

This thoughtful approach isn't popular or easy. It requires intentionality and a broader view of life—discriminating between rocks and letters. But for followers of Jesus, we know it's the just way.

Love the sinner. Hate the sin. Like the chocolate mousse. ❏

"A man was going down from Jerusalem, and he fell among robbers, who stripped him and beat him, and departed, leaving him half dead."—Luke, chapter 10

Being Spiritual

The Master told the story of the Samaritan, the stunningly godly citizen, the merciful heathen. It's a familiar parable. But as Becky Pippert points out in *Hope Has Its Reasons*, "Christian truths are unknown, because they are too well known."

I sit at a table with eleven students—nine college and two high school. It's 8:15 P.M. on Tuesday, and as our weekly custom dictates, we are writing letters. My current letter opens,

> Dear Attorney General:
> I write because I am seriously concerned about the safety of someone who has reportedly "disappeared"...

Each Tuesday night the Amnesty International (AI) chapter at Union College meets to pray, discuss world events, plan events, and write letters. AI is a worldwide nonpolitical voluntary movement with 1.8 million members in more than 150 countries who work primarily on behalf of prisoners of conscience—people who have never used nor advocated violence, who are being raped, tortured, jailed, threatened, and killed because of what they believe.

We are seldom certain how effective our letters are, though occasionally we hear of releases. Here are three older samples:

> When the first two hundred letters came, the guards gave me back my clothes. Then the next two hundred letters came, and the prison director came to see me. When the next pile of letters arrived, the director got in touch with his superior. The letters kept coming and coming: three thousand of them. The President was informed. The letters still kept arriving, and the President called the prison and told them to let me go. [Dominican Republic]

We could always tell when international protests were taking place . . . the food rations increased and the beatings were fewer. Letters from abroad were translated and passed around from cell to cell. But when the letters stopped, the dirty food and repression started again. [Vietnam]

For years I was held in a tiny cell. My only human contact was with my torturers. . . . My only company were the cockroaches and mice. . . . On Christmas Eve the door to my cell opened and the guard tossed in a crumpled piece of paper. It said, "Take heart. The world knows you're alive. We're with you. Regards, Monica, Amnesty International." That letter saved my life. [Paraguay]

Two of the students at the table often miss chapel services at our college. What astounds me is that I know people who see these two students as "less spiritual" than those who miss our AI meetings every week. *The belief persists that the supreme act of spirituality is "going to church."* This concept, of course, is foreign to Scripture. As evangelist Billy Sunday famously observed, "Going to church doesn't make you a Christian any more than going to a garage makes you an automobile."

What is the measure of true spirituality? First, we should be aware that even normative standards for measurement can be flawed. For example, basketball players are always measured from the tops of their heads to determine playing height. But, unlike soccer, no one does anything in basketball with the top of her or his head. A truer calculation would be to measure from the tip of an outstretched arm. A player five feet, nine inches tall with a short neck and long arms can be legitimately taller than a player six feet, one inch tall with a long neck and short arms. What matters is the reach.

In Christianity, the spirituality question is also one of reach. Who will reach out like the Samaritan? Many Christians seem to have lost sight of the truth that *true spirituality is found in justly, mercifully, and humbly doing acts of love.* "Going to church" is primarily important because it enables us to become better lovers in realms where people can be reached. The week doesn't prepare us for the Sabbath so much as the Sabbath prepares us for the week. And our reach should exceed our grasp, else what's a Christian for?*

Jim Wallis, editor of *Sojourners* magazine and a prophetic voice in the wilderness today, affirms, "When spirituality isn't disciplined by the struggle for justice, we can become narcissistic. Cynicism is a buffer against commitment." Three billion people live on less than two dollars a day.† Each *day*, thirty thousand children

---

*The original "altar call" was invented by Charles Finney to sign up people in church for an antislavery petition.

†Shane Clayborne says, "If the rich met the poor, we wouldn't have poor people."

die from lack of clean drinking water and starvation-related causes. How does this square with celebrity infatuation and the entertainment world's endless self-hype?

God is personal but never private. This truth can play out in surprising ways. Wallis contends, "Until we drain the swamp of injustice, the mosquitoes of terrorism will continue to breed."

Wouldn't it be horrible if our Master continued His story, "So likewise when a Seventh-day Adventist came to the place and saw him, the Adventist remained securely in the comfortable lane and passed by on the other side"?

Let us walk on the right side of spirituality. The side where we touch the world's hurt. The side of risky response. The side that moves us beyond loving mercy to doing justly.

A few years after the dismantling of the Berlin Wall, I attended a gathering of Adventist evangelists and church builders who had returned from the former Soviet Union with reports that glowed like Chernobyl bread. "The field is ripe!" exulted more than one speaker. Their stories were indeed extraordinary—thousands of baptisms, a craving for the Word of God, an inexhaustible longing for the hope, peace, and freedom of Jesus of Nazareth.

My friend Steve Case and I were talking following one presentation when a man approached us and introduced himself. In the course of our conversation, Steve mentioned that he was headed to Russia next summer.

The man's eyes gleamed as he leaned forward. "Oh! Are you going over to hold an evangelistic series?"

Steve displayed his toothiest tight-lipped smile and said, "No. I'm going over to try to *keep* the ones we're getting." The man stared at Steve stupefied.

Frankly, the Master didn't tell us to "make decisions of all nations." He actually urged us to "make *disciples . . . teaching* them to observe all that I have commanded you." The difference between a decision and a disciple is spacious. One may be short-lived; the other endures. One is easy to count; the other is as difficult to measure as true love. One builds numbers; the other builds people.

This is not to say that pursuing decisions for baptism is wrong. We need decisions. Decisions are to a spiritual life what the wedding ceremony is to a marriage. In the same sense, however, what marriage places 90 percent of its total effort on getting to the altar and tasting the cake? What would be the chances of married success? Would we scratch our heads in puzzlement as to why that marriage failed?

We must discern, as Jesus did, that the best teaching *involves* the participant. Like all good teachers, Jesus knows the learners' creed: "What I hear, I forget. What I see, I remember. What I do, I understand." We can find creative ways to keep the ones we're gaining and gain the trust of those we're keeping.

Making decisions is the first part of discipling, and it deserves applause. But without an equally committed follow through, it's the sound of one hand clapping. To make disciples, we follow Jesus' approach of involving those people close to Him. Jerry Cook put it this way: "Focus on the people you have, not the ones you hope to get. Whenever we try to build big churches, we get in trouble. When we invest ourselves in building big people, we make progress."

Here are two ideas for building big people.

1. Ministry gallery. Do you ever wonder if there's a better exit from a motivating Sabbath sermon than to shake hands, smile, and think about lunch? How many times can a person get inspired to do *something* for God—and do nothing? How many times can God's landscape be burned over with holy fire without growing new vegetation? (The answer, my friend, is blowing in the wind . . .)

What if instead, upon exiting a sermon, members encountered a menu of options to provide practical help to someone in the community? On the ministry gallery in the foyer is a list of contacts, times, and phone numbers for members to assist someone in need. A member sits behind a table to sign up people and answer questions. Possible ministries are providing car mechanic service to single moms, paying an electric bill for a month, giving Bible studies, doing yard work, intercessory praying, writing letters for Amnesty International, tutoring with the local literacy council.*

This means the church spends as much energy on finding people to help and helping them as it does in running its own programs. This may mean electing a ministry team and coordinator as regular church officers. It definitely means providing a substantial budget and involving new and young members in leadership positions.

The gallery could also be used to introduce new members or "members of the week." Allow these members to decorate their panel however they wish—with photos, wallpaper prints, medals, Bible texts—to let the church know who they are. Have some fun with it.

Our church does a pretty good job of encouraging musical artists, but *visual* artists find few church-sponsored outlets. My artist friend Conrad Christianson suggests that churches hand out blank sheets of paper one Sabbath a month to encourage artists to draw whatever comes to mind based on the sermon. The drawings would be collected at the end of the service and posted on the gallery the next Sabbath. Wouldn't you like to see what a twelve-year-old Vinnie van Gogh creates?

2. Hospital outreach. Nowhere do nonchurchgoing people contemplate eternity more often than in a hospital. With each birth, accident, illness, and death, friends and relatives slow down to reflect on transcendent truths. For many, a hospital waiting room is their church.

---

*This idea has been implemented at First Service at La Sierra Seventh-day Church.

With this in mind, develop a ministry packet for parents of newborns and for those who are grieving. Be sensitive in providing booklets and invitations and possibly a letter or a gift (such as a hand-knit baby cap) from the church, with no strings attached. Let them know that you truly care.

Tony Campolo tells a parable of touring an oil refinery where petroleum is broken down into gasoline, lubricating oil, and other products. At the end of the tour someone asks, "Where is the shipping department?"

"Oh, there is no shipping department," the tour guide explains. "All the energy generated in this refinery is used to keep the refinery going."

When most of the money and energy of the church is consumed in promoting its own programs, building its own membership, and constructing its own buildings, it becomes an end to itself. A whitewashed tomb. Another saltshaker on display.

No church is evangelizing well—or being spiritual—until it has enabled every member to be vitally involved in an ongoing, enjoyable ministry. The possibilities for member involvement—the key to true church growth—are as endless as your ideas.

Peter Benson, president of Search Institute, described a church he attended that emphasized true spirituality. "The most sacred moment of the church service," he concluded, "was when they opened the doors of the church and we walked back into the neighborhoods where we live." ❏

Why the smashee? In the end, it's a familiar story.

Peerless Pressure

If I live to be 120, I doubt that I'll forget it. There stood my freshly married sister, furiously glaring with astonishment at her equally astonished husband. Then they each stomped out of the reception hall—in separate directions. An awestruck server near me whispered, "That was the *shortest* marriage in history!"

But let's begin a little earlier.

My little sister, Janine, had agreed to marry Jim Bailey. Both were firefighter paramedics in Orange County (where few orange trees exist), California, and flocks of wedding guests had been invited. Along with my brother Bruce, I escorted Janine down the aisle. Her adoring, beaming husband-to-be waited at the end of our walk. Tra-la-la!

Now, Jim is as steady and calm and unflappable as any person I know. What I *didn't* know was what had been happening weeks before the wedding. Maybe the kneeling prayer at the ceremony should have tipped me off. Someone had painted on the bottom of Jim's shoes the message "HELP ME!"

Jim's groomsmen were mostly former fellow firefighters—rowdy, uncouth, "fun"-loving guys who really get into impractical jokes. Unfortunately, they were the last persons on earth you'd want as groomsmen. Take the bachelor party. Janine had made it clear to these guys that one degrading "traditional" activity with a prostitute would not happen or the wedding was off. The boys resented her demanding this, even though Jim wasn't remotely interested. Tensions began to build.

Apparently, the groomsmen decided to get even. After the wedding ceremony, *before* the bride and groom's pictures were taken at an idyllic spot, the guys threw Jim on the grass and mud (he had on a white tuxedo) and attempted to toss him into a pond. Wasn't that excellent? Imagine the scene: Janine hammering them with her wedding hat to make them let go, the photographer waiting, and all the guests inside the reception hall blissfully unaware of the havoc outside.

By the time Janine and Jim reached the reception, their nerves were raw. Then came the cake cutting. Janine told me later that she and Jim had been to many weddings together, and each time they saw a bride and groom mashing cake in the other's mouth they would turn to each other and say, "That's so tacky. I would never do that to you." Before the wedding they had made that vow.

First, Jim fed Janine. Groomsmen pressed forward from the front row, screaming, "Do it! Do it! *Do it!*" The guests took up the chant. I remember feeling as though I were watching a couple poised on top of a tall building with the crowd below urging, "Jump! Jump! *Jump!*" The air was electric.

Jim raised the cake to Janine's mouth and inserted it—gently. The crowd groaned.

Then came Janine's turn. She lifted the piece to Jim's lips, and as Jim said later, "I could see the devil in her eye." He looked meaningfully at her and said softly, "No smashee."

"I won't."

She did.

And he freaked. Grabbing another piece of cake, he jammed it on her head, smearing the icing over her hair and down her face as if he were mudding a seam of drywall.

They backed off each other. Janine glared at him with laser-green eyes. The crowd, which had whooped when she had cut loose, was now deathly silent. The two had jumped. I was stunned.

Jim and Janine stomped out. The crowd buzzed with amazement.

Recently I asked Janine why she did it—the smashee. Was it because of the peer pressure?

"Putting on a wedding is in itself peer pressure," she told me. "You do it so other people will enjoy themselves. I didn't think anyone was having a good time at the reception since I was outside battling with the groomsmen."

"So you betrayed your husband's trust for the chanting crowd, so they would have a good time?"

"Yep, that's right. Pretty stupid, huh?"

After Jim left the reception hall, he walked slowly back to the dressing room. *Well,* he thought, *we'll have to return the wedding gifts.* He truly believed the marriage was over.

Then peerless pressure appeared. Two of his friends, Steve and José, visited Jim in the dressing room to talk and to listen to him. They calmed him down. They assured him that the shame wasn't unredeemable. That he and Janine still loved each other. That their friendship would always remain. Jim listened and talked. At last, he and Janine met privately to apologize. They decided to go out and have a good time for the rest of the reception.

Which they did. In fact, the incident is silly and trivial to them today. They're more likely to remember the wedding ceremony, the honeymoon in Hawaii, the first house, their two sons, who are now teenagers. Years afterward, Steve and José remain their close friends. In fact, Janine claims they saved her marriage. And the other groomsmen? Well, Jim and Janine haven't seen them since.

So what do we learn from this incident? How should we respond to the chanting crowds? It's not a new lesson.

As Shakespeare said, "To thine own self be true."

As Paul said, "Don't let the world around you squeeze you into its mold, but let God re-make you so that your whole attitude of mind is changed" (Romans, chapter 12, Phillips).

As my sister said, anything else is pretty stupid.   ❏

Before strongly desiring anything, we should look carefully into the happiness of the present owner.—Francois Duc de la Rochefoucauld

---

The Epidemic of Affluenza

It was an unseen, deadly twist. In 1918, after "the war to end all wars," an insidious enemy killed more people than were killed during that war. More than twenty million died at the merciless hands of the Spanish influenza.

Now another killer lurks. I'm not referring to the predicted influenza pandemic. An enemy as insidious and lethal as the 1918 outbreak has been infecting our bloodstream for years, creating countless casualties without our even recognizing it. It's *affluenza.*

af-flu-en-za n.1. an epidemic of stress, overwork, waste, indebtedness, and misplaced priorities caused by dogged pursuit of affluence. 2. an unsustainable addiction to economic growth. 3. the sluggish, heartless, unfulfilled feeling that results from this addiction.

According to the Public Broadcasting System television program entitled "Affluenza," money plays a major role in 90 percent of U.S. divorces. By the age of twenty, the average American has seen one million commercials. Forty percent of all mail and two-thirds of newspapers are ads. Americans carry more than a billion credit cards.

And yet people complain, "I have no life." We spend our dwindling days exhausted, maintaining and purchasing things. "The good life" has sold out to "the goods life." When Vickie, a student at Union College, returned after three months in Guatemala last summer, she experienced culture shock.

"It's the shopping malls here," she told me. "The extravagance is obscene. What all this money could *do* in Guatemala! People walk through malls with eyes glazed, looking to buy, and they are the ones being sold."

Children, of course, are not immune to this selling. The kids' game "Mall Madness" promotes wanton, soulless spending. When I enter a shopping mall, I feel that I'm on the enemy's ground. You might think I'm overreacting, but I think more people pay allegiance to Satan through materialism than through Satanism, atheism, and terrorism combined. I prefer to think of the song, "Give the mall to Jesus." Otherwise we end up with shattered dreams, wounded hearts, and broken toys.

After Adventist volunteers return from short-term mission trips to impoverished regions, the volunteers' constant refrain in describing the poorer nationals is "and yet they're so happy!" Don't we get it yet? The nationals aren't happy *in spite of* their lack of overwhelming luxuries; they're happy in part *because* they lack overwhelming luxuries. Our culture conditions us to want more and more stuff we don't need. There comes a point where things start to abuse us. As Henry David Thoreau observed, "Men have become the tools of their tools." Substances can rip our priorities to shreds, and then we stuff them under *TV Guide.*

An ancient parable from India describes a wise woman who, while traveling in the mountains, found a precious gem in a stream. The next day she met a hungry traveler, so the wise woman shared her food with him. When she opened her bag, the traveler spotted the gem and asked her to give it to him. She gave it without hesitation.

The traveler left, rejoicing. He knew that the stone was valuable enough to provide security for him for a lifetime. But a few days later, he returned the gem to the wise woman.

"I've been thinking," he said, "I know how precious the gem is, and I know you know. I bring it back in the hope that you can give me something even more valuable. Give me what you have within you that enabled you to give me the gem."

Like you, I wrestle with giving. How much can I afford to give to the Pakistanis who will freeze to death next winter? How much should I give to my local church and to the local women's shelter? What could I, and should I, do without for the benefit of "the least of these"? At present, I contribute to about fifteen causes, which I monitor fairly closely. My son, Nathan, pointed out to me that these make up my investment portfolio. Still, I feel guilty at times. I'm really not *sacrificing* much. (Do you know what I mean?)

In her book *Choosing Simplicity: Real People Finding Peace and Fulfillment in a Complex World*, Linda Breen Pierce outlines ten steps toward a "recipe for simplicity." Each step involves focusing, slowing down, cutting back, or saying no. The old New England proverb could serve as our motto: "Use it up, wear it out, make it do, or do without."

After the September 11 attacks, "God bless America" became a wildly popular slogan. But what does it really mean to be *blessed* by God? The Bible paints a realistic picture of the dangers of prosperity. Chapter 8 of Deuteronomy cautions to take heed, "lest, when you have eaten and are full, and have built goodly houses . . . and your silver and gold is multiplied, and all that you have is multiplied, then your heart be lifted up, and you forget the LORD your God."

Proverbs 30 requests this blessing: "Remove far from me falsehood and lying; give me *neither poverty nor riches;* feed me with the food *that is needful for me,* lest I be full and deny thee, and say, 'Who is the LORD?' or lest I be poor, and steal, and profane the name of my God."

Of course, it's not just the poor who steal. Like publicans of Bible times, some of today's greedy corporations make gargantuan profits at the expense of people who have few options. And some do worse. With their product, U.S. tobacco companies kill more people *every day* in developing countries than the total who were killed in the September attacks. Yet in 2004, the U.S. government passed a ten-billion-dollar taxpayer-funded subsidy called a tobacco buyout. Under this buyout, no one needs to stop growing tobacco.* And amazingly, taxpayers cough up (along with their lungs) the money to these drug dealers.

Moreover, using the gross national product (GNP) as a "national health indicator" is a gross misnomer. Every oil spill, divorce, and cancer treatment enhances the GNP. On a positive note, when we consider the billions of dollars used to

---

*Plato noted, "What is honored in a country will be cultivated there."

research and treat diseases from leukemia to cerebral palsy, affluenza is one disease we can remedy by spending less, not more.

In olden days, people died from "consumption"—another name for tuberculosis. Today, we also die—spiritually, emotionally, socially, physically—from consumption. Materialism quietly kills us by the millions.

God, bless the world. Bless us with neither poverty nor riches. Save us from this comfortable scourge.

The cure for affluenza is found in one word.

Enough.   ❏

We were just supposed to talk about them, not actually do something.

Family Values

Not that long ago in the United States, talk of "family values" was all the rage. It came during a time of animated political finger-pointing, and people from all sidewalks of life joined in the discourse, each telling what was wrong with our society, our government, our schools, our homes, our children, and our pets.

After all the talk, things pretty much went back to normal. Few minds and fewer lives changed. We looked for a new banner to raise, a new media hot button to debate.

So it surprised me to wander into our friends' kitchen months *after* the "family values furor" and find tacked on their bulletin board next to the dog-food coupons a list of five specific, actual values under the heading, "Our Family Values." This was more than I could bear. Bristling to full height, I began my harangue.

"Hey!" I said, "You can't do that. You're getting way too practical here. We're just supposed to *talk* about them, not actually *do* something."

Later, however, back at home, I thought, *Could our children benefit from more specifics than the classic, "Love God and keep your room clean"?*

That evening I mentioned the thought to Yolanda, Nathan, and Geoffrey, and at my next family worship, I proposed that we develop our own values. Over the next week, each of us created a personalized list of vital traits. We put our lists together, combining where possible to produce the Blake Family Values.

Despite some outlandish complaints,* the process progressed relatively painlessly. We tried—some of us—to fit the values into five, or seven, or ten, but nine worked best. Here's what we came up with. Please view this as a sample.

---

*"You can quit editing, Dad."

Our Family Values
1. Maintain loving friendship with God first.
2. Be honest and trustworthy.
3. Work at holding a patient, cheerful, teachable outlook.
4. Deeply respect life and environment.
5. Maximize and risk God-given talents.
6. Live healthy lives.
7. Pray with all our mind, heart, soul, and strength.
8. Use time responsibly.
9. Practice courtesy, generosity, and service toward all people.

We framed and posted this list on a highly visible spot between the living room and the kitchen. At some point we may add some more values,* but we haven't caucused to discuss possible changes. We're waiting for the next political season.

Decide your own values, Christian families, even families of one.

Post them. Read them.

Live them. ❏

When they measure themselves by one another, and compare themselves with one another, they are without understanding.—2 Corinthians, chapter 10

Will There Be Basketball in Heaven?

It's best sometimes to start at the end, so let's imagine a scene in heaven. You're there (don't be shocked), and so are many old friends, including Lori and George (yes, George). You're standing around with some new friends, too: Rahab, Samson, and Paul.

As you and Lori and George are talking excitedly about having made it through Algebra II and the time of trouble (Paul says, "What's algebra?" and George says, "I never really knew either"), suddenly you remember a few of the good times.

You remember when you first met George—at a basketball game. At this point, Samson scratches his head and says, "What's basketball?" You look at him with a

---

*For example: "Leave for the father of the house at least some of the leftover casserole."

half-smile, and say, "I'll show you." Then you pull down a large, super-bouncy grapefruit and hang your halo on a tree.

At first, it's just a three-on-three pickup game: you, Rahab, and George against Lori, Paul, and Samson. The game goes well enough until you drive past Samson and slam one home. He grins, but he knows enough now about the game to be embarrassed because you beat him *bad.*

The next time Samson gets the ball, he backs you into the hoop, turns, and *rips the tree out of the ground* with the force of his slam. *Gulp.*

You move to a new tree. This Samson is one of the roughest, but you know a few tricks he's never seen before. So you fake him into another orbit and drill the ball home. But Samson is back—and this time it's personal. He tries to get around you; you plant your feet and he digs an elbow into your side and then the sky is turning and you're on top of him with Paul and George going at it too, when suddenly you look up. Jesus is standing there. And He says, "What's going on here?"

Maybe you think the above scene a little farfetched, but I left out the part where eventually teams were organized and leagues were developed and galaxies played each other and there was an A league and a B league . . .

Where competition is involved, things can get out of control. You've seen it happen. So have I.

I know basketball. Squealing shoes on hardwood. The smell of adhesive in the locker room. A zone press half-court trap. Playing before eight thousand fans.

My father was a high school and college basketball coach. Growing up, I spent more time in a gym than anyone you'll ever meet. I played on his team in high school (a school of four thousand students), and we were ranked number four in southern California my senior year. From there I played for four years on an athletic scholarship at a university.

I've lived with it, played it, refereed it, coached it. I've made last-second game winners, and I've missed one. (*Groan.*) I've played in five overtimes in one college game, and I've played in the NCAA tournament. I've guarded pro players. I'm telling you all this so you'll understand: I know basketball.

What makes competition so bad—or so good? At its essence, what is bad in competition is this: I can't do well unless somebody doesn't do as well. *My success depends on somebody else's failure.* That's bottom line.

On the other hand, what's good about competition? It often meets people where they are. That's good. And it . . . it's . . . well, the following came as a surprise to me. I wanted to list six facts that showed how competition is good. What I uncovered were six facts that exploded many of the myths we so often hear. Realistically, I don't expect these will change the world's climate; I'm just reporting what I found.

Fact 1: Competition does not prepare us for real life. In real life, we *do not* live in a competitive society. As George Knight points out in *Myths in Adventism,* "We live in the most cooperative and interdependent society the world has ever known.

We depend, for example, on countless hundreds of unknown people to produce, market, and deliver our food, clothing, shelter, and other needs. In turn, thousands of people are dependent on us. Modern society is essentially cooperative. . . .

"To prepare a young person for life, even in 'secular' society, we would do better to teach the elements and rewards of cooperation rather than competition."

Fact 2: Competition is not a good motivator. In the same way that fear is a motivator but it is not a *good* motivator, competition is a poor motivator. Competition creates too many unnecessary losers, too often encourages pride, selfishness, and rivalry. With cooperation, on the other hand, each person has a chance to excel while unselfishness is encouraged.

Paul wrote, "Let all that you do be done in love" (1 Corinthians, chapter 16). If love doesn't motivate it, it doesn't need to be done.

Fact 3: Competition does not build character. Studies show that athletes often suspend their moral judgments for the sake of sports. In pursuit of the prize, they bend rules, oppress and belittle, and do whatever it takes to win.

You may have heard the argument that competition forces you to see what you're really like. If anyone truly desires to know that, it's written in Romans, chapter 3: "There is none righteous, no, not one." Further, I've never had anyone explain to me how the "heat of competition" argument fits with our Lord's prayer: "Lead us not into temptation."

One of the worst effects on our characters that competition brings about—and I've been as guilty as anyone in this—is in creating an addiction to artificial excitement.

This is nothing new. In *The Decline and Fall of the Roman Empire,* Edward Gibbon wrote, "From the morning to the evening, careless of the sun or of the rain, the spectators, who sometimes amounted to the number of 400,000 [in the *Circus Maximus*], remained in eager attention; their eyes fixed on the horses and charioteers, their minds agitated with hope and fear for the success of the colors which they espoused; and the happiness of Rome appeared to hang on the event of a race."

Sounds like the Super Bowl, doesn't it? Today's sports teams are followed with fanatical—where the word *fan* comes from—devotion. An onlooker from another planet would conclude that the sports arenas in every major city are a type of religious temple. And she would be right.

As with any addiction, artificial excitement produces a constant craving for more. Like watching television, it never completely satisfies.

Fact 4: Competition does not enhance physical fitness. Varsity sports monopolize a school's time and equipment for the benefit of those who need exercise the least. When I first walked into an Adventist gymnasium after years of playing varsity sports, I immediately sensed something was different. *There were no bleachers.*

I asked someone about this curious absence, and the response was: We believe everyone should participate, so we don't encourage spectators.

I loved it. What an idea!

In the name of physical fitness, in competition I have had my nose broken twice, torn both Achilles tendons, jammed each finger at least twice, broken both feet, sprained my thumb, separated my shoulder, pulled muscles, torn ligaments in my feet numerous times, had a hip pointer, shin splints, a badly wrenched back that bothers me to this day, knee-cartilage damage, scars on my face when cuts required stitches, and, like a box of chocolates, assorted others. I was fortunate, though. Some people really get hurt in sports.

Fact 5: Competition does not promote fellowship. Sport by its very nature pits people against people. Just look at the fans of opposing schools during and after games. If we find fellowship in sports, it's because teammates are cooperating.

I used to play in a Christian adult softball league. The league's games were played on Fellowship Field, but the name of the field was a joke. Before each game, we prayed that no one would get hurt. Then we played, got hurt, shook hands—and that was our fellowship. I get more fellowship when I go shopping. If we're really serious about competitive fellowship, let's mix the teams and get to know our new teammates. Serve refreshments afterward. I'd like to play in a league like that.

Fact 6: Competition has brought about good results. God can bring good out of anything. People have learned self-discipline, been given hope, and even come to know God through the medium of competition. But for every person who is blessed through competition, there are ten who are cursed by it.

As always, the tough task is to weave the ideal through reality. The key thread is this: Look for *something better.* To outlaw competition is absurd unless something better takes its place. That's why I've tried to lend my time and talents to my sons' sports endeavors. At the very least, we can bring a redemptive, cooperative spirit to the games. In the end, hundreds of alternative activities and approaches—from earth games to Youth Specialties ideas—are available. Visit a bookstore. Experiment. Find something better.

It occurs to me that if all North Americans were passive to the point of sitting cross-legged on lily pads all day, I'd be saying something a little different. But many of our problems come from too much emphasis on aggression.* We see it hyped in movies, in the news, on the playing fields. We desperately need to back off.

Will there be basketball in heaven or the new earth? I don't think so. But I don't think we'll miss it.

My prayer is that we see competition for what it is and for what it does to us. May we be courageous and humble enough to admit the damage it causes to our self-esteem and to our peace. May we seek to find ways in which we can all win. In the name of the Father, our Owner; the Son, our Commissioner; and the Holy Spirit, our Coach. ❑

---

*Some of you are growing angry just from reading this. (I've been there.)

This Curve Has No Class

Of all the problems of competition, perhaps the worst takes place in the classroom. This outrage is inflicted not by students but by teachers.

You may have experienced it. The curve. That bell-shaped, powerful, *un-Christian* means of determining grades. Un-Christian? Yes, grading on the curve is un-Christian. Here's why:

1. It destroys the love of learning. With the curve, the bottom line becomes simply doing better than your rivals—your fellow students. How much or what you learn is irrelevant. Just finish at the top.

2. It is unjust. Suppose that you are taking a chemistry test. The test is tough, but you've studied hard, and you receive a score of 78 percent. However, you are in a class with lots of extremely bright students who score in the 90s. Based on the curve, you wind up with a grade of a D.

Your friend is taking the same chemistry test from the same teacher, but your friend is in a different class. Your friend receives a score of 74 percent on the test. However, the students in her class do poorly on the test. Based on the curve in her class, she receives a B. How do you feel about that?

3. It creates an atmosphere of resentment and distrust. If you've gone through the above scenario, the next time you take a subject, you hope there aren't many "extremely bright" students in your class. In fact, you studiously avoid classes with the best students. Moreover, rather than appreciating their talents, you resent those "curve busters" who always score 98 or above. And why not? They're getting in the way of your dreams.

In addition, when grading is based on the curve, you can forget helping anyone in your class—that would be like cutting your own throat. In true un-Christian spirit, it's every student for himself or herself.

It isn't uncommon for students to give out false information in an effort to get ahead: "I just don't remember what he said about that." Or, "I think I'll turn in early tonight," you announce—and then burn out your desk lamp studying till two in the morning (and hope your classmate isn't doing the same). What is it you're learning?

4. It is contrary to God's principles. In God's realm, everyone can succeed. Everyone *could* be with Him forever. In fact, to a certain degree, our prospects for being with God are enhanced as we help others to be there with us. What would happen if our success with God depended upon someone else's failure? How foreign to God's ways.

If there's ever to be a realistic reformation involving competition in Adventist schools, here's the place to start. Without fail, grading strictly on the curve ought to be prohibited in Seventh-day Adventist educational institutions. ❏

Then will I turn to the people a pure language . . .—Zephaniah, chapter 3, KJV.
Some fun for language defenders of the faith.

KO @ the Okay Corral

Characters, from Hagerstown's Review and Herald Publishing Association:
James Cavil, *head copyeditor. Fastest pen in the East. Known as "James." No amount of caviling can dissuade him from his task.*
Richard Coffen, *editorial vice president. Deadly logical. More than four thousand manuscripts have been buried with this Coffen.*
Jeannette Johnson, *acquisitions editor. Sharpshooter—fast word processor, faster tongue.*
Mysterious man, *hired wordslinger. A rogue.*
Chris Blake, *humble and earnest servant of truth and justice.*

James: All right, this meeting of the Review and Herald editorial style committee will now commence. First, let's take up a matter Chris has been contesting.

Blake: Thank you. Ladies and gentlemen—

Johnson: More precisely, "Lady and gentlemen."

Blake: I'll cut to the pith of the problem. We should change our current aberrant house style whereby we capitalize the word *okay*. Okay does not deserve to be uppercased. OK stands out and up, heralded on a page of print, yet it is the epitome of mediocrity. All lower-class words such as *okay* deserve lower-case status.

Coffen: Did you just use "upper-cased" as a verb?

Blake: With our "American" penchant for turning all nouns into verbs, yes, I did. My apologies for verbifying.

James: OK, let's speak to this issue. My position is that we keep our current usage.

Man: I concur. Some believe that OK originally stood for *oll correct*. It's a common abbreviation. If we use it so often, it must be important.

Blake: More likely it derived from U.S. President Martin Van Buren's birthplace, Old Kinderhook, New York, because he often appended his messages with O.K. But our language is increasingly riddled with trivializing abbreviations. Since we employ *and* more than *okay*, how would you like to see your pages peppered with "important" &s? & maybe some @s @ some point also? Would that be okay?

Man: What are you talking about?

Blake: & then let's abbreviate the word *television* to T.V.—a tele vision.

Johnson: Maybe that's the abbreviation for Tasteless Vacuum. We do elevate TV—and KO, too.

Blake: We should. Both are powerful enough to knock out a culture. As further evidence of our decline, just check out the 200 million mailboxes & welcome mats featuring, for example, "The Thompson's" or "The Willabur's."

Man: If the Thompson's or the Willabur's want to welcome people that way, we should let them.

Coffen: Please! Your language! Have you gone mad, Man?

James: You realize that we have changed with the times. We endured the 1970s and changed to the 1980s. We adapt our stylistic do's and don'ts.

Blake: *Do's?* Did you say *do's?* Why don't you go visit the Willabur's while you're @ it?

Johnson: Oh, no. Stand back. He's gonna empty his ammo.

Blake: — it all, let's / these flaws before we cave in completely. I'd say ½ of our churches, > or <, can't spell our own church name correctly. I passed an enormous sign B4 a stately Seventh-day Adventist hospital. It read, "Seventh Day Adventist." I could have wept.

Coffen: Well, it's understandable. With the hyphenated word, our old abbreviation should have been SA instead of SDA. Now, of course, we're Adventist.

Blake: Understandable & inexcusable. Who appears more ignorant than one who can't spell his own name?

Johnson: Fifteen million who can't?

Man: It's not that big a deal. Even 4N people know who we R. & we still receive tithe no matter if it's spelled rite or not.

Blake: Barbarism! These are the last gasps of civilization. This is about > than $. We're dealing with the currency of brains & eloquence & accuracy, not to mention _____.

Man: IC. Sounds risky 2 me.

Blake: It's time to leave the EZ comfort zone of error. What good does it do to be theologically correct if we carelessly misspell our own name & continually commit apostrophe apostasy? Faith w/o usage is dead. # 4 #, 1 of the great risk takers was Samson, who had in the end more than the jawbone of an *. We 2 must be = 2 the task @ hand.

Man: Let's Cs this MT talk. We've ,long way. Let's axN28 the +.

Coffen: Let's vote.

James: All those in favor of keeping OK upper case, as it's supposed 2B, signify by the uplifted hand. [Counts votes.] By a score of 3 2 1, with 1 abstention, the word *OK* stays up 4evR. I trust U won't harbor any hard feelings about this.

Blake: (Graciously) Y, of course. How could I possibly seek revenge? It's okay in my book. BCNU. Please XcUs me. I feel a : attack coming on . . . ❑

If you're a young adult and you're pondering what to do, this is for you.

Does the Church Really Need You?

Joy was thinking, *Why bother with this?*

The thought had come to her quite naturally. She attended—more or less—the local Adventist church, but mostly out of reflexive habit and residual guilt. When she did show up, the worship service followed a too-familiar, dragged-out routine.

"Our opening song is hymn number . . ."

"If there are any unspoken requests, please signify by the uplifted hand . . ."

"Our offering today is for . . ."

"Let us pray . . ."

"Our closing song . . ."

If she was too exhausted to attend Sabbath morning or if she was traveling or decided to do something else, hardly anyone missed her. Maybe one or two.

When someone called from the nominating committee, she would say that she was too busy. She was, actually. She wasn't terrifically interested in what they offered her anyway.

On the whole, Joy really didn't fit in. Often, she had better times with people outside the church. They were more tolerant, they enjoyed life, and some of them seemed more Christian than the Adventists she knew.

Whenever Joy talked with her young adult friends, many of whom had already left the church, they reinforced her concerns.

"Adventists think they have a lock on the truth and that everybody else is wrong."

"What gets me is the way . . ."

Overall, Joy was truly sure of one thing: This church didn't need her.

≈

Now, if you *aren't* a young adult, you're welcome to read on, but (I say this gently) the following isn't written for you. If you *are* a young adult, and you can identify at all with any of Joy's thoughts, this is for you.

First, you aren't alone in your feelings. Tens of thousands of young adults around the world wrestle with comparable doubts and shriveled hopes. Maybe that provides scant comfort as you cling to the side of the Good Ship Adventist; I don't know. One thing I *do* know, however, to the marrow of my being: Joy was assuredly wrong.

I'm going to share five reasons why I'm sure she's wrong. I pray you'll listen, because this church desperately needs you. And when you hear the word *church*, don't think of a building or an organization—think of people. We, the church, are all colors and all temperaments and all ages. *We* are the church. And we definitely need you because

1. You have energy. From beating hearts to blasting quasars to blooming violets, our universe thrives on energy. Yet, strangely, energy isn't always appreciated.

My friend Gary discovered this the first day he showed up to work in a factory. Wanting to give his all and to be accepted by the other workers, he worked up a sweat that morning. The foreman even tossed him a piece of praise. But at morning break, and again at lunch, the other workers avoided him.

During the afternoon break, Jeff, an old "lifer," ambled over to talk to Gary.

"Just startin' today, huh?"

"Yeah," Gary replied, showing his friendliest smile.

"Well," Jeff said, clearing his throat, "if you want to keep workin' here, you better slow down. We don't appreciate no hot dogs makin' us look bad." He eyed Gary a long moment, spat for emphasis, and walked back into the crowd.

Gary told me he decided right there that he would always do his best, no matter what, because he didn't want to end up as pathetically tired and vicious as those men had become. What followed was a chilling tale of persecution, including nearly being killed by his co-workers in an "accident." Eventually Gary moved on to another job. He's now a physician.

What does this story have to do with your frustrations with the church? It's probable that nobody has tried to bump you off during a frosty night of Ingathering. But you may have been bumped off a church board or a building committee.

Or you may have found it difficult to break into the decision-making circles of the church. And perhaps acceptance by the church "lifers" hasn't come swiftly or without tacked-on conditions.

While countless church members serve with astonishing spirit and energy, others have obviously grown weary. They've been fighting for decades on the front lines—as junior leader and Investment coordinator and deaconess and 122 jobs without a title. They're tired, and they wish they weren't, but they know they have to stay involved to stay spiritually alive.* So now they fight—sometimes at your expense—to maintain their involvement. Involvement *is* the key to feeling needed. And energy is one involvement essential.

You have energy. For discussing difficult questions with patience and tact. For forgiving. For trying new ideas. For standing up for our youth. For smiling warmly. For following the Holy Spirit.

That kind of energy is profoundly needed.

2. You see through the sham. Life magazine carried an article entitled "Why Are We Here?" The editors asked forty-nine famous and not-so-famous people to share their views on the meaning of life.

Of all the views, I like Garrison Keillor's most. It soared and whistled and smacked its lips all at once. He began, "To know and to serve God, of course, is why we're here, a clear truth that, like the nose on your face, is near at hand and easily discernible but can make you dizzy if you try to focus on it too hard.

"But a little faith will see you through. What else will *except* faith in such a cynical, corrupt time? When the country goes temporarily to the dogs, cats must learn to be circumspect, walk on fences, sleep in trees, and have faith that all this woofing is not the last word."

He concluded, "What keeps our faith cheerful is the extreme persistence of gentleness and humor. Gentleness is everywhere in daily life, a sign that faith rules through ordinary things: through cooking and small talk, through storytelling, making love, fishing, tending animals and sweet corn and flowers, through sports, music and books, raising kids—all places where the gravy soaks in and grace shines through. Even in a time of elephantine vanity and greed, one never has to look too far to see the campfires of gentle people. Lacking any other purpose in life, it would be good enough to live for their sake."

Garrison Keillor knows what's genuine and what's not. So do you.

As a church, we need you to *tenderly* peel back the conventional blinders we wear. For example, you can mention to us, at the peak of our certainties, that Jesus is also certainly the Lord of surprise. And that while He was on earth, the people who knew Him best were the people He surprised most.

---

*They are right about that.

You can tell us when we're worshiping our organization above our God.

You can call attention if our focus is on programs instead of people, if we're stuck in ruts of ineffective or counterproductive evangelism.

You can let us know if we're sending the wrong message—that people aren't wanted or supported unless they behave.

You can help us to do justly, reminding us that "the kingdom of God does not consist in talk but in power" (1 Corinthians, chapter 4).

You can see that it's not all bad out there in "the world"; in fact, tremendous good exists. Incredible love. Rich wisdom. Blazing dedication. Perhaps many of us don't have to be afraid of contamination so much as of growing stale.

In short, because you see problems, we need you to stay with us. We want to listen to you; we need you to humbly point us again in the right direction. As Ellen White candidly observed, "We have many lessons to learn, and many, many to unlearn."

3. You can reach other young adults. I remember many years ago sitting and waiting in front of a television set, where a young man was reading my future on a ping-pong ball. It was the first televised draft lottery. Winners received a free trip to Vietnam.

You don't remember Vietnam, of course. Perhaps instead you were weaned on the Gulf War or Enron or a hundred corrupt political scandals. You may have grown up as I did, with a daring distrust of almost everything. Especially organizations. Now you live in a slick culture. Style is substance. It's a multiple-choice society, and whatever gets you ahead is a good choice. Or so they say.

Maybe because the foundations aren't as secure, the rumbling news bulletins don't jolt you as much as they once did. You can relate to the anchorless shifting of the ground, the shifting and groaning of the planet. More than that, you can identify with other young adults, the *twentythirtysomething* crowd who grew up in an atmosphere of superchange. You relate to the money panics, the work hassles, the striving to do more than survive and often just surviving. You definitely know what it means to be too busy.

You show brilliant flashes of wit and warmth, as well as soul-numbing binges of selfishness and materialism. There are too many choices. You sometimes feel paralyzed by an overload of information.

But because you feel it, because you've lived it, you're able to reach other young adults. You can touch them with realistic hope as nobody else can. You can point them to the Foundation that never shifts.

We need you for that.

They need you too.

4. You can remind us how to have fun. Fun has an undeserved bad reputation in religion. In *Who Switched the Price Tags?* Tony Campolo wrote, "There isn't anything frivolous about having fun. Learning how to have fun is one of the most serious subjects in the world.

"Without fun, marriages don't work. When jobs aren't fun, they become intolerable and dehumanizing. When children aren't fun, they are heartbreaking. When church is not fun, religion becomes a drag. When life is not fun, it is hard to be spiritual."

According to David Augsburger, Jesus made three strange promises to His disciples: "They would be absolutely fearless, they would be in frequent trouble, and they would be absurdly happy."

At socials, in worships, during board meetings, on ball fields, an undercurrent of healthy fun unites us and nudges us gracefully along the godly path.

The best teachers make learning fun. The best leaders make serving fun. Yours is a fun generation. We need you to help us keep the fun in our fundamentals.

5. *You need us.* At some point you've sensed the futility of corporate ladder climbing. You've glimpsed the bland landscape at the end of the yuppie rainbow. You know what it's like to pour every ounce of your energies into education/friends/work/entertainment. It isn't enough.

You need us. The church can help keep you on track, especially as you help keep us on track. The church calls you to be disciplined in the true sense of the word—as a disciple of Jesus Christ. The church calls you to be tolerant, even of the intolerant.

The church calls you to use your time in seeking the best, not merely the good. The church calls you to a higher, nobler influence. The church calls you to commitment instead of postponement, to the important instead of the urgent. The church calls you to peace of mind.

Among her many gifts, Ellen White possessed the gift of common sense, uncommon as it is. She demonstrated this when she wrote, "God teaches that we should assemble in His house to cultivate the attributes of perfect love."

Where else but in the church do you find so many opportunities to cultivate love and forgiveness and acceptance? Where else do you meet regularly with people so incredibly different from yourself?

As Tony Campolo tells it, "At its best, there is no fellowship on earth that is crazier than the church. At its best, the church befriends people we would never get to meet within the sterile confines of our class-structured society. In the church, we are ushered into loving relationships with people who otherwise would be strangers. In the church, Democrats can get to know Republicans, pacifists can get to know soldiers, punk rockers can get to know lovers of Bach."

You need us—the church—for that.

And in the end, if you ever doubt that you are needed, please remember this: There is always room for one more Joy.

> **"What Can I Do?"**
>
> Of all the misconceptions of church life possible, the most treacherous is revealed in the following lament: "But I don't hold any church offices. I can't do anything."
>
> The truth is, even if you don't hold an official church position, there are googol* ways you can do justly, love mercy, and walk humbly with your God. Here's a sampling of ideas from projects already being done.
>
> Sheryl heads up a puppet ministry for children.
> Debbie and Sergio share themselves in Big Sister/Big Brother programs.
> Monte travels with Maranatha on short-term mission projects.
> Kathy tutors in a Teach a Kid program.
> Prem serves in the downtown soup kitchen.
> Emilio attends Amnesty International meetings and writes letters.
> Warren steps out with The Walkers, a young-adult walking group.
> Sarah volunteers for an Adventist Volunteer Services position overseas.
> Courtney organizes baby showers and other social events.
> Leslie watches over the neighbors' kids for free once a week.
> Thang Van conducts an upbeat Bible study during lunch at work.
> Jennifer directs a children's cherub choir. ❏

I would I could stand on a busy corner, hat in hand, and beg people to throw me all their wasted hours.—Bernard Berenson

---

His Life for This

One night a platoon of soldiers were moving through the jungle. As they reached a clearing, the enemy jumped out of the brush and ambushed them. Many of the combatants were killed; the survivors retreated into the undergrowth.

Dead soldiers from both sides littered the ground in the clearing between the two enemy platoons. Suddenly the soldiers heard moaning. One of their men wasn't dead. But it was certain death to go out there and bring him in.

The wounded soldier moaned for long minutes in the blackness. Eventually, the sergeant, a young man respected and loved by the platoon, said he was going out to get the wounded man. The others tried to discourage him but finally agreed to cover him as he got out in open fire.

---

*This is an actual number, you know.

He made a dash into the clearing, lifted the wounded man, and dragged him back toward the jungle. Bullets flew from the enemy. Just as he was tossing the wounded soldier toward the waiting medics, the sergeant caught a bullet in his back. He was killed instantly.

The wounded soldier survived, and when he was released from the hospital, he returned home. A little after the war ended, the sergeant's parents contacted him. They said that the young sergeant had been their only son and that they would like to see the young man he had saved. The soldier let them know when he would be in their area, and they set up a time to meet.

The parents of the sergeant prepared a lavish feast for the soldier. They wanted everything to be right—he was a guest of honor. When the young man arrived, however, he turned out to be a braggart, undisciplined, obnoxious, and self-absorbed. He was flippant and insensitive in his approach to them. After a short time, the parents couldn't wait for him to leave.

Finally, he moved toward the door. As the father closed it behind him, the mother burst into tears and cried out, "To think that our precious son gave his life for that!"

When I consider this story, I think of my response to being saved. Am I ever rude and selfish? Am I undisciplined? Am I self-absorbed?

Ah, to be *constantly* living a life of justice and joyful gratefulness to God. For indeed, He has sacrificed so much to save me.

May my life, my next minute, be lived so that the Father God lifts His lips into a smile and says while pointing at me, "My Son gave His life for that." ❑

When it is our duty to question or protest, to remain silent is a sin.

When Silence Is Wooden

The students in this classroom were perfect.

Every eye focused on the speaker. Each gesture, intonation, and expression was duly noted. For the entire period, the atmosphere was reverently hushed. Almost tomblike.

The students in this classroom were failing.

Oh, they were pulling good grades, all right. Mostly As and Bs. But they were failing nonetheless. Like pinned specimens, they were perfect only when they appeared to be dead.

There are two types of people who fail—those who cannot do what they are told, and those who can do nothing else. Here are three reasons why we as students—from high school and college classes to adult Sabbath Schools—are failing to speak out, to be responsive, to wed learning to life. Ultimately, as a tragic result, we are failing to act justly.

REASON 1: We have been taught to believe that being good means being quiet. If this is as far as it goes, it is wrong. Consider the lament one of Garrison Keillor's characters made to his parents:

"You taught me to believe in quietness as sign of good character, that a child who sat silently with hands folded was a child who has overcome temptation. In fact, I was only scared, but being a nice quiet boy, I was offered as an example to other children, many of whom despise me to this day. . . . I learned that quietness could be used to personify not only goodness but also intelligence and sensitivity, and so I silently earned a small reputation as a boy of superior intellect, a little scholar, a little sunbeam in this dark world, while in fact I was smug and lethargic and dull as a mud turtle."*

From infancy we are taught that we should be good and quiet. We *can* be good and quiet, but the two aren't necessarily the same.

REASON 2: We are not encouraged to ask questions. The question on the elementary math test read: "A tree on the edge of the road fell across the road. The tree was twenty-two feet long. The road was fifteen feet wide. How far beyond the road did the tree extend?" Marvin scratched his head. He didn't know how he should answer. Why? Because he didn't know whether the tree fell straight across the road or at an angle.

Susan looked long and thoughtfully at the examination question that read, "State the number of tons of coal shipped out of North America in any given year." Then her brow cleared and she wrote, "1482—none."

I like those stories. They have life in them. They probe beyond what is "correct."

Teachers must be self-assured to ask students an open-ended question, one that goes beyond right or wrong. Conversely, a teacher who is threatened asks questions—laden with peril—in a multiple-choice format that implies the following correct answers:

A. What you think the teacher thinks.
B. (See A.)

This type of "discussion" stunts growth, splinters community, and smothers innovation. We loose interest in the life of the mind.

REASON 3: Increasingly, our world of technology is creating passive spectators. We are content to watch. When we see depictions of trouble on TV, we expect it all to be resolved, more or less, within the hour. We come to expect clear-cut, add-water-

---

*From *Lake Woebegon Days.*

and-stir conclusions, and when these don't occur in reality with appetizing regularity, we believe something is wrong with our lives. Or with reality.

So what directions do we take? Here is "C. What I think."

Believe that God's friends ask questions. Interaction is the essence of Christianity. When you read the Bible, notice how often God's friends ask questions of Him. Look at Job, Abraham, Moses, David.* Then ask yourself, Why are they His friends? Are God's angels silent, or are they asking questions this very second?

No doubt these words can be misapplied. Some people need to sit back and reflect longer before responding, and they could interpret these words as giving license to their thoughtless, knee-jerk reactions. But I am more concerned by the vast numbers of pinned specimens who are not responding, not asking, not interacting.

We have often been encouraged to be more than mere reflectors of others' thoughts. Mere reflectors, however, are still one step ahead of mere absorbers. ❏

There is a sanctuary in heaven, the true tabernacle which the Lord set up and not man. In it Christ ministers on our behalf, making available to believers the benefits of His atoning sacrifice offered once for all on the cross. He was inaugurated as our great High Priest and began His intercessory ministry at the time of His ascension.—Fundamental Belief 23

The Other Sanctuary Doctrine

It was 1980, and the Seventh-day Adventist Church was in upheaval. Appearing on the apocalyptic stage alongside Daniel and Revelation were Desmond, David, Walter, and revelations. Ford, Davenport, and Rea—"FDR"—brought their new deals, and the resulting furor led thousands to depart Adventism.

One of the most controversial stances was Dr. Ford's questioning of the doctrine of the heavenly sanctuary and the investigative judgment, challenging whether there are two literal rooms in heaven, a Holy Place and a Most Holy Place, where Jesus now ministers for us.† For years after the eruption, many applicants for positions in church employment were asked, as evidence of their orthodoxy, whether they believed in a literal sanctuary in heaven. A friend of mine, interviewing for a youth pastor assignment, was asked, "Do you believe there are two rooms in the heavenly sanctuary?"

He replied, "In my Father's house are many rooms."

The interviewers laughed. "Fair enough," they concluded. He got the job.

---

*See Job, chapters 3, 7, and 10; Genesis, chapter 18; Exodus, chapters 5 and 32; and Psalms 6 and 13.

†See Hebrews, chapter 9.

Others weren't so fortunate. In August of 1980, 111 chief Adventist scholars and administrators convened at Glacier View Ranch in Colorado to decide whether Dr. Ford's dissonant views were legitimate. They determined that the traditional Adventist doctrine of the sanctuary should remain, and scores of pastors, including Dr. Ford, eventually lost their ministerial credentials.

This sanctuary doctrine has distinguished Seventh-day Adventism from nearly every belief system on earth. However, the basis for this doctrine appeared well prior to 1980 or 1844. Scripture devotes thousands of words to the sanctuary, beginning with Exodus, chapter 25: " 'Let them make me a sanctuary, that I may dwell in their midst.' "

Over the next six chapters we read intricate descriptions of God's designs for the sanctuary, or tabernacle, in the wilderness, including astonishingly precise measurements and materials for the ark ("Then you shall make a mercy seat of pure gold; two cubits and a half shall be its length."), the table ("You shall make the poles of acacia wood, and overlay them with gold."), the lampstand ("The base and the shaft of the lampstand shall be made of hammered work; its cups, its capitals, and its flowers shall be of one piece with it."), the curtains, veil, altar, court of the tabernacle, oil for the lamp, garments for the priesthood, ordination ritual, sin offering, burnt offering, sacrifice of ordination, altar of burnt offering, altar of incense, offerings for the tabernacle, bronze laver, anointing oil, incense, and appointment of the workers.

The sanctuary has been a big deal to God for a long, long time. The heavenly sanctuary fulfills one transaction. But another sanctuary would accomplish an equally important enterprise.

≈

A Google mouse hunt for *sanctuary* produces an astonishing yield. Following the Sanctuary Records Group (with artists Lynyrd Skynyrd and The Tubes), I encountered sanctuary sites for tigers, farm animals, elephants, donkeys ("over 11,000 rescued in the UK and Ireland"), koalas, fish, seals, bats, seabirds, and (to amen choruses from porcine-pure Adventists) potbellied pigs—replete with recipes for "compassionate cuisine."

I also find through Google a different brood: Stalking Victims' Sanctuary, Borderline Personality Disorder Sanctuary, and The Cynic's Sanctuary, which boasts in its hall of fame Aesop, Voltaire, Mark Twain, Dorothy Parker, and Jesus of Nazareth.

Then I chance upon *Without Sanctuary: Lynching Photography in America*, and my search ends. The book's photos fill me with horror. Nearly 150 photos depict an incomprehensibly gruesome legacy. In a righteous, festive atmosphere, crowds pose next to their human quarry as though they just landed a prized catfish. Adding to the stark, shocking truth, many of the photos were transformed into postcards complete with a "Place Stamp Here" print on the reverse side, suitable for handling by the United States Postal Service.

In his online review of the book, Joe Lockard laments, "At least the German civilians forcibly escorted through the death scenes of extermination camps in 1945 had the decency to weep and protest unconvincingly that they did not know. Americans photographed these horrors of tortured, mutilated and burned bodies as an advertisement for white supremacism and popular 'justice.' "

Between 1882 and 1950, the Tuskegee Institute reports, 3,436 lynchings took place throughout the United States, with likely a greater number unrecorded. When these lashing storms of mindless rage, fear, and pride blew humanity apart, no harbors of justice and mercy appeared. Without sanctuary, the "good old days" weren't good for anybody.

≈

Something wonderful happened. Jesus arrived, bringing with Him a new interpretation to the sanctuary. He announced, " 'The kingdom of God is within you' " (Luke, chapter 17, KJV). Paul picked up this thought in 1 Corinthians, chapter 3: "Do you not know that you are God's temple and that God's Spirit dwells in you?" (The church in Corinth, apparently, did not.) He continued in chapter 6, "Do you not know that your body is a temple of the Holy Spirit within you, which you have from God? You are not your own; you were bought with a price. So glorify God in your body."

Paul reinforced this doctrine in his next letter to the Corinthians: "We are the temple of the living God; as God said, 'I will live in them and move among them, and I will be their God, and they shall be my people' " (chapter 6).

Hebrews describes the new covenant of God, one enacted on "better promises" (chapter 8). God declares, "I will put my laws into their minds, and write them on their hearts, and I will be their God, and they shall be my people." The succeeding two chapters outline the eternal heavenly sacrifice of Christ, and the superiority and finality of Christ's sacrifice and the new covenant, concluding with "I will put my laws on their hearts, and write them on their minds."

In the light of this new sanctuary doctrine, we can see Jesus' desires for us more clearly. The Sermon on the Mount, for example, is a sanctuary sermon: Create a safe space in your minds and bodies for God and for His creation, including your enemies.

The typically termed "Lord's Prayer" is a sanctuary prayer: "Thy kingdom come, Thy will be done, on earth as it is in heaven" (Matthew, chapter 6). Is heaven a safe place? God wills His kingdom on earth to be a safe place.

The promise of the Holy Spirit is a sanctuary promise, as Jesus plainly stated at the Last Supper: " 'I will pray the Father, and he will give you another Counselor, to be with you forever, even the Spirit of truth, whom the world cannot receive, because it neither sees him nor knows him; you know him, for he dwells with you and will be in you. . . . If a man loves me, he will keep my word, and my Father will love him, and we will come to him and make our home with him' " (John, chapter 14).

The mystery of the ages is a sanctuary mystery. It is "the mystery hidden for ages and generations but now made manifest to his saints. To them God chose to make known how great among the Gentiles are the riches of the glory of this mystery, which is Christ in you, the hope of glory" (Colossians, chapter 1).

A sanctuary is a holy place—a safe haven. We are each of us called to be a sanctuary, a refuge for God and His creation. Breathing, laughing, singing, running, walking, talking sanctuaries.

What makes us safe? The same thing that makes the heavenly sanctuary safe, the same attribute that makes Jesus safe: grace. The kingdom of God is within us when we lead gracious lives—forgiving, accepting, and sharing lives based on the better promises of graceful love.

$\approx$

My thirty-year-old musician friend doesn't go to church much anymore. We sit over curry and rice at The Oven while I ask him what would make church more attractive.

He reflects a moment. "Instead of 'Where you been?' I'd like people to say 'Glad to see you.' And there ought to be more choices in the middle. I mean, you're either a Pathfinder leader or . . ."

"An infidel?" I suggest.

He breaks into raucous laughter. "Right. Is there anything between Pathfinder leader and infidel?"

I assume a thoughtful expression. "A conference president, perhaps . . ."

Without human sanctuaries, the remnant becomes an exclusive club instead of an inclusive gathering.

To many people, Adventist institutions have mouthed mercy and goodness, fairness and love while treating their employees as disposable information carriers—easily ignored, crushed, or discarded. The stories are legion. Countless former members have bolted because they felt belittled and betrayed. Will Campbell could have been describing Adventist institutional blindness (or *hypermetropia*—farsightedness) when he quipped, "Jesus talked about a cup of cold water. But right off, we have to be about installing a global sprinkler system." In our haste to spread the gospel "into all the world," we neglect our own family. Dag Hammarskjold concluded, "It is more noble to give yourself completely to one individual than to labor diligently for the salvation of the masses."

Without human sanctuaries, ironically, those who cry out that we should "finish the work" may be doing just that.

Adventist schools and churches become converted into safe houses when they care more about kindness and acceptance than they do about behavioral purity and being right. When the bullies, gossips, and truth squads are allowed to attack virtually unchecked, education becomes fearfully stunted.

What does it mean for the church to be a safe place? It means our church sanctuaries are actually sanctuaries, and the human sanctuaries that comprise the church are free to wonder and probe without fear, generous in interpreting others' aims, open to consider different views, steadfast in defending and nurturing freedom, secure in the knowledge of agape love. So it is in heaven and shall be on the new earth.

Without human sanctuaries, we grow afraid to risk true learning; our truncated education makes us wise as doves and gentle as serpents.

The African-American female quintet Sweet Honey in the Rock sings "Would You Harbor Me?" about diverse peoples: Koreans, Jews, heretics, AIDS sufferers— those who are on our society's edges. Adventists have created harbors for people groups. For example, the Association of Adventist Women was developed to provide a sanctuary for Adventist women. Adventist Peace Fellowship nurtures an asylum for believers in the historic Adventist stance of noncombatancy. At Faith and Science Conferences, theologians and scientists enjoy a safe forum for discussing creation issues.

Without human sanctuaries, truth and freedom cannot flourish.

The Giraffe Society, based at Andrews University, is a grass-roots service network that pledges in its mission statement to "risk standing up and sticking our necks out against any form of negligence or mistreatment of Seventh-day Adventist youth or young adults, including inadequate financial support, guarded self-interest, and worst of all, non-involvement." Even in board meetings and nomination committees, giraffes provide healthy sanctuaries for youth and young adults.

In March 2003, two weeks before the invasion of Iraq, the Union College Humanities Division sponsored a "learn-in" titled "Between Iraq and a Hard Place," in which students, faculty, and staff could listen civilly to others' opinions. One-fourth of the student body (230) voluntarily showed up to give and hear fifty-two speeches on topics ranging from "Is a just war plausible?" to "What are the alternatives?"

Without human sanctuaries, the young may be devoured.

Finally, as is the case in the earthly and heavenly sanctuaries, within each human sanctuary arises a ministry of intercession. In His mountaintop sermon, Jesus announced, "Blessed are the peacemakers." Peacemaking, like love, is an active venture. "If any one is in Christ, he is a new creation; the old has passed away, behold, the new has come. All this is from God, who through Christ reconciled us to himself and gave us the ministry of reconciliation; that is, in Christ God was reconciling the world to himself, not counting their trespasses against them, and entrusting to us the message of reconciliation. So we are ambassadors for Christ, God making his appeal through us" (2 Corinthians, chapter 5). If Adventists don't enter this world with dependable, discerning, courageous, liberating action, it doesn't matter whether we are "declared righteous."

First Service at La Sierra University Church concludes its Friday night worship service each week by encouraging attendees to sign up at the tables in the foyer for Christian activism. Helping people obtain financial assistance, proper housing, and adequate health care moves pro-life beyond pre-birth. To care for the environment, to speak out against racism and the moneyed interests of tobacco, to guard the rights and lift the hopes of the downtrodden is to be a temple for the living God.

Without human sanctuaries, reconciliation and peace are rarely achieved, and spiritual pronouncements seldom meet practical concerns.

Through the transforming power of God's gracious love, our bodies become incarnational tabernacles with two compartments. We move from the Holy Place to the Most Holy Place, from our metaphorical heart to our metaphysical mind, from propositional truth to relational healing, from desire to application. We move from "the true tabernacle which the Lord set up and not man" to the true tabernacle which the Lord set up within man, from outer space where "Christ ministers on our behalf" to inner space where we minister on Christ's behalf. As trustworthy sanctuaries for God and His creation, we become gilded inside with pure gold, our acacia wood overlaid with gold, with the lampstand's cups, capitals, and flowers hammered into one piece (integrity). He has engraved His laws of love upon the holy ark of our brains.

Nobel laureate Roger Sperry observed that in the brain "there are forces within forces within forces, as in no other cubic half foot in the universe that we know." Dr. Paul Brand added, "I have been inside a human brain on maybe a half-dozen occasions. Each time I have felt humble and inadequate, a trespasser entering where no man was meant to. Who am I to invade the holy place where a person resides?"

Without this sanctuary doctrine, the seed of the heavenly sanctuary encounters no soil, finds no purchase, germinates no growth. Unless the Seventh-day Adventist Church prioritizes and practices this doctrine, the remaining doctrines never materialize. Without sanctuaries here creating safe space and making intercession, we are forever wandering, incessantly seeking shelter, eternally expecting and fearing the physical, emotional, and spiritual lynchings that will inevitably descend.

Jesus, Prince of Peace, brings the most radical spiritual assertion. The sanctuary—the kingdom of God—is within you. Is among you. Is you. ❏

It only takes a spark, remember, to set off a forest fire. A careless or wrongly placed word out of your mouth can do that. By our speech we can ruin the world, turn harmony to chaos, throw mud on a reputation, send the whole world up in smoke and go up in smoke with it, smoke right from the pit of hell.—James, chapter 3, The Message

While the World Held Its Breath

The school bell continued ringing. I knew the childhood drill well. Instead of walking out calmly, single file, to the playground to get away from a possible fire, we stayed in to hide from a possible firestorm outside. Crawling under desks, we knelt toward Armageddon instead of Mecca, burying our heads between our skinny knees and covering our brainstems with tiny clasped hands. "Civil defense" we called it, though our prospects were decidedly less than civil. Had an actual nuclear attack occurred, we would have been toast.

Like thousands of concerned citizens, Yolanda's father built an underground bomb shelter with cinderblock and concrete. It measured about ten feet by ten feet, featured one bed, and was stocked with canned foods and water. Years later, I climbed down the steel ladder into the dank darkness and realized I would have had difficulty weathering three days down there, much less the six weeks experts recommended.

The world was abjectly aware of the horrific possibilities. One commentator described our planet's condition: Everyone is standing in a room knee-deep in gasoline while half a dozen people hold boxes of matches. People argued over whether we were capable of blowing up the world a thousand or two thousand times. One night as a teenager, I awoke to a giant boom and a blinding flash across the western sky over Los Angeles. I thought, *Well, they did it. They bombed us. This is going to change my life.**

Evan Thomas's *Robert Kennedy: His Life* details the thirteen extraordinary days of the Cuban missile crisis in 1962. What makes the narrative particularly riveting is that much of the material comes directly from secret tapes recorded by U.S. President John F. Kennedy. Though the U.S.S.R. had sworn not to place offensive weapons in Cuba, aerial photos that October revealed that Soviet nuclear missiles were indeed in Cuba. Everyone at the highest levels of the U.S. government viewed this as an intolerable threat. How should they respond?

"President Kennedy was under considerable pressure from the military to strike. Meeting alone with the president on Friday morning, the Joint Chiefs of Staff virtually bullied the president to begin bombing. . . . 'You're in a pretty bad fix,

---

*In typical teenage solipsistic fashion. (It turned out to be a thunderstorm, by the way.)

Mr. President,' said the ever-bellicose Air Force chief of staff, Gen. Curtis LeMay. 'What did you say?' asked Kennedy, taken aback. . . . 'You're in a bad fix,' repeated LeMay, almost as if he was enjoying his civilian master's discomfort. Kennedy mumbled a joke, but he was not amused. 'Those brass hats have one great advantage in their favor,' JFK groused to his aide, Kenny O'Donnell. 'If we . . . do what they want us to do, none of us will be alive later to tell them they're wrong.' "

With the exception of decisions made in the Gardens of Eden and Gethsemane, Kennedy's decision would affect the lives of more people than had any decision in history. Had he decided to bomb, more than one hundred million lives would have been immediately lost, with the cataclysmic effects of a nuclear winter to follow. All fourteen hundred of the country's nuclear bombers went on twenty-four-hour alert. U.S. strategists discussed evacuation possibilities for major cities.

"The top White House officials were handed envelopes to be opened in case of attack. Inside were directions to landing sites from which helicopters would supposedly whisk them to a mountain cave in Virginia. 'I'm not going,' RFK told his aide Ed Guthman. 'If it comes to that, there'll be 60 million Americans killed and as many Russians or more. I'll be at Hickory Hill [home].' "

Fortunately, the nuclear holocaust was averted. " 'In order to save the world,' Premier Nikita Khrushchev had declared to the Soviet Presidium, 'we must retreat.' "*

My mouth hung open as I read: "Only the Joint Chiefs were dejected. 'We lost!' Gen. Curtis LeMay bellowed at President Kennedy. 'We ought to just go in there today and knock 'em off!' "

What an incredible, infantile perspective! To avoid "losing," let's kill 120 million people! To their credit, the Kennedys comported themselves like adults during this crisis: "JFK steady and reasonable, RFK urgent and probing."†

Of the many lessons to learn from this account (including that we must pray for political and military leaders, no matter how much we deplore their ways), here is one for the ages: To act as an adult is to refuse to raise the risk, to decline to heighten the mounting hysteria, even when we know we are in the right. No matter how tormented by goading, whining, sniping, or bullying, we will not respond in like manner.

This lesson is applicable in community services and church boards. This lesson is germane to families, between parents and children, husbands and wives. Too much is at stake here. One life is too much to hazard with adolescent bellowing or

---

*He eventually lost his position over the incident, proving again that doing what's right doesn't mean gaining the world's applause.

†In the interest of fairness, we should note that the Kennedys didn't always comport themselves as responsible adults.

sulking or finger-pointing. One bomb of nuclear words may destroy a child, a pastor, a church family. It's happened before.

Instead, we are called to self-discipline, to justly fight back the urge to rain general destruction on our target. "Put away all malice and all guile and insincerity and envy and all slander."* Supplement "knowledge with self-control, and self-control with steadfastness."† Do the right thing always, "and the God of peace will be with you."‡

The days of the Cuban missile crisis are past, yet lives still hang in the balance. How are we behaving? ❏

Why "evolution" and "exodus" are close neighbors.

Revival Isn't Enough

Where are the youth? I thought. While visiting a Seventh-day Adventist church, I had decided to look in on the youth Sabbath School class. Soon after receiving vague directions, I was walking down a hall and peeking in open doors.

The first room held the cradle roll department. Colorful chairs, posters, felts, drawings, and charts spotted the décor. Spinning mobiles hung from the ceiling. The inviting room was large and airy, and the many children were drawn from their seats (or propelled by hunched, careful parents) toward the activities.

Next appeared the kindergarten department. Here the room was smaller but still as bright and cheery as a Sesame Street set. With tongues pushed out in serious concentration, the students worked at tables. Then came the primary department, the junior department, the earliteen department. Oddly, as the physical size of the students increased, each room progressively grew smaller, less colorful, less animated.

When I reached the end of the hall, I could see no more rooms. The hall took a right turn to an outside door a few feet away. *Where are the youth?* Retracing my steps, I asked for more specific directions. The youth, I was told, were located "at the end of the hall."

Somewhat perplexed, I walked to the end of the hall again, found nothing, shrugged my shoulders, and turned for the exit.

Then I saw it. My heart sank. It was the youth department.

---

*1 Peter, chapter 2.
†2 Peter, chapter 1.
‡Philippians, chapter 4.

At one time it must have been a janitor's closet; it was much too cramped to be a regular classroom. Dark paneling and antiquated wallpaper covered the area. One poster, one small window, one fake plant in a corner, and one basket over-flowing with leftover *Insight* magazines completed the décor. Wooden, straight-backed chairs faced each other, their backs pressing against the walls in a kind of mute standoff.

The room was empty. After inquiring, I was told that the youth were meeting today with earliteens because "so few had attended."

How symbolic is that hallway. In the beginning, when youngsters can least ap-preciate it, we bombard them with extravagant space, design, and activity. As in-fants mature and their tastes and needs develop, we offer them less and less until finally (like adults) they are "grown up" enough to be deprived of anything that stirs their senses.

We know that many youths are leaving the church, because you and I know them personally. Their names are Jennifer and Emilio and Shawntae and Matthew and Robyn. We see them at church off and on, but then we don't see them any-more. And the greatest tragedy is that when they leave the church, they often also leave behind their God.

So what's the answer to the youth challenge? Is it larger Sabbath School class-rooms? Is it a corps of dedicated youth volunteers? Is it a division-wide "spiritual revival"?

All of these are needed, but they aren't enough. I believe the answer for our youth is found instead in the following two allegories.

Allegory 1: Hike the Ball

Picture youth as members of a football team ready to play the game of life. The field is mowed and freshly lined; the stands are crammed with spectators. The quarterback, devoted and capable, huddles the team to exhort them.

"Let's win this one for Jesus!"

The rest of the team hollers, "Yeah!"

"Are we gonna score a touchdown for God?"

"Right on!" the players respond, slapping each other on the back. They are fired up! With a shout, the team races to the line of scrimmage. Upon arriving, they look up into the stands, beckoning others to join them in the game, and some spectators actually climb out of their seats to join the team.

Then the players get set in their stances, waiting for the snap. Waiting. Waiting. Readjusting their stances. Waiting. Nothing is happening.

The quarterback calls a time-out and everyone huddles up. The quarterback implores them, "Don't you *want* to make progress in this game?"

"Yeah!" the players shout.

"Is this gonna be *God's* team?"

Each player replies, "Right!"

"Then let's go out and get 'em!"

The team breaks huddle and races again to the line of scrimmage. From there they look up toward the stands, wave, and dig in, each eager to do his or her part. They wait for the snap. And wait. Looking at each other, then back at the quarterback, they remain determined. And they still wait. Waiting. Waiting. Waiting. At last, frustrated, the quarterback calls another time-out. Time to huddle up again.

"We're not making much progress," the leader observes.

The players silently nod their heads in agreement.

"I get the feeling sometimes," he continues, "that you don't really care. That you don't love Jesus enough to play the game for Him."

That hurts. They know Jesus died for them. They know their loved ones are counting on them.

"Maybe if we each signed a pledge to truly live for God, we could make some real progress," the quarterback concludes.

The players agree, and with tears and earnest, fervent encouragement, they all sign the pledge. No more of that old no-progress game—they're headed for the end zone. The huddle breaks, and the players walk to the line of scrimmage. Some of them glance over toward the stands and notice all sorts of fascinating activities going on. Then it's down in the stances again.

Eventually, after another huddle, a few players drift off the line and head for the bleachers. This prompts some well-meaning people on the sidelines to begin yelling advice to the quarterback: "Just tell the center to hike the ball!" So, after a few more interminable huddles, the ball is hiked. In the ensuing confusion, the opposition totally overwhelms the team. It's a staggering loss, one that people say never should have happened—and had *better not* happen again.

Now, *what's the solution to the youth team's lack of progress?* At this point, amazingly, some people still insist that what's needed is for the team to hold another reviv . . . er, huddle. But that's not the answer, is it?

No. This team needs some *plays* to run. They need prepared, detailed patterns. They need organized role assignments. They need to see themselves making real, measurable progress in the game of life.

How do we get youth excited about their church? *Involvement.* Meaningful, active, risky, practical, Spirit-filled involvement.

In 1 Corinthians 12, Paul likened God's church to the human body. If any part of the body is not involved, it will atrophy, become infected, and will need to be cut off before the entire organism is stricken.

Seventh-day Adventists can point with pride to our educational and Sabbath School systems, saying, "The youth are learning about God. They are being fed the best spiritual food we can provide." But we aren't doing enough for our children when we merely feed them. Have you ever felt so stuffed after eating that all foods seemed repugnant? Even people fed the most nourishing food in the world will grow fat and lazy if they don't exercise. What's more, *they'll begin to hate that food, no matter how good it is.*

Moreover, when we focus merely on getting people excited about God, we enter a microwave relationship: Take it out of the freezer, thaw it, revive/zap it, place it back in the freezer. After a couple sequences, the product becomes as tough and tasteless as leather. That's how religion tastes to inactive youth.

Whatever their appearance, most youth want to be involved, to run plays, to enjoy spiritual exercise. It's the church's job to provide worthwhile, imaginative channels for their involvement.

Allegory 2: Excuse Me?

I'm sitting in a jet airplane at thirty-one thousand feet watching the sun ease down. Traveling west, I'm able to enjoy this sunset longer than usual. The "landscape" is different too. Miles of vermilion cotton stretch below, replete with ridges, alleys, and plains. Each moment the picture changes hue. *Breathtaking.*

One hundred years ago, this scene was unknown. People living then enjoyed no air-conditioned comfort six miles up, no view of the top layer of clouds while traveling five hundred miles per hour. No matter how beautiful the sunset appeared, they couldn't see it from this perspective.

For thousands of years, human beings have been enthralled by sunsets, and for those same thousands of years, human beings have been encumbered by a span of life called adolescence. But the perspective has changed for both. Today we hear talk that teenagers, like sunsets, are not what they used to be. Are today's youth *different* from adolescents in the past? The answer is yes—and no.

A *Newsweek* special edition entitled "The New Teens: What Makes Them Different" concluded, "Today's teenagers face more adult-strength stresses than their predecessors did—at a time when adults are much less available to help them." However, in the same issue, author Judy Blume, who receives thousands of letters from young people every year, reveals this about today's youth: "They write about their most immediate concerns—family, friends, love, loss, sex, school. They wish their parents would acknowledge their feelings and take them seriously. They wish for unconditional love."

Just as we did when we were growing up.

So how should we treat them? It's easy to say "Let's help our youth" and "I support them." Everyone can and seemingly does say that. The *difficult* part, the only worthwhile part, appears as we try to translate our noble sentiments into day-to-day actions. To understand this difficulty fully, first imagine that you need to go to a certain clothing store. You can't go somewhere else: This is the only clothing store around.

As you enter the store, a young man with spiked hair, multiple piercings, and tattoos gives you an appraising look. He's wearing torn jeans and a fluorescent T-shirt spattered with the words "Powered by the King." Glancing around the store, you notice that everyone in the store is dressed in bizarre fashions. You feel some-what out of place in your conservative dress, and after browsing for a while, you realize that there's absolutely nothing in this store in your style. Approaching Spikey, you politely ask to see the manager.

"I'm the manager," he says.

"Excuse me?"

"That's right; I'm the manager. Let me get you one of my salespersons." He hollers over his shoulder, "Yo! Got a customer!"

To your astonishment, out from the back slouches a girl no more than sixteen years old. "Fix this one up," the boy says. Then he rolls his eyes and adds, "If you can."

The girl looks you over carefully with obvious distaste. "OK," she says at last, "first the hair. Let's mousse this baby to the sky!"

"Wait a minute. I—"

"Then, you *gotta* change your gear. Whew! And the way you act, too. You gotta chillax. Here, for starters, stick this gum in your mouth."

"But I don't *mmmbpt*—"

"You'll get the hang of it. We'll fix you up with some Jimmy'Z, some Ops, and some slaps on your feet."

"Young lady," you sputter, "that isn't *me.*"

"Then there's the way you talk," she continues. "It's gynormously generic! You gotta change your rap. See, like, that's the only, like, way to, like, do it."

Suddenly you realize: *This store is run entirely by teenagers,* and you have no-where else to go.

How do you feel? A bit uncomfortable? That's how many youth feel when they enter our churches. They feel criticized, alienated, manipulated.

Moreover, what makes adults critical and unsupportive may be merely a differ-ence in taste, and taste is not a matter of right and wrong. That you don't like Jimmy'Z, or Brussels sprouts or onions, for example, doesn't make you *wrong*, and you wouldn't appreciate being criticized over the matter. The same is true for many tastes and expressions of youth. And lest we think it's a small matter not worth our concern, consider the following excerpt from a plaintive letter we once received in the *Insight* offices. The writer asked, "Why does it seem that older people in the Adventist Church are always looking down on us? Not only that, but the church, aside from schooling, seems to ignore us. I've thought of leaving the Adventist Church because of how we are treated."

We may find reasons to disagree with this young person, but she shares her honest perspective. Should we take her seriously?

Translating intentions to practical involvement is difficult because we all must cross the treacherous terrain of tastes. Let's face it, adult tastes are not the same as those of youths.* The apostle Paul gave the best advice for crossing this terrain when he wrote, "Be careful . . . that the exercise of your freedom does not become a stumbling block to the weak."†

Today we need to redefine who are "the weak." Are they those rigid, easily offended members who insist that their tastes are honored, who stick with the church no matter what, and who complain all the way? We often think so. That's who we most often bend over backward to please when we design our services, our socials, and our outreach so as not to offend these "weaker" members.

These people aren't the weak. They are as strong and durable and inflexible as steel. At times, their uncompromising nature is a wonderful godsend to the church; we need them to help us stay the course. But they are not our weaker members. *The weaker members today are our youth.* They don't complain in front of church boards or rant about changing standards or threaten to withhold their tithe of $138. They just leave. All too often, they don't come back.

Generally, we adults who "run the store" exercise our freedom and authority to accept only our own tastes and styles. If we bend for others, it's for the strong-as-steel among us, whose tastes usually run opposite of, like, you-know-who.

We need to treat our youth as our weaker brethren. We need to use our freedom wherever possible to bend and adapt to *their* tastes and needs. That, of course, is a staggering thought. Briefly, we need the following:

A. Livelier worship. Many Sabbath mornings it seems we include the Holy Spirit only if He's listed in the program. We can and should schedule times in our morning worship for spontaneity and rejoicing. We can sing songs that are less funereal and more alive. We can encourage audience participation. We can point to how worship prepares us for possibilities to serve during the week.

Most important, we can involve youth in every aspect of our worship service, from song service to Scripture reading to children's story to the sermon. Many have been amazed at what youth can do when given regular opportunities, especially with respect to creating technological audiovisual presentations.‡ Computer

---

*To which both sides add, "Thankfully!"

†1 Corinthians, chapter 8, NIV.

‡The Australasian Division is the best I've seen at this.

terminals were their umbilical cords—let's take advantage of their superior expertise.

B. Friendlier fellowship. Because youth are socially motivated, they require much personal contact with all ages. Have them mentor younger children, be mentored by someone older, adopt a grandparent. Create wildly fun activities (see Adventist books and Youth Specialties for ideas). Enable them to enjoy a safe sanctuary with each other and to provide one for visitors. Let them know that we love them with unconditional love. Write them letters. Be there for them.

Some superb avenues for involving youth in high-energy, social, and spiritual fellowship are Youth to Youth conferences sponsored by our church. Adventist Youth to Youth involves teenagers in helping other teenagers stay drug-free. These conferences also include seminars on self-worth, spiritual growth, and leadership training. (To find out more, contact Adventist Youth to Youth on the Internet or through Andrews University.)

C. Riskier evangelism. Serving in soup kitchens, holding public seminars, and going on short-term mission projects are all life-changing forms of evangelism for youth because they involve an element of risk. Youth need to be shaken out of their self-centered lifestyles and comfortable perspectives just as much as their parents do. They need to know that selfless service is more fulfilling than entertainment. They need to see themselves making a tangible difference in people's lives. They need to make progress in the game by demonstrating God's love.

≈

Even when we personally commit to involving youth in these three ways, we will face obstacles that test our patience, endurance, and sanity. Here are seven tips to overcome those obstacles:

1. Focus on the positive. When our son Nathan was in the second grade, he brought home a math paper that nearly made me cry. It was a test comprised of one hundred problems, and circled in red at the top was –2. At that moment I realized that for the rest of his schooling, our son would be facing –2 instead of +98, and that he would face that perspective all his life.

We don't have to give in to negatives. After that day, when Nathan brought home a sheaf of papers and said, "In all, I missed sixteen," he knew what to expect. Dad was going to make him count all the ones he got *right*. He complained, but he counted every one. And when I asked, "How many did you get right?" and he said, "Five hundred and eighty-three," his smile was worth it all. Catch them doing something right.

A positive outlook involves carrying joy with us. When I talk to parents about how to raise young people, I say, "It matters more that you enjoy your religion than that you are right about it. Young people don't care so much about whether you are right. They care about whether it *works.*"

We can live joyfully and cast the best possible light on situations and motivations. Let's give them the good to remember.

2. Don't push for perfect performances. Where have we gotten the idea that God is interested only in perfect performances? Perfect *love,* yes, but perfect performances? Look no further than the book of Mark to discover the truth. Consult Mark, chapter 9, in the Revised Standard Version to see how Mark begins nearly every sentence:

Verse 1: "And he said to them . . ."
Verse 2: "And after six days . . ."
Verse 4: "And there appeared . . ."
Verse 5: "And Peter said . . ."
Verse 7: "And a cloud . . ."
Verse 8: "And suddenly . . ."
Verse 9: "And as they were . . ."

And you get the picture. You can also find the same word beginning verses 11, 12, 14, 15, 16, 17, 19, 20, 21, 22, 23, 25, 26, 28, 29 . . .

Now, as any respectable English teacher can tell you, that's far from perfect writing. Mark could have done much better just leaving out 95 percent of the *ands* (as many modern translations have done for him). His writing style doesn't approach the eloquence of Isaiah's, Paul's, or Dr. Luke's.

But somehow God thought it was good enough to include in His library. He wanted Mark in there, *ands* and all. That's how God is—giving us His work to do when He could do it much better—to perfection, in fact. God is infinitely more interested in our youths' involvement than He is in perfect performances because He knows that's the way His children grow. They make mistakes. *And* just as we did, they learn from them.

3. Accept them as they are. Our lives will be immeasurably richer if we learn this lesson: *Acceptance does not mean agreement.* Jesus accepted the woman caught in adultery ("Neither do I condemn thee.") when He didn't agree with her behavior ("Go, and sin no more."). His acceptance was the catalyst that changed her life.

Acceptance is not endorsing ideas or behavior. Acceptance is affirming the infinite worth of another person, no matter who she is or what he has done. Acceptance is keeping our feelings, our mind, and our hands open. Acceptance is simply listening without comment. Our youth desperately need acceptance.

4. Offer them a religion that makes sense. At some point in this piece you may have wondered, *Which are matters of taste, and which are bedrock standards?* That's a good question. We should ask ourselves that question often.

Somehow we must communicate to our young people that wearing torn jeans is not as important as healing torn relationships. They already know that, of course, but they have to know that *we* know that. Our beliefs make wonderful, joyous, liberating sense, so let's communicate them in that way.

5. Give them ownership. A few years ago, a car commercial was aimed specifically at younger drivers. It used the slogan "This is not your father's Oldsmobile." Our task is to help our youth understand, "This is not your father's religion." Johann von Goethe noted, "What you have inherited from your fathers, earn over again for yourselves, or it will not be yours."

A thirteen-year-old who gets baptized is a full-fledged member, entitled to the rights and responsibilities of members who have been in the church sixty years. In Christ, there are no old-timers and not-ready-yets.

6. Be committed to youth ministry. The most fearful obstacle you will face is that you may read this piece or others like it and do nothing.

Along with abundant good news, I hear horror stories concerning treatment of youth. Whenever we hear these stories, let's resolve to stand up for these weaker brethren. For many of them, this will be the most crucial time in their lives. In *Gospel Workers,* Ellen White wrote, "The youth need more than a casual notice, more than an occasional word of encouragement. They need painstaking, prayerful, careful labor. . . . There must be more study given to the problem of how to deal with the youth."

7. Point them in the right direction. True or False: Our youth are our greatest hope for the future.

The correct answer is False. Our youth are not our greatest hope. Our returning Savior and Friend is. We must never forget that. Whenever we're with youth, we can point them to God and joyfully show how much we love Him. That love will be the best thing we can give them.

Christian youth ought to understand between a weather vane and a compass. Both point out direction, but only one is not subject to the breezy currents of remorseless pandering, willful ignorance, and careless deception. Christ is the compass.

Let's work together on these ideas and involve our young people. Give 'em proper coaching, give 'em plays, and give 'em the ball. Truly, they are not second-class members on this forever flight. It's time we treated them with first-class care.   ❑

If you're pleased with the general current of Adventist writing, skip this one.
Really. If you're not, read (and write) on.

Writing Wrongs

Years ago, I was asked, "How do you feel about the future of Adventist writing?" I gave an upbeat response, layered with charity and cheer, and soon headed out the door. The question, however, lingered in my head long afterward. Maybe I'm mostly alone, but I am concerned. Perplexed. Annoyed. I take no pleasure in mentioning this.

For eight years I worked in an Adventist publishing house, and frequently my experiences there were fulfilling and encouraging. At other times I witnessed a shrinking from difficulty, a slouching toward mediocrity. Too long we've waited and hoped and prayed for a change in the current. It's time to swim against it.

Marketed mainly (as one publishing administrator framed it) for "conservative, white, fifty-five-year-old housewives,"* many Adventist articles and books today constitute a bland soup. Readers are held hostage to shrill doomsayers or merchants of safe passage, while writers often appear self-congratulatory and predictable, introducing characters and themes, as Dorothy Parker once wrote, that run "the gamut of emotions from A to B."

Must it be this way? Balderdash! Bring on the Brobdingnagian brouhaha! Adventist publishing needs to do two things to wake from its slumbering near-life experience and approach life's nuanced realities with honesty and grace to woo new readers.

First, we must grow a backbone. Will criticism come as a result? Of course it will. At what point did "receives no criticism" become a merit badge of Christianity? Most assuredly, cowardice, obtuseness, and expediency are not the stuff of heroism. We can look to historic Adventist pioneers such as H. M. S. Richards Sr., who stood hip-deep in the current—brave, bright, deep and true—and worked their way upstream. These days I relish the balanced depth of Alden Thompson, the clean phrasing of Andy Nash, the pithy resonance of Beatrice Neall, the audacious voice of Nathan Brown, the prophetic messages of George Knight.†

But for every shining Knight piece we find forty dull and bloodless ones—elastic, vacuous, bloated, devoid of breath, brains, bones, and bowels—narrow fellows in the grass. Propelled by flagging clichés, they pile on testimonial platitudes like syrup-laden flapjacks and chase them with a bromide. A sweet surfeit reigns.

---

*I don't mean to disparage housewives, who are a truly noble species.
†I'm leaving out many, many people.

My friend Gary Krause, an excellent writer, chose to write an assigned news commentary spot about the tendency of American soldiers in Iraq to listen to raucous music laced with vicious killing images. Gary opined that perhaps, from a life-enhancing angle, their approach was not optimal.* The article was rejected by the *Adventist Review* on the basis that it might offend some people. I have to say I'm not offended by their response, but I am angered. And I'm even angrier that soldiers I'm supporting with tax dollars blithely enter real situations as if they are playing video games.

How in the world can Adventists "do justly" when we do not communicate justly?

It's also the case that Adventist publishing (including the *Adventist Review*) has gone forward in courageous ways, printing articles and books that do not portray Adventism in a necessarily positive light. At times our publishers have boldly pushed the envelope of ideas. I recall a book committee deciding whether Alden Thompson's *Inspiration* should be published. Normally at the Review and Herald Publishing Association, about a dozen people appeared for book committee to discuss about fifteen book proposals over ninety minutes. This day, however, twenty-five people showed up to spend two hours discussing one book, which was eventually and overwhelmingly approved.

In the course of the conversation, speakers questioned the prudence of publishing material that showed the Bible as infallible but not inerrant—though this *is* the official Adventist stance, and though no one challenged the veracity of the book's material. The question, "What might this do to the faith of people in the pews?" hung in the air.

Then the counterarguments began. Intrepid speakers assured, "The people in the pews can take the truth. In fact," they submitted, "that's the only thing we should be giving them." Old Duncan Eva said little until the end, when he made a statement that rang bells for me.

"If you would defend a lion," he said, "let it out of its cage."

As I'm tapping out this jeremiad, I recognize that I also fall short—I launch these words from level ground and aim them back at myself. What is our principal problem? Sloth.† As humans, we look for more efficiency—no invention ever came about from being satisfied with carrying sticks on our backs. Yet our efficiency bent can lead to damaging shortcuts—in reasoning, documenting, writing. When we grow lazy, we become sloppy.

Good writing is hard work. Enrique Poncala observed, "When something can be

---

*He wrote, "Of course we wouldn't expect warriors to be playing 'I Know That My Redeemer Liveth' from Handel's *Messiah* or, for that matter, to 'I Just Came to Praise the Lord' from the Heritage Singers. But is it too naïve to hope that, if war is fought and innocent lives lost, there should be more sobriety and less bravado?"

†My confession: I am so slothful that I push "99" on the microwave instead of "130" for a minute and a half, because I don't want to move my finger one more time. Pathetic, isn't it?

read without effort, great effort has gone into its writing." Abraham Lincoln once said of another lawyer's windy brief, "He got to writing and was too lazy to stop."

A conspicuous fruit of lazy writing is religious cliché. I read continually in Adventist journals of "the mission of the church," but I couldn't say exactly what that is. Is it to reveal the character of God? To evangelize the world (whatever that means)? Is it to make everyone Adventist? To love as Jesus loved? Spread the three angels' messages? Is it all of the above or none of the above? We act as though we all know what we mean, but we have merely the foggiest idea. If you asked ten Adventists what "the mission of the church" is, you would likely get eleven opinions, including your own. The same holds true for jargon such as "finish the work," "praise the Lord," and "have a burden for." "You can't 'outgive' God" sounds like a heavenly dictum, but it can bring hell to a home if spouses don't agree.

Another little-known effect of sloth is legalism. We lazily devolve to a checklist mentality, unwilling and eventually unable to think in complex, godly ways. When a life is ingeniously enjoyed, great thought has gone into it.

Poet William Carlos Williams wrote,

It is difficult
to get the news from poems
yet men die miserably every day
for lack
of what is found there.

Art adds to our lives sublimity, texture, and a sense of proportion.

In the summer of 2006, Eugene Peterson, perhaps best known as author of *The Message* version of the Bible, gave a talk entitled "What Are Writers Good For?" to a group of authors and publishing industry executives at the Tattered Cover Book Store in Denver, Colorado. Peterson noted, "More often than not, when the word *God* is used in our society, it is reduced to a piece of information, impersonalized into a mere reference, debased into blasphemy, or inflated into a hot air balloon of puffery. The dreaded godtalk."

Because our culture depersonalizes and functionalizes language, he asserted, "as writers we learn the art of indirection—not explicitly telling people what is going on by objectifying and isolating it, but hinting at, drawing readers and hearers into participation obliquely." Using Emily Dickenson's phrase "tell all the truth but tell it slant" as a text, Peterson went on to describe two useful metaphors for writers: Samaria and manure.

Jesus spent the first three years of His public ministry in Galilee and the last week in Jerusalem. To get from Galilee to Jerusalem, one has to travel through Samaria (in the King James Version, "must needs go through Samaria"). While Matthew and Mark rush to Jerusalem as quickly as possible, Luke devotes ten chapters—more than one-third of his Gospel—to telling the Samaria portion of the story.

The most prominent feature in this section of Luke is a gathering of ten parables mentioned nowhere else. The walk through Samaria reveals Jesus as a master storyteller. Unlike Galilee and Jerusalem, Samaria wasn't "home turf" to Jesus and His Jewish companions. Peterson observed,

> Luke gives us Samaria as a metaphor for the way Jesus uses language with people who have very little or maybe no readiness to listen to the revelation of God, and not infrequently are outright hostility. This is the way Jesus uses language when He isn't, as we would say, in church. . . .
>
> Samaritans then, and Americans now, have centuries of well-developed indifference, if not outright aversion, to God-language—at least the kind used by synagogue and church people. They have their own ideas on God and how to run their lives, and cool and thinly veiled contempt for outsiders. Samaritans are well-defended against the intrusions of God-language into their affairs, particularly when it comes from Jewish (or Christian) lips. So as Jesus goes through Samaria He is very restrained in His use of explicit God-language. Preaching and teaching are not eliminated but they do recede to the margins. Jesus circles around their defenses. He tells parables. A parable keeps the message at a distance, in the shadows, slows down comprehension, blocks automatic prejudicial reactions, dismantles stereotypes. A parable comes up on a listener obliquely, on the "slant." The Samaritan listens, unsuspecting. And then, without warning, without the word being used: God!

Then Eugene Peterson referred to the parable of manure.* For three years a fig tree has produced no fruit, so the farmer orders the gardener to cut it down. The gardener says, "Hold on, not so fast. Wait a minute. Give me some more time. Let me put some manure on this tree." Peterson continued,

> In the context of the Samaria metaphor, I see that gardener as a writer. Our culture wants to get things done as quickly as possible: action, efficiency, immediacy. Solve the problem in the quickest, which is also the most impersonal, way. Writers interrupt and say, "Give me some time. Let me write a novel, let me write a poem, give me a chance to get this soil . . . restored, revitalized. Let me dig some manure into the imagination of my community." . . .

---

*Found in Luke, chapter 13.

Manure is a slow solution. Still, when it comes to doing something about what is wrong with the world, Jesus is best known for His fondness for the minute, the invisible, the quiet, the slow—yeast, salt, seeds, light. And manure.

Manure does not rank high in the world's economy. It is refuse. Garbage. We organize efficient and sometimes elaborate systems to collect it, haul it away, get it out of our sight and smell. . . . But the observant know that this apparently dead and despised waste is teeming with life—enzymes, zygotes, microorganisms. It's the stuff of resurrection. . . .

Throughout these several days that Jesus is walking with His disciples, parables are His primary language of choice. We know that the end is coming: crucifixion and resurrection. We know that there is not much time left before Jesus leaves His disciples and they are going to be left to carry on in His place. Every step they take through Samaria increases the urgency. This is the last time Samaritans are going to see Him, listen to Him. Why in the world is Jesus telling unpretentious stories about crooks and farmers and manure? Why isn't He preaching the clear word of God, calling the Samaritans to repentance, offering them the gift of salvation in plain language? As the end approaches, His language becomes less and less, not more, direct. . . .

The intensity of the language [we use] can reduce our attentiveness to the people to whom we are speaking—he or she is no longer a person but a cause or a problem. Impatient to get our message out we depersonalize what we have to say into rote phrases or a programmatic formula without regard to the person we are meeting. As the urgency to speak God's word increases, listening relationships diminish. We end up with a bone pile of fleshless words—godtalk.

At Union College, I teach a course I created called Modern Christian Literature. Students spend our first class on a field trip to Christian Family Stores, meeting all manner of marketed manna—which means literally, "What is it?"* Afterward, we spend two weeks disabusing ourselves of the notion that "Christian" is a worthwhile and accurate adjective. It isn't. We can no more have Christian literature than we can have a Christian still-life painting.†

"Christian" is best used as a noun. You're a Christian, I'm a Christian, she's a Christian. This grammatical distinction generally shocks students, particularly given the course name, but it's our grappling with the question that matters. Must all "Christian literature" contain a reference to God? Then the book of Esther is

---

*For a treatment of items in this store, see "Beyond WWJD."
†Sorry, painting glowing light sources or hidden crosses doesn't qualify.

out. Should all "Christian literature" end on a happy note? Strike most biblical histories, along with much of wretched human history. The class considers literature that is *life-enhancing*—does that qualify? Could we possibly encounter a life-enhancing text from the Quran? Would it be Christian literature then?

Unfortunately, we often extrapolate adjectivally into other realms—"Christian music," "Christian politics," "Christian dry cleaners," "Christian fiction."* Deliver me. If we watch a self-proclaimed "Christian film" that turns out to be trite, agenda-driven, and fundamentally dishonest, should we question our Christianity? Must we make a choice between "Christian" and art with integrity?

Excellence and relevance ought to be the aims of Christians, especially in dealing with current life. When I see someone walking alone in a group of friends with a mobile phone slapped to her face, I can't help but wonder, *Is she that bored and dissatisfied with her present existence?* When our writing continually neglects newspaper realities, I wonder, *Are we so bored with the present that the sum of our soul nourishment consists of pressing an ear to the dial tone of a heavenly mansion?*

After we grow a backbone, we must acquire new eyes. We can see as God sees, finding the holy and thrilling in the commonplace. This doesn't mean substituting gynecology for romance, inserting gratuitous gun/sword/fist/kick fights, or (no matter how many millions it generates) marrying off Jesus and Mary Magdalene. It means dealing honestly and intelligently with reality. It also means helping others to see.

When Jacob awoke from his dream, he said, "God is in this place, and I wasn't aware of it." Through our clumsy middle-school years, our parents' shattering divorce, our desperate efforts to avoid chronic loneliness, in all our ineffectual rage and sadness, God was in that place and we weren't aware of it. Christians look a little longer. We focus on GODISNOWHERE until we see past "God is nowhere" to notice "God is now here."

God is here. Now. As you read these words. He yearns to open our mind to unseen realities and unimagined potential. Augustine wrote, "God is nearer to us than we are to ourselves." The prophet Elijah prayed, "O LORD, open his eyes that he may see," and his servant-friend discovered the mountainside "full of horses and chariots of fire" (2 Kings, chapter 6). Good writers invite the horses and fiery chariots into our rooms, for every space on the planet is "charged with the grandeur of God." In reality there is no secular and sacred.†

Good writing shows what is hidden, like the arrow in the FedEx logo, so that

---

*What a monstrosity of theological and artistic garbage the Left Behind series has produced. This shameful sham did accomplish one good thing, however. It helped introduce the bumper sticker, "When the rapture comes, can I have your car?"

†Carole King's "You've Got a Friend" is a deeply spiritual song, *Groundhog Day* is a profoundly spiritual film, and the checker at the grocery store is a sacred vessel for God. The song "Let the Bodies Hit the Floor" is also spiritual, but it's the wrong spirit.

we never again miss it. Good writing points out what is absent, like the period in Dr Pepper, so that we stop seeing what isn't there. Good writing admires the ballet of banana slices curling from a knife. Good writing caresses a scalloped coral shell on fine white sand. Good writing cares about every sacred molecule in creation.

Good writers also know that every hero hides warts and every villain plays out noble moments. Life is an intricate interplay that goes beyond false distinctions of "good" and "bad" people. Fiction can be truthful—full of truth—and nonfiction can present a glazed, distorted view of reality.

Good writers approach spiritual themes from fresh perspectives. Anne Lamott, Brennan Manning, Terry Tempest Williams, Dallas Willard, Sue Monk Kidd, Rob Bell, Kathleen Norris, Philip Yancey, Annie Dillard, Tony Campolo, Donald Miller, Shane Clayborne, Walter Wangerin, Brian McLaren, Ravi Zacharias, and dozens more are showing the way.

Good writing turns the obvious on its head. Our family still giggles about an academy graduation motto: "The past is behind us, the future lies before us." Now *there's* a stirring insight! What would be better mottos? "The future isn't what it used to be" or "The present is the past of our future" or "The best way to make our dreams come true is to wake up."*

Good writing moves beyond formulaic constructions. One of my favorite writing descriptions is found in *C. S. Lewis at the Breakfast Table*. It says of Lewis's writing, "There would be no platitudes, no shallow optimism, . . . there would be nothing stereotyped; whatever he said would have a welcome freshness, a new viewpoint, an attractive difference of approach."

Creating a new viewpoint doesn't mean leaving behind all the landmarks of the past. That would be preposterous. We recognize, along with John Brunner: "There are two kinds of fool. One says, 'This is old, and therefore good.' And one says, 'This is new, and therefore better.'" Yet changing old thinking patterns can extricate us from the sucking tentacles of malignant stereotypes.

For example, what would happen if we decided to never again use the terms "conservative" and "liberal"? Seriously, would we have to start actually analyzing ideas on their merits? Would we stop mindlessly and instantly boxing, branding, and rejecting people? Would we find common ground spreading across mythical boundaries? I've decided to cease using the terms "conservative" and "liberal"— they cause too much damage, carry too much baggage. Instead, I'll use the terms "classic" and "innovative."

Classic. Innovative. Yeah, much better.

In Paul's letter to the church at Philippi, he instructed, "Finally, brethren, whatever is true, whatever is honorable, whatever is just, whatever is pure, whatever

---

*Maybe I should stay out of the school motto business, but you get the point.

is lovely, whatever is gracious, if there is any excellence, if there is anything worthy of praise, think about these things." Is this a call to avoid everything else? If it were, we should become sequestered monks, and even that wouldn't do it. Jesus sends us into the same world He inhabited—the lying, dishonorable, unjust, impure, ugly world. Paul urges us here to *find the good* in every situation, in every piece of literature, in every person, and to *think about that good.*

Good writing doesn't explain overmuch. For example, flight attendants are required to explain on each flight exactly how to use a seat belt, but do you really think anybody doesn't know?* We buckle up on our first ride home from the hospital. And if by some infinitesimal chance one didn't know, would that sleight-of-hand demonstration from the front help? Just say, "Buckle your seat belts." We'll figure it out.

For those times when we can't figure out or fix life, we just have to laugh at it. Once, on a flight, I had the window seat, Yolanda was in the middle seat, and a big guy was hogging the armrest from the aisle seat. About an hour into the flight, the guy fell asleep and turned toward Yolanda, breathing detestably bad breath on her, and we started laughing.

"Switch seats with me!" she implored.

I laughed like a madman. "No way!" She laughed harder, the silent, shaking, out-of-control, intemperate laugh I love.

Fine writing also requires economy and tautness of language. A good writer will not write, "I thought to myself" any more than she would write, "I ascended up the stairs." There simply is no other way to think or ascend. Nor will a precise writer succumb to writing "not to mention" and then go right ahead and mention it. A good writer understands that the word *very* acts as a de-emphasizer.[†] And instead of a "near-miss collision," I generally prefer a near-collision, unless I'm colliding with butterscotch pudding. Writers (including biblical ones) often use the term "free gift." To append the word *free* here assumes that some gifts are not free. Despite advertisers' braying claims, all gifts are free, including the incalculable gift of God's grace.

"But, Chris," you suggest, trying your best to be sensitive and tactful, "that's not the way most of the world does it."

"True," I respond, "but [insert your mother's voice here] if most of the world jumped off a cliff, would you do it?"

Finally, a good writer recognizes bad writing by developing what is rightly called a "crap detector."[‡] Adept communicators possess this detector and direct it primarily at

---

*While I'm on the subject of flight attendants, the primary definition for "momentarily" is "for a moment." Thus, "We'll be landing momentarily" is far from comforting.

†See Theodore Cheney's book *Getting the Words Right* for more writing and editing tips. Countless excellent writing resources—from E. B. White on style to Howard Zinsser on simplicity—are available.

‡This is actually a gentler euphemism.

themselves. This capacity unmasks vague sentimentality, punctures bloated posturing, burnishes grubby, indistinct images, and breathes life into syntactically deflated lungs.

My friend George Gibson is fond of jesting with people. He recently sidled up to a former Adventist union president in an Adventist Book Center and said in a stage whisper, "I sure hope you're not reading anything heretical!"

"Oh, no," the man assured him earnestly, "I read only books written by Adventists."

Unfortunately, that's too often the case. If it's produced by Adventists—whether *Adventist Review*, Uncle Arthur, 3ABN, or Pacific Press®—people view uncritically whatever is shown.* The black-or-white corollary, of course, is that everything produced *outside* the Adventist sphere is highly questionable and irredeemably suspect.†

Good eyes in writing necessitates using many people's eyes. Before reaching the first page, you can usually find one difference between an average book and an excellent book. Look at the acknowledgments. In a superb book, the author will thank at least a dozen people for their helpful feedback in the writing process. Whenever I teach writing, I teach this concept: You must use other eyes. Skeptical eyes.

Mark Buchanan points out that our age is less one of skepticism than one of credulity. The literal meaning of the word *skepticism* is "to look into a matter closely, to scrutinize, to study with great care." Based on this definition, modern culture needs more skeptics, not fewer. People say they don't believe in the Bible, but when asked if they have studied it, they explain, "No. As I said, I'm a skeptic." A refusal to investigate thoroughly, to inspect closely and inquire deeply is the opposite of skepticism.

The following is a twenty-one-gun salute to healthy skepticism and precise critical appraisals.

≈

"Your manuscript is both good and original; but the part that is good is not original and the part that is original is not good."—Samuel Johnson

"The running time is 115 minutes; the walking-out time is much earlier." —Kenneth Tynan, on a movie

"The scenery was beautiful but the actors got in front of it."—Alexander Woollcott

"When Mr. Wilbur calls his play *Halfway to Hell* he underestimates the difference."—Brooks Atkinson

"He maintains a gravelly, rasping note, hammering at you until—after two hours without an interval—you rush out thankfully to listen to the traffic."—John Barber on an actor's performance

---

*Ellen White's writings are best used to open discussion, not to close it.

†I wonder what Jesus meant when He said, " 'He who is not against us is for us' "? (Mark, chapter 9).

"Wagner's music is better than it sounds."—Mark Twain

"The TV has gone into the 'coming shortly, but just before that, and stay with us because after that we have . . . right then, let's talk about the next thing we're not going to do' routine, where everything stops before it's started."—Keith Floyd

"Instead of being disarmed, the reader is likely to arm at once."—Eudora Welty

"A novel whose moments of brilliance are obscured by reams of tiresome exposition, hokey plot twists, and astonishingly opaque characters."—Michiko Kakutani

"It may be that this autobiography is set down in sincerity, frankness, and simple effort. It may be, too, that the Statue of Liberty is situated in Lake Ontario."—Dorothy Parker

"Only a mediocre writer is always at his best."—W. Somerset Maugham

"The stately blandness of its manner is quite at odds with the fusty triviality of what it has to offer: It condescends from a great depth."—Kenneth Tynan

"Circumlocution, n. A literary trick whereby the writer who has nothing to say breaks it gently to the reader."—Ambrose Bierce

"This book fills a much-needed gap."—Moses Hadad

"People who like this sort of thing will find this the sort of thing they like." —Abraham Lincoln

"Very nice, though there are dull stretches."—Antoine de Rivarol, on a two-line poem

"Many a best-seller could have been prevented by a good English teacher." —Flannery O'Connor

"The book is full of people behaving in ways that humans never behave." —Dorothy Einon

"This is smoke, wisps with substance, and welcome to entertainment and celebrity in the twenty-first century."—Rick Kushman

"From the moment I picked up your book until I laid it down, I was convulsed with laughter. Some day I intend reading it."—Groucho Marx

"The need for mystery is greater than the need for an answer."—Ken Kesey

When Bible prophets rail against comfortable compliance and unseeing eyes and unfeeling hearts, they have in mind creating a better future. How does the future of Adventist writing look?* (Fortunately, the future lies before us . . .) New spinal columns and new eyes are required if Adventist publishing is to experience a renaissance. In humility, I offer a few suggestions to Adventist writers.

1. Write for a broader audience than Adventism. Avoid religious jargon (godtalk).

---

*I tend to consider "Adventist" an apt adjective as well as a noun, as it refers to a more defined membership and carries less judgmental baggage than does "Christian."

2. Read excellent books. Travel broadly. As H. M. S. Richards Sr. surmised, one who is known as a person of the Book is generally a person of many books.
3. Turn the expected on its head. Appreciate mystery. Explore new angles.
4. Enlist many eyes, especially skeptical ones.
5. Be candidly honest. Always speak the truth in love.

Adventist writing is not doomed to a future of the bland leading the bland. Hope is the melody of our song. In the end, we find realistic hope whenever someone with backbone discerns and points out the truth, says it aloud, mentions the elephant in the room.

Let's sing and start shoveling. ❏

The Son of God, Jesus Christ, whom we preached among you, Silvanus and Timothy and I, was not Yes and No; but in him it is always Yes. For all the promises of God find their Yes in him.—2 Corinthians, chapter 1

Yes, I Don't "Abstain"

They're Seventh-day Adventists. They don't drink, smoke, or eat meat!"
My friend Richard was introducing our group—nine Union College students and me—to the local Amnesty International chapter. He seemed genuinely astounded by our existence, as if we could well qualify for a circus sideshow. ("Step right up! See the amazing Adventists!") We stood awkwardly with half-smiles, wishing we could be known in some other fashion, but soon we were making friends and together planning ways to help people around the world. Later, the students and I laughed about the incident as we discussed what alternative introductions we would choose.

"They love God and they love all people!"
"They give Christianity a good name!"
"They are honest, brave, peaceful, and intelligent!"
"They're the friendliest, most helpful people I know!"
"They proclaim the three angels' messages!"*

For weeks afterward, I kept returning to Richard's words, thinking about what I yearned to share with him and other friends for whom Adventism is mystifying. I don't want to communicate that I merely *avoid* unhealthy or "naughty" things. That's way too tame. I hold strong sociopolitical, proactive reasons for my lifestyle choices.

---

*All right, this one didn't come up.

"I don't abstain from drinking alcohol—I *boycott* it." Alcohol is the number one drug problem in the world. In the United States, alcohol is a factor in about half of all human tragedies. One-half of all homicides, one-third of all suicides, one-half of all rapes, 72 percent of all assaults (including spousal abuse), 70 percent of all robberies, and one-half of all child-abuse cases are alcohol-related.* Really, I don't even care if the new wine of the New Testament is fermented or not. *Why would I support something that today is implicated in this much carnage and misery?*

"I don't abstain from smoking tobacco—I *boycott* it." Smoking is slow suicide. Beyond that, no enterprise is more corrupt and deadly than transnational tobacco. The tobacco industry's violation of public health, human rights, and the environment is mind-boggling and soul-sucking.† Compared to big tobacco, big oil is merely a baby monster.

Tobacco currently kills more people worldwide than HIV/AIDS, alcohol, drug abuse, fires, murders, suicides, drowning accidents, and car crashes *combined*—about four million a year.‡ If twenty-seven airplanes, each filled with four hundred passengers, crashed every day of every month, would it make headlines? Yet the U.S. government recently gave tobacco farmers a bailout of ten billion dollars. I'm reminded of Joseph Stalin, who stated, "A single death is a tragedy; a million deaths is a statistic."

"I don't abstain from eating meat—I *boycott* it." Fewer than half of Adventists are vegetarian, but I became a vegetarian before I became an Adventist. I did so for four reasons listed briefly here.

- Curbing starvation. We can feed ten times as many people on a vegetarian diet as we can on an omnivorous diet.§ This matter—feeding starving people—matters greatly to me.
- Living healthfully. It's true, I have more energy now than when I was playing ball and eating meat. As scientific research documents, vegetarians are also less susceptible to dozens of diseases. This doesn't of itself make me more "spiritual"; Adolf Hitler was a vegetarian. It does help me to be more productive.
- Helping the environment. As a lover of God's creation, I do my balanced best to be a responsible caretaker. (Creation care is a relatively new evan-

---

*From *Facts About Alcohol; Alcohol and Health: Sixth Special Report to the U.S. Congress;* and *Alcohol Health and Research World.*

†See http://www.bigtobaccosucks.org.

‡The World Bank predicts that by 2030, the toll will more than double to ten million deaths per year, with most of the increase in people from developing countries.

§No human being is a carnivore. Eating bread or ketchup or fries or tortillas or ice cream in addition to meat makes one an omnivore.

gelical trend.) According to ecological experts, becoming a vegetarian is the best thing one can do to heal the environment. Imagine that.

• Treating animals with respect. I don't support all of PETA's tactics and aims, but I do believe that on the new earth we won't be eating our sentient "pets." Jesus certainly ate fish, but the fish weren't caged, shot up with chemicals, and killed without ever seeing the sky, as is the case with some veal and poultry.

I don't abstain. I boycott. I boycott because I'm pro-life, and pro-life is pro-health, pro-peace, and pro-planet.

Jesus is about saying yes. Yes to respect for life. Yes to justly living life to the fullest. Yes to courageous love. Yes to swimming against the current. Whenever we can be known for what we *do* in a life-enhancing way instead of what we *don't* do, it seems to me that yields a better introduction and the best conclusion. ❏

"Our lives begin to end the day we become silent about things that matter."
—Martin Luther King Jr.

If there is no place for civil disobedience, then the government has been made autonomous, and as such, it has been put in place of the living God.—Francis Schaeffer

There can be no more conclusive evidence that we possess the spirit of Satan than the disposition to hurt and destroy those who do not appreciate our work, or who act contrary to our ideas.
—Ellen White*

Loyal Dissent

She is a hero now, renowned as the mother of the civil rights movement. In her day, she was vilified and threatened.

With one act of refusing to give up her seat for a white man and move to the back of the bus, Rosa Parks grew into a civil rights icon. But she wasn't the first black woman in the South to be jailed for refusing to move,[†] nor was hers a hasty, abrupt decision. Prior to her protest, she had been active for twelve years in the

---

*From *The Desire of Ages*, p. 487.

[†]A Seventh-day Adventist woman, Irene Morgan, did the same thing eleven years earlier in rural Virginia (access "The Freedom Fighter a Nation Almost Forgot" in the *Adventist Review* online edition, written by Carol Morello of the *Washington Post*). Morgan's little-known defiant act of civil disobedience led to "a landmark 1946 decision striking down Jim Crow segregation in interstate transportation."

local NAACP* chapter, serving as its secretary. She had attended civil rights training workshops where Septima Clark, a longtime activist, mentored her. She had diligently studied effective nonviolent means in an effort to eliminate the noxious blight of discrimination. Far from acting alone, she was part of a civil rights *community* in Montgomery, Alabama.

When some suggested that she hadn't wanted to move because she was tired after a long day of work, Rosa Parks responded, "The only tired I was, was tired of giving in." Millions followed her example as Dr. Martin Luther King Jr. led a nationwide movement to end segregation. Remembered and loved for her courage and humility, Rosa Parks died October 25, 2005, amid a torrent of tributes.

Less than five months later, another giant fell. Desmond Doss, the first conscientious objector to receive the Congressional Medal of Honor (for his service during World War II), died March 23, 2006. His story is legendary with Seventh-day Adventists and advocates of peace. Doss always referred to himself as a "conscientious supporter," maintaining that his patriotism and devotion to duty were never questionable in his mind. He would heal the wounded, but no one could make him kill.

Others, however, viewed him as a coward. When Doss knelt to pray beside his bunk in his barracks, soldiers taunted him and threw boots at him, scorning his simple faith. Their disdain turned to outrage when he refused to train or work on the Sabbath. One soldier promised to act when combat began. "I'll kill you myself," he said.

In 1945, Doss rescued soldiers repeatedly on the islands of Guam and Leyte, displaying amazing courage and receiving the Silver Star. On the next island, Okinawa, his company assaulted a heavily fortified, four-hundred-foot cliff, sustaining heavy losses. On May 5, while enemy fire peppered the area around him for five hours, Doss lowered about seventy-five injured soldiers down an escarpment. Throughout that time, he held only one thought: *Lord, help me get one more. Just one more!*

For his actions, Doss received the Medal of Honor—the United States military's highest award for bravery. Not all heroes carry guns.[†]

May 5, 1945, was a Saturday—the Sabbath.

Loyal dissent takes many forms. If we remain loyal to our principles, to love and justice and redemption, we eventually will encounter resistance. Martin Luther King Jr. certainly knew that. He was a master in pinpointing problems and offering a perceptive countercurrent perspective.

---

*National Association for the Advancement of Colored People.

[†]More print information is available on Desmond Doss via book or Web. Or view the film *The Conscientious Objector.*

On nonviolence:

- Nonviolent resistance is not a method for cowards; it does resist. If one uses this method because he is afraid or merely because he lacks the instrument of violence, he is not truly nonviolent.
- Nonviolence is a powerful and just weapon, which cuts without wounding and ennobles the man who wields it. It is a sword that heals.
- Nonviolence means avoiding not only external physical violence but also internal violence of spirit. You not only refuse to shoot a man, but you refuse to hate him.

On "inconvenient" justice:

- The Negro's great stumbling block in the drive toward freedom is not the White Citizen's Councilor or the Ku Klux Klanner but the white moderate who is more devoted to order than to justice.
- Never forget that everything Hitler did in Germany was legal.
- The time is always right to do what is right.

On misguided aims:

- A nation that continues year after year to spend more money on military defense than on programs of social uplift is approaching spiritual doom.
- Our scientific power has outrun our spiritual power. We have guided missiles and misguided men.
- The chain reaction of evil—hate begetting hate, wars producing more wars—must be broken, or else we shall be plunged into the dark abyss of annihilation.

Like his Master, Dr. King preached that violence breeds violence. Revelation, chapter 13, announces, "If anyone slays with the sword, with the sword must he be slain. Here is a call for the endurance and faith of the saints."

Somehow, though, that enduring faith gets muted and transmuted. Rod Parsley, pastor of the World Harvest Church in Ohio, issues actual swords to those who join his Center for Moral Clarity, and he urges his followers to "lock and load" for a "Holy Ghost invasion." This sort of messianic militarism confuses onlookers about the true nature of the Prince of Peace, giving credence to factions who see violence as the best option for resolving conflict.

U.S. President (and General) Dwight D. Eisenhower lamented, "Every gun that is made, every warship launched, every rocket fired, signifies, in the final sense, a theft from those who hunger and are not fed, those who are cold and are not clothed. The world in arms is not spending money alone. It is spending the sweat of its laborers, the genius of its scientists, the hopes of its children."

I'm not so naïve to think that the nonviolent approach is without cost. After all, John the Baptist ended up with his head on a platter. The world has more than enough sociopaths,* and courting their good side can be like trying to make a pet of a shark. Feed it, caress it, care for it, call it cutesy names such as "Finny." It doesn't matter. The first time you bleed in the water, you're what's for dinner.

"Nonviolence is a flop," admits Joan Baez. "The only bigger flop is violence." That's why Revelation calls for endurance and faith. Passivism is not passivity. Proactive involvement helps us conquer our fears.

Paradoxically, people both hate and crave being afraid. Witness the popularity of horror movies and adrenaline-rush activities such as skiing, car racing, and weather chasing. To some degree, we're afraid of not being afraid.

Media outlets and politicians can manipulate this loathe/like fear relationship. They may use a perpetual "war on terror" to stimulate fear and press a nervous electorate's buttons. In the United States, the odds of being killed by a terrorist are *far* less than those of being killed in an automobile collision. Which prospect frightens the average citizen more?

As C. S. Lewis points out, "The demon inherent in every [political] party is at all times ready enough to disguise himself as the Holy Ghost." Absolute commitment to any political party irrespective of issues and candidates is, it seems to me, imprudent.† However, this does not mean that we should stay clear of all politics. We shouldn't allow fear of corruption to nix our involvement in politics any more than we should allow fear of drowning to prevent us from learning to swim. Politics is like electricity—of itself, it is neither good nor bad. It is raw power. What effect it has depends on how we use it or how it uses us.‡

Whether we use the crawl, backstroke, breaststroke, butterfly, sidestroke, or dog paddle, we pledge our allegiance by actively swimming with or against the current groupthink.

Though the United States didn't officially outlaw slavery for more than 180 years, early Adventist Church officials spoke against it from pulpits and in the press. Listen to Ellen White: "When the laws of men conflict with the word and law of God, we are to obey the latter, whatever the consequences may be. The law of our land requir-

---

*In her book *The Sociopath Next Door*, Martha Stout maintains that perhaps one in every twenty-five people has no conscience and can do anything without feeling guilty.

†I'm a registered Independent.

‡As Adlai Stevenson mused, "Your public servants serve you right."

ing us to deliver a slave to his master, we are not to obey; and we must abide the consequences of violating this law. The slave is not the property of any man."

Curiously, though Adventists claim the Bible as "the only rule of faith and practice," the Bible is silent on the subject of abolishing slavery. Not a word. Yet today, one would be hard-pressed to find any Christian who believes that slavery is an acceptable institution. Though the Bible doesn't condemn it and may even be interpreted as condoning it in places, the inherent *wrongness* of slavery is self-evident.

What will future believers look back and determine to be *today's* slavery issue for Adventists? Although not as egregious as slavery, it could be the ordination of women. I may be playing Captain Obvious by stating that this is a divisive subject; it has fomented extensive debate and official General Conference votes. The world church has spoken. Yet, in the scope of history, what are we saying about justice?

Ellen White was a fully ordained minister. I've seen a copy of the official credentials, dated December 27, 1887, in Battle Creek, Michigan, signed by George Butler, president of the General Conference, and Uriah Smith, secretary. The ordination precedent was set long ago. Are we bent on denying "fullness" to half our members—similar to denying full citizenship? (I'm just asking here.) Could our church be saying in essence, "Of course, you, as a female, are a full member of this church. However, we won't allow you certain privileges"? Can we understand why some members might feel slighted?

Years ago, when Sears and Roebuck (with employees in the hundreds of thousands) was struggling for solvency, outside consultants spent many months to come up with one piece of advice for turning the company around: *Take care of your own people. Listen to them, reward them, respect them.* This, the consultants declared, will translate to loyalty and effective, knowledgeable changes. Guess what? It worked! Sears followed their suggestion, and the company was transformed.

What if the Seventh-day Adventist Church followed that model? *First, take care of your own people.* When the good shepherd left the ninety-nine to go after the one, do you think he left the ninety-nine to the wolves? No, before leaving on his evangelistic mission, he secured them in a safe place. A healthy place. That approach made him a good shepherd.

Recently, an exasperated female student said to me, "Why doesn't the church give women the same privileges as men? I would much rather go to a woman pastor with my problems." Her comment followed an interpersonal communication class in which we discussed the fact that females typically are better communicators than males. Males generally communicate to establish hierarchy; females generally communicate to establish connections.* Which type of communication from a pastor leads to healthier, more caring relationships in the church?

---

*See Deborah Tannen's books for researched evidence of this; in particular, *You Just Don't Understand.*

Some administrators caution, "Let's wait and see what happens with this." However, the very nature of waiting can determine the outcome. As the ban continues, women are not as willing to enter pastoral ministry—who will hire them upon graduation? Thus, we continue to find fewer women pastoral candidates and role models. "Waiting" creates a self-perpetuating condition.

This approach reminds me of a conversation between two of my friends. Married to one another, they already enjoyed two sons and fulfilling careers, but the husband wanted another child.

"No way," the wife said. "Two is plenty. You need to get a vasectomy."

"How about this?" he countered. "Let's try for a baby for one week and *then* I'll get a vasectomy. That way we'll find out if God really wants us to have another child."

"I've got a better idea," his wife offered. "To *really* know God's will for us, get the vasectomy first. Then we'll try for a week."

How can we know God's will on women's ordination? Future generations will judge us on our loyalty to God's principles. The inherent justice of the issue appears self-evident.

≈

A strange wind blows through our world. The whelming current tugs at us. If we listen closely, we catch whispers of George Orwell's *1984* Ministry of Truth: "War is peace." "Freedom is slavery." "Ignorance is strength."

Brian McLaren describes the kingdom of God as "a revolutionary, countercultural movement—proclaiming a ceaseless rebellion against the tyrannical trinity of money, sex, and power." Instead, we see evangelical Christianity, lured especially by power, sliding into the maw of greed and deception. Lobbyists line the walls and wallets of legislatures and large churches. Randall Balmer observes, "Corporate interests are treated with the kind of reverence and deference once reserved for the deity."

Have we lost our capacity for independent cultural critique? Swimming against the current isn't easy. The poet e. e. cummings alleged, "To be nobody-but-yourself—in a world which is doing its best, night and day, to make you everybody else—means to fight the hardest battle which any human being can fight; and never stop fighting."

It is possible to break through creatively, to dissent, to be one's own person. My son Geoff described to me a U2 concert he attended. The U2 lead singer, Bono, is an intrepid and innovative Christian who plays in "secular" venues. At the conclusion of the concert, with all the lights turned down, Bono shone a spotlight at everyone in the crowd, then he set the light on a stand pointing straight up to the sky, to God, and the band walked off the stage. "It was cool," said Geoff.

Adventists have long advocated separation of religion and government, God and Caesar. More and more, though, it seems that the two may be growing together in some minds. Currently, in the United States, patriotism is often equated with God's desires. I've heard Adventists shift seamlessly from "God bless our armed forces" to appeals for *Liberty* magazine and separation of church and state.* Oddly, the historic Adventist stance that the beast from the earth in Revelation, chapter 13, represents the United States of America is being heard less often the closer we get to "the end of time."

In his book *God's Politics: Why the Right Gets It Wrong and the Left Doesn't Get It,* Jim Wallis tells what a just and consistent pro-life position entails. Explaining the position in *Christianity Today,* he declared, "Christians can't say, 'All we care about is someone's stance on abortion. I don't care what they do to the economy, to the poor, I don't care what wars they fight, I don't care what they do on human rights.' It's almost like we care about children until they're born and then after that, they're on their own. We're cutting health care, cutting childcare for moms moving out of welfare. No, you can't just care about a child until they're born."

The brand of semantic gymnastics he was opposing, like a fiddler dancing from string to string, reminds me of a joke. It was the new clerk's first day on the job in the fresh produce section of a supermarket. A woman came up to him and said she wanted to buy half a head of lettuce. The boy tried to dissuade her, but she persisted. Eventually, he said, "I'll have to go back and talk with the manager."

He walked to the rear of the store to talk to the manager, not noticing that the woman was following him. When he reached the back of the store, he said to the manager, "There's some stupid old hag out there who wants to buy half a head of lettuce . . ."

When a look of horror appeared on the manager's face, the clerk turned around, saw the woman, and added, ". . . and this nice lady wants to buy the other half. Will it be all right?"

Relieved, the manager said, "That would be fine."

Later in the day, the manager complimented the boy on his quick thinking and asked, "Where are you from, son?"

The boy said, "I'm from Toronto, Canada—the home of beautiful hockey players and ugly women."

The manager replied, "My wife is from Toronto," to which the boy said, "Oh? What team did she play for?"

In an official church statement titled "A Seventh-day Adventist Call for Peace,"[†]

---

*Surely we desire God to bless everyone on earth, so the requested blessing is defensible. My point is the relative ease with which we invoke God to back "our side" exclusively. (See "The War Prayer" by Mark Twain.) I pray unabashedly for peace.

[†]Dated January 10, 2006.

the Adventist Church proclaimed, "While it is inevitable that nations and people will try to defend themselves by responding in a military way to violence and terror—which sometimes results in short-term success—lasting answers to deep problems of division in society cannot be achieved by using violent means. . . . From both a Christian and practical perspective, any lasting peace involves at least four ingredients: dialogue, justice, forgiveness, and reconciliation."

This statement makes me proud of my church. Again.

We are not automatically traitors when we disagree with our church or country. Indeed, we can be the most loyal members and citizens when we do so.* Lending our support through our voice, time, and money, we don't ever give up, though we may change approaches and sometimes our minds. We support, strive, and dissent—all for redeeming love.

Jesus showed us examples of loyal dissent. Never a sell-out, He stood strong and true always. Moreover, He was magnificent in modeling nonviolent dialogue, justice, forgiveness, and reconciliation.

Perhaps His most astonishing lesson on loyalty revolved around the destitute widow and her meager yet enormous offering. She gave a huge percentage of her income to one of the most corrupt organizations in history, the one that fostered the killing of the Son of God—and Jesus praised her?

Maybe loyalty isn't so easy to figure out.   ❏

The Lord is not slow about his promise as some count slowness, but is forbearing toward you, not wishing that any should perish, but that all should reach repentance.
—2 Peter, chapter 3

Why I Don't Pray for Jesus to Come "Soon"

About a year after my Christian conversion, I heard a gifted singer perform a soulful rendition of Andre Crouch's "Soon and Very Soon." After the service, I thanked her for her inspiring offering and commented off-handedly, "He can't come soon enough."

She looked at me oddly. "I still have loved ones who aren't ready," she said.

Yes, I am aware of Jesus' promise, "Behold, I come quickly." I am aware that three times in the final Bible chapter, God trumpets, "I am coming soon." I'm also

---

*Were Rosa Parks and Desmond Doss loyal people?

aware that *quickly* and *soon* cry out for definition, because those words were written more than nineteen hundred years ago.

When applied to Christ's second coming, *quickly, soon* and *near* obviously mean something other than literal time. If *soon* means one hundred or nine hundred or fifteen hundred years—frankly, when more than one hundred years passes, the word *soon* loses its significance for me.

Briefly, how do we account for apparent time disparities? Common wisdom says, "How long a minute is depends on which side of the bathroom door you're on." Does a similar relativity hold true for heaven's door?

I believe *soon* is the beat after my next heartbeat. Christians ought always to connect *soon* with *only-a-beat-away.* Everyone understands the proximity and suddenness of death. Scan today's newspaper, and you'll discover at least twenty people who were surprised by death's knocking. When a person dies, Christ comes a blink—a "twinkling of an eye"—later. Soon enough.

The nearness, in terms of days and years, of Christ's second coming does mean something to me, much as a sign that reads "FALLING ROCK, DETOUR AHEAD" tends to focus my attention. But "soon-saying" in terms of any measurable time or dates carries at least three dangers.

1. We place listeners in danger of hearing untimely cries of "wolf" too often, and we are left sheepishly discredited.
2. A runner who sprints for a mistaken finish line will have nothing left for the actual ending that looms 400 meters ahead.
3. We are in danger of spiritual immaturity. The Brazilian psychiatrist Keppe describes our basic human disorder as "the disease of theomania—the desire to be God, . . . the desire to be the playwright instead of the actor in the drama." Let God be God, and leave the timing of soon-saying to soothsayers.

Our imploring Christ to come *now* smacks of thumb-sucking selfishness, especially when so many "aren't ready," as the singer rightly put it. Spiritual maturity can reveal itself most clearly in our attitude toward prayer—not in getting what we want but in wanting what we get.

Do we imagine that God isn't suffering a trillion times more than we? Every flyspecked starvation, every screaming torture and rape, every suicidal pain, every unbelievably bleak loneliness hurts a child of His. Every one. Every *second.* What arrogance we fashion when we beg Jesus to come now because of our situation.

Much as I long for Christ—my breath, my blood, my everything—to come "soon" so that I might see His eyes, His hands, that I might hear from His warm lips His words for me, that I might watch His spreading smile, that I might feel His sinewy arms squeeze me as I sob shuddering tears of relief and joy and gratitude, that I might smell and taste an atmosphere uncorrupted and deathless, I trust His timing.

Because I want others, particularly my close loved ones, to see and hear and feel and smell and taste God for themselves, Jesus can take His good time. That's part of the good news. He knows what time is best.

Come, Lord Jesus, when You're ready.   ❑

When you find your work hard, when you complain of difficulties and trials, when you say that you have no strength to withstand temptation, that you cannot overcome impatience and that the Christian life is uphill work, be sure that you are not bearing the yoke of Christ; you are bearing the yoke of another master.—Ellen White

No man is happy unless he believes he is.—Publilius Syrus

Fred Flintstone and Joy

When I was at our friends Mark* and Linda's house, they handed me a magazine that had been mailed to them unsolicited.

"Have you seen this?" Linda asked.

I hadn't, though I had previously read many anti-Adventist sites and writings. Perhaps you have seen them, too. The ardent reclaiming ministries, the accusations of suffocating legalism, the expunging testimonials, the siren calls to "Come out of her, my people."

"Mind if I read it?" I said.

"Take it, please," she replied.

So I read the May–June 2005 issue of *Proclamation!* published by Life Assurance Ministries, Inc. The kicker under the logo read, "For Former Adventists, Inquiring Adventists, Sabbatarians, Concerned Evangelicals." Maybe I qualified on the last three—I have yet to meet an unconcerned evangelical.

I tried to weigh justly the concerns expressed in the magazine. At times I agreed; other times, the gaps in logic left me discombobulated, my mind spinning like Fred Flintstone's legs. What follows is not any "official" response, just a Christian trying to make sense of things.

The allegations are legion, so I'll try to boil them down. Two of them can be dispatched quickly. These are two of three charges I found I agree with wholeheartedly. In other words, brothers and sisters, they have a point here.

---

*I have many Mark friends—Mark R., Mark S., and Mark F.—which I find remarkable.

1. Adventism is imperfect. Seventh-day Adventism is an imperfect belief system with an imperfect governing structure populated by imperfect people. Yep, yep, and yep. Everything human is imperfect, and we qualify on both counts.

Adventists can make the mountains ring or the angels cry. We are capable of enchanting good and astounding bad. Our fingers itch and our thoughts whistle and bubble while we break cookie jars and hearts—and Jesus loves us, anyway.

In addition, we believe in present truth, which suggests that truth and knowledge are progressive—a journey, not a destination—so we are at once and ever departing and arriving.

2. People can find freedom and security and peace outside Adventism. I am genuinely happy for those people. Heaven will likely be filled with more than 144,000 people who were never Seventh-day Adventists—most will have never heard of Adventists. Some of them will not have heard of Jesus.

3. Christians are no longer "under the law." The Ten Commandments do not save anyone. Jesus alone saves. His grace redeems us and is our only solid reason for total trust. (You might be tempted to skip over the Bible texts, but take a close look at them.)

"Now we are discharged from the law, dead to that which held us captive, so that we serve not under the old written code but in the new life of the Spirit" (Romans, chapter 7).* "No man is justified before God by the law" (Galatians, chapter 3). Christians are no longer under the curse of the law; the law can neither save nor enslave us. Absolutely. It's right there, permeating Romans and Galatians.

"There is therefore now no condemnation for those who are in Christ Jesus. For the law of the Spirit of life in Christ Jesus has set me free from the law of sin and death"† (Romans, chapter 8). "If you are led by the Spirit you are not under the law" (Galatians, chapter 5). We are not under the law's condemnation if we are led by the indwelling Holy Spirit.

As you may be aware, on this point Adventists have sometimes not been as forthright and focused as we ought to be. We have taught, for instance, that our character determines our destiny. We should have taught that our destiny determines our character. We bear fruit because we are saved, not in order to be saved. This resembles the difference you feel when you are served by a salaried salesperson who simply wants to help as contrasted with a salesperson who is working "on commission."

Moreover, keeping the Sabbath should never be viewed as a kind of Pathfinder merit badge. "By grace you have been saved through faith; and this is not your own doing, it is the gift of God—not because of works, lest any man should boast" (Ephesians, chapter 2). Sabbath observance is no cause for boasting.

---

*In the Bible, "the law" at times refers to more than the Ten Commandments.
†Hooray! Ma man! Splendid! (Or however you express great joy.)

The Bible and Adventist fundamental beliefs are eminently clear and congruent on this matter. We are saved only by grace through faith in Jesus.

In my reading, I also ran across three charges with which I disagree. Because it's best to work with definite, existing content (rather than making up counterpoints), I'll use quotes from the magazine. I'm aware that whenever we attempt this type of polemical approach, we risk becoming too caustic.

1. *The new covenant declares that the Ten Commandments (in particular, the Sabbath) are no longer applicable to true Christians.* What a load of twaddle.* Or as the apostle Paul says in some versions, "God forbid!"

"What then shall we say? That the law is sin? By no means! Yet, if it had not been for the law, I should not have known sin" (Romans, chapter 7). *If the law no longer applies, then who needs grace?* "So the law is holy, and the commandment is holy and just and good" (Romans, chapter 7).

Those eleven commandments† are all about love—how to love God and love people. In that respect, we do desire to be "under" them and to "continue" with them, just as we desire to be under and to continue with love. When we're following God's Spirit, living by the commandments liberates us. In the end, they aren't restrictions God thought up to oppress us—they are how love works on the third rock from the sun. They are "holy and just and good." God gave these guidelines for our benefit—emotional/mental/social/spiritual laws every bit as dependable for humans as God's physical laws. We can argue and chafe against them as we can against the law of gravity, but in the end, reality wins. We don't break the commandments as much as we break ourselves upon them.

"What then? Are we to sin because we are not under the law but under grace? By no means!" (Romans, chapter 6). We are not *saved* because we avoid lying, killing, coveting, and taking God's name in vain. These behaviors are simply how godly people act. Candidly, I don't care if they're the first or second or seventy-seventh covenant—the commandments help me love better.

I found that the crux of the magazine's complaints is really legalism—specifically, "observing the Sabbath." Writers go to tremendous lengths, arguing with mind-bending linguistic gymnastics, to prove that the Sabbath is not applicable, is not credible, is not salutary today. One writer confides, "Although we could clearly state that we knew we were secure in our salvation apart from the Sabbath, there lurked a fear behind our bold assertions: What if Adventists were right? What if

---

*H'mm. My Caustic Sensitivity Indicator is beeping.

†Including Jesus' words in John, chapter 13: "A new commandment I give to you, that you love one another; even as I have loved you, that you also love one another. By this all men will know that you are my disciples, if you have love for one another."

Sabbath really was significant? . . . We had to throw all of ourselves—even our fears—on His mercy. We had to give up our tradition of Sabbath observance."*

Using a similar rationale, I think I could give up my "fears" about breaking other commandments. I know they aren't part of my salvation, so I could throw all of myself on God's mercy and go on a "liberating" spree of . . . whatever.† Then a new legalism—the old antinomianism—rears its head: We are sanctified by what we can do. But, funny thing, when the apostle Paul states that we are "justified by faith apart from the works of law," he follows up with, "Do we then overthrow the law by this faith? By no means! On the contrary, we uphold the law" (Romans, chapter 3).

So, here's the question: Is the Sabbath significant today? Critics claim nine of the Ten Commandments are supported in the New Testament, but not the Sabbath. So forget Jesus' counsel to "pray that your flight may not be in winter or on the Sabbath" (forty years after His death, at Jerusalem's fall). Don't think about the unholy mess that the apostle Paul would have stirred up had he actually told believers not to observe the Sabbath. Ignore the fact that if he *did* say that, apparently nobody got it, for Christians faithfully kept the Sabbath for more than a century after Christ's resurrection.‡ Avoid considering the Sabbath's existence *before* the other nine were given to Moses (see Exodus 16). Perhaps those can all be explained away. Let's talk in practical terms.

Do you in your wildest dreams imagine we need the Sabbath less today than did the children of Israel? Were their lives more frenetic and materialistic than ours? Did they experience more ambivalence and diversion than we do? Was God's existence and creative genius more in doubt? Or is this a time in earth's history when we *most* require the calm, uplifting, clear focus the Sabbath provides?§

Sabbath is an antidote to legalism. In a culture that weighs our worth by how much and what we produce, quantity and quality, on this day God says, "Produce nothing. Now, hear this: I love you just as much today as on any workday. You are worth the world to Me just as you are because of who you are. My child, take a break from your striving."

Musician and Bible student Michael Card now keeps the seventh-day Sabbath. He reflects, "We started out of this desire for simplicity and this appreciation for rest. But I think, really, the thing that pushed me over the edge was a Seventh-day

---

*Page 2.

†One writer recognized the potential here: "When we look at the Biblical facts that indicate the Ten Commandments did not exist before Moses and are not to continue after the Cross, we are not opening up the floodgates to anarchy or wickedness" (page 1). Somehow I don't find this comforting.

‡As detailed in Samuele Bacchiocchi's *From Sabbath to Sunday.*

§For more benefits of the Sabbath, see the chapter "I Got No Time for God" in *Searching for a God to Love.*

Adventist brother who said, 'God didn't change any of the other commandments, so He hasn't changed that one.' The rationale behind that argument, I thought, was pretty airtight."

Rob Bell, in *Velvet Elvis,* rhapsodizes about Sabbath:*

> Sabbath is taking a day a week to remind myself that I did not make the world and that it will continue to exist without my efforts.
>
> Sabbath is a day when my work is done, even when it isn't.
>
> Sabbath is a day when my job is to enjoy. Period.
>
> Sabbath is a day when I am fully available to myself and to those I love most.
>
> Sabbath is a day when I remember that when God made the world, he saw that it was good.
>
> Sabbath is a day when I produce nothing.
>
> Sabbath is a day when I remind myself that I am not a machine.
>
> Sabbath is a day when at the end I say, "I didn't do anything today," and I don't add, "And I feel so guilty."
>
> Sabbath is a day when my phone is turned off, I don't check my e-mail, and you can't get ahold of me.
>
> Jesus wants to heal our souls, wants to give us the shalom of God. And so we have to stop. We have to slow down. We have to sit still and stare out the window and let the engine come to an idle. We have to listen to what our inner voice is saying.

So when I read that we should "give up the Sabbath for Jesus," I think, *What was that?* That's like giving up ice cream for Ben and Jerry—except that Ben and Jerry didn't actually invent ice cream.

"I would not lower the righteousness of Christ to that of 'living the Ten Commandments,' " contends one writer. "I believe His life exemplifies a much higher level."[†] Suppose we applied the same reasoning to a different realm. "I would not lower myself to rely on the twenty-six letters of the English alphabet to communicate. I believe communication occurs on a much higher level than mere letters. Mor ov r, in th futur , I will find fr dom by l aving out c rtain l tt rs, b caus I'm fr !"

Naturally, Christ *is* more than the ten or eleven or fifty commandments He gives. But like letters of the alphabet, these basic commandments enable us to put love into practice and to complete the picture. Just as we wouldn't set up false distinctions between the alphabet and language, we shouldn't propose false distinc-

---

*On page 117.

[†]Page 1.

tions between Jesus and His commandments. That simply doesn't make sense.

2. We can celebrate Sabbath rest every day of the week. Sure, and we could celebrate Thanksgiving, Christmas, and the Resurrection every day of the year. Why celebrate these only on limited "special" days?* Are we not thankful every day for what God provides? Are we not daily grateful for the Incarnation? Do we not appreciate day-by-day our hope in the risen Christ? Hey, why bother with silly commemorations?

Because celebrating at certain times helps those blessings grow in our esteem. God knows that. That's why God set up festivals and feasts and jubilees.

God also knows we need a respite and reminder every week; a marvelously meaningful sanctuary in time. This doesn't mean we don't experience Jesus every day of the week. In fact, the Sabbath is meant to prepare us for that daily experience.

One writer confesses, "I reasoned that the pastor had to know about the Sabbath, but he was tricking his congregation into believing it was okay to worship on Sunday!"† I happen to think it's fine to worship on Sunday—and Monday and Tuesday and Wednesday and Thursday. . . . Celebrate the risen Christ all day every day. The choice isn't between worshipping on Sunday or not.

Other examples of false dilemmas abound.

"Jesus, not a day, is our true Sabbath rest."‡ Most assuredly, Jesus is. We rest in Him every moment of every day. We also rest in His guidelines for living life justly, mercifully, and humbly. Those guidelines include speaking the truth, feeding the hungry, and enjoying Sabbath. And what is meant here by "true"? Legitimate? Real? Reliable? Honorable? Is the Sabbath rest any of these? I would say yes. The fact that Jesus is true doesn't make Sabbath false.

Another writer asserts, "What matters is not observing laws but becoming new creations."§ This is an either/or fallacy—limiting a choice to two exclusive options when other options exist. Consider these parallel constructions: *What matters is not eating food but growing up. What matters is not breathing but living godly lives. What matters is not walking or riding a bus or a bicycle or driving a car but traveling somewhere.* Where do we meet reality? At some point, even Fred Flintstone's rotating legs have to connect with solid ground.

Glittering generalities such as "becoming new creations" aren't worth the glitter they are sprinkled with until the *how* is addressed. I thought, *After we become born again—a new creation filled with God's Spirit, how shall we then live? Could "observing spiritual disciplines" be one approach?*

---

*Lent actually does extend recognition of the Resurrection to forty days. And I suppose one could say retailers extend recognition of the Incarnation when, with somewhat less than noble motives, they begin Christmas advertising around August.

†Page 4.

‡Page 2.

§Page 2.

3. *Every Adventist must leave Adventism to find freedom, security, peace, and joy in Jesus.* This is a stunningly narrow stance. Many Adventists are authentic, born-again Christians who live by the Spirit.

In reality, people who leave a legalistic, cultic system don't leave Adventism—they leave its twisted, sick cousin. Thousands of former Adventists have returned to the fold when they discovered the beautiful Jesus behind the beliefs. Using the straw-man fallacy, critics shift the argument and erect a "straw" position that is easily torn down. Distortions may emerge through exaggeration, abbreviation, or obfuscation, by suggesting implausible scenarios or characterizing Sabbath merely as a minefield of restrictions.

"I didn't know how I could get as excited about being an Adventist as Christina was about Jesus," one writer exclaims, "but I wanted to be open-minded."*

Okay, we can play that word game, but this time let's insert the name of the author's new church. "I don't know how I could get as excited about being a Trinity Evangelical Free Church member as I am about Jesus, but I want to be open-minded." Who on earth thinks like that? Again, we are provided with a false, misleading set of choices: church membership or Jesus? It is possible to seek both.

Here are other first-person testimonials from the magazine, with my thoughts.

"I was just about to turn 21—when God in His grace plucked me out of Adventism." *Sincerely glad you're doing well. Sincerely sad your experience with Adventists was so ungracious, because Adventism is really all about grace.*

"By the time I was in academy I knew I would never be 'good enough' to make it to heaven."[†] *While you may have been taught something else in academy, you don't have to be "good enough." You will never be good enough. Only Jesus is good enough.*

"I neither understood nor cared about the doctrines."[‡] *Too bad. Knowing what we believe can prove extremely helpful.*

"Our desire is that you risk releasing all that you have known and cherished and take hold of Jesus."[§] *Well, um, what if Jesus and His teachings* are *all I have "known and cherished"?*

At last, I put the magazine away. Frankly, I can't imagine devoting my life to being against an organization, whether it's anti-Presbyterian or anti-Amway or anti–North Korea. Focusing on negatives leaves a bitter taste. My sense is that the "anti-Adventist" people don't see it this way. They view themselves as focusing on the good news of the gospel.**

---

*Page 4.

[†]Page 3.

[‡]Page 3.

[§]Page 2.

**What I don't get is if they are so *over* Adventism, why do they spend so much of their time talking about it?

Anyway, somehow these former Adventists missed the freedom, missed the assurance, missed the joy. It's true that Adventists are partly to blame. Humbly walking with God, we ought to be free, secure, and joyful. Too often we are not. Too often we have distorted the picture of God into an image unrecognizable. Too often we have been distant, dark, unimaginative, and controlling. Too often we have turned away good-hearted believers. God have mercy on us, and on them.

I guess I could feel the same about Christians in general, who are often arrogant, narrow, militaristic, hypocritical, and self-serving. *Forget it,* I could conclude. *This Christianity stuff is too weird and restricting.* Millions, of course, do just that.

Instead, I cherish my assurance in Christ. His grace alone saves me. I find freedom and challenge and rest and hope in my life as an Adventist. I also find frustrations, but I find those everywhere. As an Adventist, I live by grace, in peace, for love, with joy. Joylessly serving God is like peeling a grape—so little return for so much effort. Even Fred Flintstone, stuck working in a mythical Paleolithic pit, still manages to create a vibrant, exuberant life.

Once when I was at Elmshaven, the former home of Ellen White, I listened to her granddaughter, Grace Jacques, reminisce about worships with "Grandmother" when Grace was a girl. "They were never boring, never long, never something we simply endured," Grace said, her eyes twinkling. "Grandmother laughed often, and she insisted that worship time be something the children enjoyed."

Maybe that's why Grandmother could write that if we find the Christian life uphill work, saddled with discouragement and complaints, we are wearing, not the light, easy yoke of Christ, but the yoke of another master.

"Be not afraid, for behold, I bring you good news of a great joy which will come to all the people."*

"For the kingdom of God is not food and drink but righteousness and peace and joy in the Holy Spirit."†

"May the God of hope fill you with all joy and peace in believing."‡

"The joy of the Lord is your strength."§

"Joy," submits Leon Bly, "is the most infallible sign of the presence of God."**

One more selected message to members of the Seventh-day Adventist Church: If you don't enjoy it, you don't have it. ❑

---

*Luke, chapter 2.
†Romans, chapter 14.
‡Romans, chapter 15.
§Nehemiah, chapter 8.
**Or as Fred would say, "Yabba-dabba-doo!"

In a time of deceit, telling the truth is a revolutionary act.—George Orwell

Doing Justly

On March 16, 1968, Hugh Thompson was flying his helicopter over My Lai in Vietnam when he saw Charlie Company butchering the villagers with no "enemy" in sight. Thompson landed his helicopter between the remaining civilians and his fellow soldiers and ordered his crewmates to ready their machine guns with orders to fire on any American who refused the order to halt the massacre. Though outranked by other officers, he told the soldiers to back off. He then radioed two other helicopters flying nearby to pick up eleven wounded Vietnamese villagers for medical assistance.

Here is an example of loyal dissent. Whatever our station in life, we can speak up and step in.

In the true "trial of the century," the Nuremberg trials determined that no one is exempt, even under orders, from treating humanity justly in all circumstances. All is not fair in war or in love or in church. Martin Luther King Jr. contended, "Injustice anywhere is a threat to justice everywhere." Note that Micah specifically spoke of *doing* justice, not merely *believing*. Lacking a living bridge of action, justice is "just ice." Cold and dead.

"Doing justly" seems extremely risky, but as Malcolm Muggeridge noted, "Christianity is not a statistical view of life." Christians are called to take the unpopular stance, the difficult path, the contrary current. Often we lose a battle and find ourselves.

This is not the risk-taking of the "second gold rush" in California's Silicon Valley—staking claims to invisible dot coms and investing in etherized dreams. Rather, we risk our love. Simply, we stake our claims to the pursuit of truth. Always, we invest in people. This investment means we *will not* take advantage of others, particularly those who are vulnerable.

When Adventist General Conference president Jan Paulsen visited the Solomon Islands in 2001, he said Christians "have an interest in all the issues and all the elements that deal with quality of life." Thus, we Adventists should pursue justice beyond the realms of religious liberty and temperance. "We are actively interested," he said, "in everything that shapes the way we live."

≈

Justice has at its foundation the trait of honesty. In *Searching*, I highlighted the paramount need for honesty. As a church, we don't spend nearly enough time on this vital matter. Without an undeviating commitment to honesty, we lack a true north—our spiritual compass is constantly spinning. I have a friend who is desperately concerned about the spiritual condition of his son, who cannot be trusted. "He has a divided heart," my friend concluded sadly.

In church, this problem comes to light whenever we twist the Bible to say anything we want. Honesty is regularly trampled on church platforms—it happens to an astounding degree—when speakers neglect to give credit for their borrowed ideas and words.* I know of a pastor who "borrows" notes, sermons, and articles incessantly without giving credit. He is not alone in this tendency to take shortcuts. "The will to win," announced Bobby Knight, "is not nearly as important as the will to prepare to win."

As an example of the will to do justly, in April and May 2001, Harvard University students sustained a twenty-one-day, nonviolent protest against the injustice of low wages earned by staff workers at Harvard. The students had learned during the course of their education about the importance of looking out for the underprivileged, and they wondered why a school with more than a billion dollars in endowment wouldn't pay its cafeteria workers and gardeners a living wage. In students' minds, the school had an obligation to go beyond what was *legal* to do what was *right*. The students won, and the living-wage movement is still alive. One person commented, "Today, the students are the ones doing the teaching."

After I wrote about that stand in the *Adventist Review,* someone wrote a letter to the editor claiming that raising the minimum wage actually harms minimum-wage earners because ultimately the raise hurts the economy. This brought to my mind Abraham Lincoln's observation that though he often heard arguments from people who maintained that slavery was a good thing, he had never met anyone who wanted to try out this good thing by becoming a slave himself. Ask any of today's minimum earners if they care to give up a wage increase for the sake of "the economy." For the same reason, every employee should, I suppose, also voluntarily reduce our incomes. You first.

A just balance is called for. R. C. Sproul observed, "Social ethics must never be substituted for personal ethics. Crusading can easily become a dodge for facing up to one's lack of personal morality. By the same token, even if I am a model of personal righteousness, that does not excuse my participation in social evil. The man who is faithful to his wife while he exercises bigotry toward his neighbor is no better than the adulterer who crusades for social justice. What God requires is justice both personal and social."

Doing justly is also standing up for women, minorities, youth, seniors, and whoever needs defending, without the courts weighing in. This must be our con-

---

*"Selected" in church bulletins doesn't actually denote credit. It really means, "We stole this one."

stant mind-set as Christians. It is reported that U.S. President George H. W. Bush would occasionally pause in the middle of a cabinet discussion to ask, "What if we just wanted to do what was right?"

"The just shall live by faith," Paul explained to the Romans and Galatians. We *must* live by faith because in this life injustice prospers, deceit sells, and bullying triumphs. We must believe that ultimately justice wins.* In her prefatory note to *The Poisonwood Bible,* Barbara Kingsolver thanked her parents, who were medical and public-health workers in the Congo, for their having "brought me to a place of wonders, taught me to pay attention, and set me early on a path of exploring the great, shifting terrain between righteousness and what's right."

On occasion, I'm asked how one can work for the church and do justly. My answer is that no one should ever work for the church. Though I've been employed by the church for nearly thirty years, I've never worked one second for the church, and I hope I never shall. I work for God, which in turn makes me a better employee for the church.† Moreover, when the church lets me down (and they will), that doesn't affect my faith in God. Please, don't ever confuse the church with God. Recognizing that distinction would have saved and will save tons of agony.

We may never need to plant ourselves between soldiers and civilians, but we can plant ourselves between bullies or gossipers and their victims. We do justly by saying, "I don't think that's right" or "Let's change the subject." At times, that's as difficult to do as what Hugh Thompson did at My Lai, yet in doing so we are being loyal to our true Leader.

Cover and fill us with Your righteousness, Jesus. Help us to know and do what is honest and right, no matter the cost.   ❏

---

*We get a sneak preview in Revelation.

†Even when no one is watching or I'm "off-duty," I'm still working gratefully for The Boss. (See Colossians, chapter 3.)

Love Mercy

'Tis not love's going hurts my days,
But that it went in little ways.

—Edna St. Vincent Millay

We were shafted, with no hope of escape—until somebody showed up from the outside.

So While We're Stuck

M y mind struggled to remain clear and calm, but I felt the panic rising. We were trapped, stuck, packed like pickles in a jar.

"I can't breathe!"

"Help, *somebody!*"

Every Christmas season my College Writing classes enjoy high-spirited holiday fun the final Friday of the semester. We nibble treats from Conroy's Bakery, dance the Blakestep to "King of Kings," and sing carols throughout the five-story administration building.

Generally, we begin on second floor, bellowing "Joy to the World," "Deck the Halls," and "Away in a Manger." One of my favorite carols, with which we often end our unrehearsed concerts, is "We Wish You a Merry Christmas," because I particularly like the verse, "O bring us some figgy pudding!"—though no one has ever brought us some, not even President Smith, who keeps it to himself, likely.

One December 10, the eleven-thirty class and I wandered the halls spreading our outlandish joy. While many students opted to walk the stairs between floors, others filled the elevator and sang lustily, their voices ascending the shaft to the very portal of heaven. At times I joined them, punching all the floors and caroling at each stop as the doors opened and closed on amused onlookers.

We had finished serenading the first-floor Advancement office (alas—no figgy pudding) when someone yelled, "Let's go to the computer lab on third floor!" It was 12:17 P.M. as I passed the elevator, and I heard squeals of laughter and voices beckoning, "Mr. Blake, get in!"

With nary a glance, I stepped blissfully into what was a *quite* crowded elevator. Then two more burly guys squeezed on. We shifted to make room. Someone pressed 3. The doors closed two inches in front of me. I remember thinking, *Man, this thing is packed! It would be terrible to be stuck . . .*

The elevator *sank* four feet. And stopped.

Screams and nervous laughs erupted. We pressed the basement button to continue down. The elevator didn't stir. We pressed all the floors. Nothing. I pried the doors until they parted three inches—enough to reveal the first floor at the level of my chest. More screams.

To understand precisely what we were facing, you should know that afterward I paced off the dimensions of our elevator: six feet wide and three-and-a-half feet deep—twenty-one square feet. Incredibly, into that tiny area we had crammed *nineteen college students and one idiotic professor.*

When the space began heating up considerably, students started dropping their winter coats to the floor. One student suggested that we could raise our arms over our heads to create more room. *Bad idea!**

I asked if anyone felt claustrophobic. Daisy and Kayla, two of the shortest girls (previously at armpit level), moved to the front to inhale fresh air from the three-inch space. They would remain there for the duration.

Peering up, I noted that, despite what the movies depict, we had no way to open the ceiling without a Phillips screwdriver and an acetylene torch. However, a pink phone hid behind a panel in the corner. Nathan Helm picked it up.

"Hello," he said evenly, "we're stuck in the elevator in the Dick Building. Send someone to get us out. . . .Yeah. . . . We're stuck. . . . We tried that. . . ." After hanging up, he told us that the switchboard operator—a desk worker in the women's dorm—didn't sound reassuring. "And," he added without a trace of irony, "she didn't speak English very well."

Through it all we remained calm, though we weren't singing. We could hear voices from the other side, and every time I pried the doors apart for air, I noticed more legs in the lobby. Apparently, news had gotten out.

About ten minutes into the ordeal, a note fluttered from the opening: "We called plant services." *Hooray!* But with advancing terror I remembered that, despite Adventist insistence on the Sabbath starting Friday at sunset, almost everyone who works at our college leaves on Fridays at *noon.* I decided not to share this epiphany.

Then, after seventeen minutes/hours had passed, we heard someone from the outside working a coat hanger into the elevator's opening mechanism.The doors parted. We climbed out while a boisterous crowd counted incredulously, ". . . eighteen . . . nineteen . . . *twenty!*" †

I've thought of this episode many times, of how much it was like our experience as human beings. How we are stuck on this crowded planet. How we must not panic. How we should look out for one another, showing mercy to those who need it most. How we could hear voices from the other side, but ultimately we were hopelessly trapped—until plant services was called and a Carpenter set us free. Glorious freedom!

Wouldn't it be absurd to choose to stay on the elevator?

Today I carry that fluttering note in my wallet: "We called plant services." I never want to forget it.

---

*I made a mental note to flunk that student, should we survive.

†Afterward, I discovered that the actual key to the door was an hour away in Omaha. A former student of mine who worked in plant services rescued us. (Thanks, Philip.)

I'll also not forget that on the final exam the next week, where students could describe the elevator incident, Kayla titled her short essay, "Too Much Figgy Pudding." ❏

Have you ever wondered if God adequately comprehends the magnitude of our suffering?

What Breaks His Heart

What hoopla! What a party!

For more than forty topsy-turvy months—three and a half years—the backers and handlers have waited and ached for this chance to trumpet it from the rooftops, to sing it down the narrow streets. Now the moment is here.

Or more precisely, *He* is here.

Because He's different on this day. This is not the He they've known. This isn't He of the tell-the-truth-even-if-it-hurts pronouncements. Not He of the let's-avoid-the-crowds-today communiqués. Not He of the don't-pander-to-public-adulation perspective.

He welcomes the public worship. He encourages the roaring approval. He graciously receives unrestrained praise. It's as though He has finally announced, "I accept the nomination!" and instead of brightly colored balloons dropping from the ceiling, palm branches are laid before Him like a carpet. Through the streets the procession surges with singing, shouting, laughter, and joyous dancing. Everything is different now. *Hosanna! This is our King, our wonderful, marvelous King!*

Then the moving celebration stops.

At the crest of a hill overlooking magnificent Jerusalem, all eyes focus on the city. The temple gleams in the sunlight, resplendent in marble and gold, the pride of the Jewish nation. At that point, as Ellen White describes in *The Desire of Ages*: "All eyes turn upon the Saviour, expecting to see in His countenance the admiration they themselves feel. But instead of this they behold a cloud of sorrow. They are surprised and disappointed to see His eyes fill with tears, and His body rock to and fro like a tree before the tempest, while a wail of anguish bursts from His quivering lips, as if from the depths of a broken heart."

Jesus cries for the people who wouldn't accept Him and His life-giving gift. "Jerusalem had been the child of His care, and as a tender father mourns over a wayward son, so Jesus wept over the beloved city. . . . One soul is of such value that, in comparison with it, worlds sink into insignificance; but here was a whole nation to be lost."

Jesus knew He was about to be humiliated and murdered. Yet unlike most of us, Jesus cried only for others, never for Himself.

The Bible records two instances when Jesus wept—this one and at the grave of His friend Lazarus. But as God, He had wept before.

When Adam and Eve, His first children, chose death over life, He must have cried.

In Noah's time, the flood of a rejected God's tears covered the planet.

When David's son was killed, God cried with His friend.

As mothers of Bethlehem wailed because the insanely furious King Herod had their children slain in front of them, God wept.

At a billion billion times for a billion reasons Jesus has wept, and He continues to weep today. Just pick up a newspaper to find out why.

Four teenagers die when hit by a drunk driver.

An airplane carrying festive passengers home for Christmas explodes into flames, killing all on board.

Under the onslaught of a mudslide, a village is buried.

Every minute at least twenty-five children starve to death.

Most tragedies don't ever appear in the newspapers, though. The stories aren't sensational enough; they happen every day. If they did appear, they'd read like this:

Lonely girl becomes pregnant, chooses abortion, is left by boyfriend, tries to pick up shattered life.

Boy is taunted unmercifully until his will to succeed is gone.

Former friends decide not to forgive each other; forfeit God's forgiveness.

Love of money and possessions takes over young person.

Family gets caught up in amusing themselves, decides to throw away friendship with God and eternal life.

Jesus weeps over these tragedies. Whether or not the participants weep, Jesus weeps. And He asks us to cry too. What breaks God's heart should break our hearts. As people continue to be stomped on in this life, He asks us to feel mercy for them.

More than that, He asks us each to do our little something to relieve the suffering. As C. S. Lewis asserts, Christians believe that "a great many things have gone wrong with the world that God made and that God insists, and insists very loudly, on our putting them right again."

Christ weeps with those who weep.

There's a lot of crying going on.

Throughout eternity, Jesus will remember with sadness the agonies of His children, many of whom chose to reject Him. We know Jesus will remember because of the scars that will remain on His hands. (One soul is of such value.) But He will also never forget because of the hidden scars—the ones that cover the broken heart that killed Him.

Yet we all—Christ included—harbor a hope that holds and lifts us. It's a forward-looking view of sadness. We look forward to the fresh world described in Revelation, chapter 21—where God's people will live. "God himself will be with us; he will wipe away every tear from our eyes, and death shall be no more, neither shall there be mourning nor crying nor pain any more, for the former things have passed way."

What a world that will be.   ❏

Not long ago when I was languishing in the hospital, I learned a lot about my church.

The Key to Life

Following a brutal racquetball game with Gary "Killer" Krause, my right knee swelled like a menacing puffer fish. Unable to run, I called Nebraska Orthopedic to make an appointment with Dr. Strasberger.* After evaluating tests, he told me what the problem was and how we could proceed.

The good doctor took his time, defined his terms, and patiently answered all of my questions. In other words, he treated me with utmost respect. He could have said, "There's an injury. It's your knee. Let me fix it." Instead, he described a probable torn medial meniscus, how others have responded to arthroscopy, and what my recovery would probably entail.

Two days later, I walked briskly into Bryan Hospital cradling two crutches under my left arm, because the hospital insisted that I bring crutches. (Apparently, someone knew I would be in worse shape for a while before I got better.) Yolanda, my friend and life partner, accompanied me. I wasn't nervous, probably because this was my third surgery—the first was a C-section, and the second made a *vas deferens* in my family's future. I was, however, uncomfortable with the hospital's peculiar "dress code."

After I had slithered into a thin blue dress with a scandalous slit, two nurses approached. One was clearly brand new to this start-an-IV-on-a-real-human procedure; she fairly trembled with apprehension. Over decades I have donated gallons of blood, but I found myself looking away as the young nurse tentatively applied the tourniquet and, needle in hand, began searching for a vein to love.

That's when the experienced nurse spoke up. I will be forever grateful to her, for she kept a running commentary of encouraging advice, even stepping forward to assist at one point. As nearly as I can remember, she spoke these words in calm, soothing tones: "There, that looks like an excellent place to start. . . . That's it. . . . Good. . . . Try not to stick the needle all the way *through* the arm. . . . Now pinch it with your thumb and slip it out. . . . Here, let me try—this is kind of tricky."

---

*He sounded vegetarian.

How I wish I could transplant her patience and tact into Christian churches. She helped just enough to ensure success (I lived) while still assuring the other nurse of her value and trustworthiness. We must instill that confidence into youth and other "inexperienced" Christians.

Following visits from a grinning pastor and two smirking colleagues bearing a sensitive, compassionate get-well card ("Snap out of it!"), I was wheeled on a gurney to a cavernous, cold, tiled room. I scooted onto the chilled operating table, and wished I had worn a faux fur coat with my dress. Then a nurse covered me with a heated blanket. *O rapture!*

Dr. Strasberger (who looked less vegetarian now) explained in detail what was going to happen. Amazingly, *every person* who contacted me while I was in the hospital, from the receptionist on, explained what he or she was doing and what would happen next. I wouldn't hesitate for a moment to go back for treatment.

When I sat up to receive the huge spinal-block needle in my vertebrae, I must have transmitted my concern.* A nurse placed the fallen warm blanket across my far shoulder, held it there, and asked, "Are you feeling a little anxious?"

I could see only her eyes. I smiled and admitted, "A little." I can't explain to you how much I appreciated her question right then.

After the cutting portion of the surgery, Dr. Strasberger led me on a guided tour of my knee. Someone pulled back the curtain across my chest so I could watch with sedated interest the monitor while the doctor intoned, "Here's your ACL. . . . Here's where the patellar chondromalacia was, and here's . . . the frontal lobe of your brain, which appears remarkably empty."

One prominent, throbbing, all-important lesson emerges for the body of Jesus. It's a lesson I constantly teach. It's one I'm continually learning afresh.

Communication is the key to life.

More to the point, communication is the key to your church's life.

Church Communication Guidelines

1. Take adequate time, define terms, and answer all questions.
2. Always treat everyone with utmost respect.
3. Plan for people to be in worse shape before they get better.†
4. Explain what is happening. Clarify peculiar codes.
5. With patience and tact, encourage independence and confidence.
6. Mercifully cover signs of discomfort with encouraging warmth.
7. Occasionally ask, "Are you feeling a little anxious?" ❏

---

*I was, in fact, praying.
†Remember the Israelites after Moses returned to Egypt.

What energizes you? Have you thought about it?

Batman Has Landed

On two occasions one summer I found myself surprisingly motivated.

Scene 1. The first occasion took place at Tsali State Park in North Carolina, on one of the nation's top mountain biking trails. I was riding with local mountain men Steve and Bill, attempting to coax my flatlander legs to keep up.

The previous day I had climbed a different trail fairly effortlessly before careening downhill with sheer abandon. At Tsali, we climbed gradually for eight miles on rugged single-track, bumping over rocks and roots. I was doing all right, I thought. Then the *real* climbing began. We ascended the next three *steep* miles, and I discovered in a soulful, intimate way the meaning of a relatively new word.

bonk (bongk), *v.t., v.i.* Slang. to become exhausted, depleted of energy: "run out of gas," "hit the wall," "stick a fork in me; I'm done."*

I bonked at mile ten. *No más.* I couldn't *walk* my bike up the incline. My driving pistons had morphed to Play-Doh. Bill handed me two Power Bars, and I munched them slowly, bending over, wheezing and gasping. I threw down the bike like a bad habit, staggered to an old rotting tree stump, and sat on it. *No way* I'd be moving anywhere for a long, long time.

In less than eight seconds I was up, kicking and yelling and jumping around like a cross between a Turkish dervish and a teenager pogoing in a mosh pit. *Boundless* energy captivated me. Exhaustion was the last thing on my mind.

What happened? No, the Power Bars didn't kick in for another fifteen minutes. Instead, I had become energized by dozens of giant red ants that were racing up my legs like the start of the New York Marathon.

Scene 2. The first week of August, our family enjoyed family camp at Camp MiVoden in northern Idaho. Late one evening, I was reading on the cabin bed with my back propped against two pillows before an open window. The cool mountain air whispered about us. Yolanda sat knitting beside me, and our sons rested, reading and talking. A tranquil, happy scene.

I felt something light on my hair and carelessly brushed it forward. A black bat landed on my chest, wings spread, its weasely eyes fastened on me.

"Yoww!" Instantly, I broke the world's record for the sitting long jump. Yolanda performed even better. She spurned the law of gravity as she flew across the room

---

*Aussies and Kiwis, just work with this version.

and out the door. I have never seen her so inspired. The room emptied in approximately 0.3 seconds.*

What is it that energizes us? Some of us are energized to exercise by a fold of fat around our middles. Others are energized to buy eyeglasses when we can't read a map.† What we see in our dominant reality as our immediate need motivates our response.

However, most people tend to see only what they're looking for. Hairstylists spot uneven bangs. Dentists detect receding gums. Baseball scouts pick out curveball weaknesses. Police officers notice suspicious behavior. Christians see . . . *what?*

Christians need to see with new eyes. To look for inner beauty, listen for hidden cries. These motivations are literally everywhere. In addition, we need to train our noses for the scent of angel wings.

O, that we could be energized out of our comfort zones not by the ants and bats of hell, but by the love of God. The apostle Paul wrote, "Do you not know that God's kindness is meant to lead you to repentance?" (Romans, chapter 2).‡

What will energize us on the new earth? No more terrors then. How about adrenaline-addicting deadlines? Probably not. Showing up an adversary? No. Without fear or hatred, what will be our motivation? The same motive that should drive us now: love for a kind God and His creations. Love is the one and only godly motivation.

When I was much younger, cleaning slimy, disgusting dishes grossed me out. What could be worse than sticking your hands into someone's crusted leftovers? Then Yolanda and I had children. Amazingly, at that point I *chose* to clean their soiled diapers. Virtually nothing grosses me out after that. I have been to the valley of the shadow of death. As John tells us in his first letter, "There is no fear in love, but perfect love casts out fear." Love set me free.

Ron Whitehead told me that after he had led a family worship about the Second Coming, he was tucking his son in for the night when his son whispered, "Daddy, I want to fly."

This is my prayer.

Daddy, I want to fly. Let me be energized, motivated, and lifted by Your pure love.   ❑

---

*In stark contrast to the forty-five minutes required to get the bat out of the room, highlighted by my waving a broom at the rafters like a maniacal cleaning man.

†Not that I've had these problems myself. (What's the deal with pants shrinking in winter and four-point fonts in different colors?)

‡Apparently they didn't.

Can you recall a vivid picture of love and courage?*

The Most Mature Thing I've Ever Seen

Every student at Monroe High School knew about it. Nobody did it. Nobody. Lunchtime at Monroe High School was consistent. As soon as the bell that ended the last morning class started ringing, the students swarmed toward their lockers. Then those who didn't eat in the cafeteria headed with their sack lunches toward the quad. The quad was a large, treeless square of concrete in the center of campus. It was the meeting-and-eating place.

Around the quad the various school cliques assembled. The druggies lined up on the south side. The punkers were next to them. On the east side were the brothers. Next to them were the nerds and brains. The jocks stood on the north side next to the surfers. The rednecks were on the west side. The socialites were in the cafeteria. Everybody knew their place.

This arrangement did create some tension. But all the tension generated on the perimeter of the quad at lunchtime was nothing compared with the inside of the quad.

The inside was no-man's land.

Nobody at Monroe walked across the middle of the quad. To get from one side to the other, students walked around the quad. Around the people. Around the stares.

Everybody knew it, so nobody did it.

Then one day at the beginning of spring, a new student arrived at Monroe. Her name was Lisa. She was unfamiliar to the area; in fact, she was new to the state.

And although Lisa was pleasant enough, she did not quickly attract friends. She was overweight and shy, and the style of her clothes was not . . . right.

She had enrolled at Monroe that morning. All morning she had struggled to find her classes, sometimes arriving late, which was especially embarrassing. The teachers had generally been tolerant, if not cordial. Some were irritated; their classes were already too large, and now this added paperwork before class.

But she had made it through the morning to the lunch bell. Hearing the bell, she sighed and entered the crush of students in the hall. She weaved her way to her locker and tried her combination three, four, five times before it banged open. Standing in front of her locker, she decided to carry along with her lunch all of her books for her afternoon classes. She thought she could save herself another trip to her locker by eating lunch on the steps in front of her next class.

---

*This account was initially published in *Insight* and *Chicken Soup for the Teenage Soul.*

So Lisa began the longest walk of her life—the walk across campus toward her next class. Through the hall. Down the steps. Across the lawn. Across the sidewalk. Across the quad.

As Lisa walked, she shifted the heavy books, alternately resting the arm that held her light lunch. She had grabbed too many books—the top book kept slipping off, and she was forced to keep her eye on it in a balancing act as she moved past the people, shifting the books from arm to arm, focusing on the balanced book, shuffling forward, oblivious to her surroundings.

All at once she sensed something: The air was eerily quiet. A nameless dread clutched her. She stopped. She lifted her head.

Hundreds of eyes were staring. Cruel, hateful stares. Pitiless stares. Angry stares. Unfeeling, cold stares. They bore into her.

She froze, dazed, pinned down. Her mind screamed, *No! This can't be happening!*

What happened next people couldn't say for sure. Some later said she dropped her book, reached down to pick it up, and lost her balance. Some claimed she tripped. It didn't matter how it happened.

She slipped to the pavement and laid there, legs splayed, in the center of the quad.

Then the laughter started, like an electric current jolting the perimeter, charged with a nightmarish quality, wrapping itself around and around its victim.

And she lay there.

From every side fingers pointed, and then the taunt began, building in raucous merriment, building in heartless insanity: "You! You! You! YOU!"

And she lay there.

From the edge of the perimeter a figure emerged slowly. He was a tall boy, and he walked rigidly, as though he were measuring each step. He headed straight toward the place where the fingers pointed. As more and more students noticed someone else in the middle, the calls softened, and then they ceased. A hush flickered over the crowd.

The boy walked into the silence. He walked steadily, his eyes fixed on the form lying on the concrete.

By the time he reached the girl, the silence was deafening. The boy simply knelt and picked up the lunch sack and the scattered books, and then he placed his hand under the girl's arm and looked into her face. And she got up.

The boy steadied her once as they walked across the quad and through the quiet perimeter that parted before them.

The next day at Monroe High School at lunchtime, a curious thing happened. As soon as the bell that ended the last morning class started ringing, the students swarmed toward their lockers. Then those who didn't eat in the cafeteria headed with their sack lunches across the quad.

From all parts of campus, different groups of students walked freely across the quad. No one could really explain why it was OK now. Everybody just knew. And if you ever visit Monroe High School, that's how it is today.

It happened some time ago. I never even knew his name. But what he did, nobody who was there will ever forget.

Nobody.   ❏

She bore me and bore with me, but she has never bored me.
My tribute to an amazing woman.

Mother, May I?

Giving birth to this book was a snap compared to giving birth to me. At least, that's the story I've heard from someone else who was there. And to hear other tales from the same source, things didn't get any easier later on. But let's not dwell on that. Instead, I'd like to share some stories about my mother, if I may.

My early memories of Mom often revolve around food. For example, while some families learn not to talk with food in their mouths, we learned not to talk when food was *not* in our mouths. Mom believed we ought to trust her. This was simply accomplished. If we were foolish enough to ask what we were going to eat, there was always one answer: "Poison."

"What's for breakfast?"

"Poison."

"What's for lunch?"

"Poison."

"What's for supper?"

"Poison."

Not exactly a well-balanced diet. I could visualize myself some day writhing on the floor, gurgling and clutching my throat, my lips blackening, and Mom shrugging and muttering, "Well, don't say I didn't warn you!"

Mom also had the habit of saving unused food. To this day, if I find a drinking glass with a quarter of an inch of milk in the refrigerator, I know she's in the house.

This penchant has led to some culinary peculiarities. I well remember the left-over homemade ice-cream mix, mistaken for nonfat milk, that ended up in the world's sweetest scrambled eggs. Half-used cans of stewed tomatoes flourished in forgotten recesses behind last week's asparagus. People would invite us over to see their flowers blooming and we'd say, "That's nothing. You should see our tomatoes," and then we'd lead them to our refrigerator.

Another area that stirs memories is running. When I was a child, Mom and I would race to the backyard wall and back. The races faithfully followed one format. I sprinted to an early lead, touched the wall, turned around, and lost the race. For there, approaching the wall, was my mother, giggling and puffing and making all the movements that in others accompany speed.

I knew I was doomed if I looked at her, but I couldn't help myself. Glee and incredulity would grab me so that I'd double over laughing, struggling for balance and breath, turned to stone by a modern Medusa. Mom passed me on the stretch every time. The moral here lies somewhere between the tale of the tortoise and the hare and the experience of Lot's wife.

However, don't get the idea that Mom couldn't be fazed. She didn't come by her family nickname, The Great Inhaler, for nothing. For instance, *never* steer close to another car if Mom is a passenger. Minutes later, when you can again draw breath, you wish you had hit the car. Less trauma on the lungs.

Her best inhale took place the time I came home from college (four hours away) unexpectedly. I had set it up ahead of time with my brother, Bruce, so that Mom was in her bedroom when I sneaked into the house. I knew a telephone number whereby one could ring one's own house, so I placed a handkerchief over the mouthpiece (for that faraway sound) and called from the kitchen.* Mom picked up the phone in the bedroom, and we talked for fifteen minutes, or until the phone bill might be running high. Then we hung up, and I waited.

Enter Mom. Oh, what an inhale! Windows buckled. Curtains flapped. The oxygen was suctioned from my body. Airplanes soaring overhead lost altitude. They'd blame it on "turbulence," but it was all Mom.

At fifty-three, Mom really took to running. She began training, entered 6K races (about four miles), and worked up to running a half-marathon (thirteen miles) at age fifty-seven. The past two years, she has won her division in the 5K Turkey Trot held in Dana Point, California. She looks to take first again next year, though an eighty-year-old whippersnapper is close on her heels. Mom works out every day. And I have to tell you a secret: She isn't any faster than when we raced to the wall.

Maybe running is in my mother's blood. Growing up in Greensburg, Kansas, whenever she spotted black clouds boiling in the distance, she ran home before the fine dust stung her arms and legs. It seeped through cracks and covered the kitchen linoleum until she couldn't see the pattern. "Dust pneumonia" whistled through shuttered houses. At night, her family slept with wet cloths draped across their faces.

My mother lived through the dust bowl and the seven years of drought of the Great Depression. In 1936, her father ("He was a wonderful dancer," she recalls.)

---

*For the young people who are reading: This was before mobile phones existed—but after electricity was discovered.

experienced severe abdominal pain. Before antibiotics and sulfa drugs, he lay for a week in the veterans' hospital, waiting for a surgeon. By the time they opened him up he was filled with gangrene—his appendix had burst. He died in that hospital, leaving his thirty-five-year-old wife with no income and five children, ages three to eleven. The children had to be shipped to relatives in other states for a year until my grandmother found a job at the post office.

As fast as she ran, my mother couldn't avoid the sting of losing her father when she was eleven, and then, decades later, her husband to cancer. After he said No to dialysis, our family gathered about his bed and watched him die.

"Are you okay, Jim?" she would ask. He wasn't, of course, and would never be again in this life. Whether he grunted or smiled weakly or closed his eyes in resignation, she remained close by, tending to his every need.

After Dad died, Mom started running in a different way. When people came to visit her, they rarely found her at home. She might be at aerobics class (at sixty, she became an instructor), or wandering through a museum, or substitute teaching. She figured she had spent enough of her life at home raising four kids,* so she ran around visiting friends and relatives from Kansas to Finland, Mexico to Alaska.

Three years later my mother married Jack, a highway engineer with the World Bank. That was when I found out something else about my mom. She is a fabulous dancer. For thirteen years she and Jack skipped across the ocean like a stone—dancing in Barbados, Paris, Rio, Madrid. Well into their seventies they were the buoyant, shimmering stars of every dance floor, even teaching West Coast swing dancing on jazz cruises.

Then, suddenly, a stroke felled Jack. For months he lay in bed partially paralyzed, his chest a pale washboard of bones, as my mother cared for him. She wakened every night at his slightest whimper. When he could walk a little, she helped him to the bathroom and back to bed. One night he fell in the bathroom at 3 A.M.

"It took me an hour and a half to get him up!" she told me over the phone, laughing. "I thought I might have to call 911."

"Mom, you're seventy-six," I said. "Call for help next time."

My mother laughs easily, as if nothing more could crush her. Most mornings after her workout she organizes laughter-filled Scrabble games with people half her age at Metro Java coffee shop, and she often wins.†

I saw her and Jack as they appeared together at a family reunion in Kansas City. Wan and gaunt, Jack shuffled with the distinctive slow, listing, stuttering gait of a stroke victim. His left hand curled inward like a scorpion's tail. On the afternoon of the second day, my mother had been playing favorite old tunes on a keyboard

---

*Those other three were a handful.
†They all cheat like mad.

when I noticed her staring at Jack. She left the keyboard and walked purposefully across the floor.

"Come on, Jack," she said, extending her hand. "Let's dance."

What in the world is she doing? I thought. *He can scarcely stand.*

Jack took her hand and stood tremulously. Gently she led him to the center of the floor. He seemed baffled, dazed, tottering. I readied myself to retrieve him.

As the music started, my mother began dancing—stepping lightly, sliding, swiveling, bending, smiling—all the while holding his hand. And then the most amazing alteration took place.

Jack became transfigured. He watched her with wonder and love. His lips curved up. His eyes glowed. His body straightened and swayed with the beat. He raised his arm, and graceful movement spilled from his fingers like quicksilver.

He was dancing through my mother.

Many cannot dance for themselves. Constrained by their own crippled flesh or by crushing distress, they can now savor life only through others.

God calls us to dance for one another. Behind closed doors, ordinary people sponge bed-soured skin, lift flopping limbs, resurrect downed spirits, and spend tedious hours holding the vulnerable heads of their beloved above the brackish water. These life-givers are the world's silent celebrities.

I think of and thank my mother who, at eighty-two, still dances and has always danced.

For Jack. For my father. For her father. For me.   ❏

Many years ago, two simple choices formed a treasured tradition for all of us.

Fabulous Family Night

Our family started a great tradition. One night each week we celebrate what we call Family Night.

Now, don't get me wrong. Every night of the week our family enjoyed family worship together. Along with a lively story we often sang a song or three (since Geoffrey was three), and we generally stuck with the classics: "Wide As the Ocean," "This Little Light of Mine," and of course, for our wee men, "Zacchaeus."

Friday night, as we welcomed the Sabbath, was special. On Friday night we sang six songs (since Nathan was six), read through the Sabbath School lesson and the memory verses, and for supper, by flickering candlelight, we ate homemade bread and soup.

These traditions are important to us. In fact, these shared nights establish spiritual bonding. But the newest tradition I want to tell you about takes place on Tuesday night. On this night, on a rotating basis, one member of the family gets to choose: (A) what we eat, and (B) a special activity. Simple, huh? But I've been amazed at the way we look forward to this night. We enjoy loads of involvement and laughter. Here are some examples of what goes on:

Nathan often chooses to make the meal himself. One memorable salad included pineapple, shredded carrot, raisins, and yogurt on a bed of lettuce. It was . . . interesting. And, I must admit, it was pretty tasty.

Yolanda often chooses not to make the meal herself. So two weeks ago on her night, we ate spaghetti at Rocky's.

Geoffrey enjoys basic fare—vegeburgers or hot dogs. He gets exotic, however, when it comes to dessert. He orders Toffuti.

I generally ask Yolanda what she thinks I ought to want.

When it comes to activities, Nathan usually opts for a game of Memory, where we try to pair up seventy-two cards. We play in teams—Nathan and Mom (boo!) versus Geoffrey and Dad (yea!). So far, I think my team's won-lost record is 1–22. That may be one reason Nathan likes this game. Of course, by now he's marked some of the cards with creases and peanut butter. I'd pick them up myself if I could remember which goes with which.

Yolanda sometimes chooses to go for a ride or to visit the park, or she may read a special story. And although I can't understand it, she sometimes chooses to play Memory.

Geoffrey had a few nights when Chinese checkers were a hit. I was secretly glad when he got off it until he mentioned the replacement—Memory. I've got to talk to that boy.

I've done some special worships (with the family as costumed characters), played all sorts of games except one (the name escapes me), and visited our insurance agent. In truth, the visit with our insurance agent, Diane, turned into a delightful time. She had her two girls, ages seven and four, in the office, so we made friends with another family.

Some nights we take on secret missions of mercy. I'd give you more details, but providing them might cause me to break an ironclad rule: Recipients cannot know that we were the ones who helped. Suffice to say that we employ the cover of darkness. Nathan and Geoffrey revel in it.

We mark on our calendar three months in advance whose night it is each week, and we look forward to it. It provides for each of us a sense of freedom and authority. As the boys grow older, the selections will change ("How about enchiladas and parasailing in Puerto Vallarta?"), but I'm looking forward to some changes.

I hear the memory can start to fade. ❏

Sublime Sabbath, serene Sabbath, serendipitous Sabbath, stunning Sabbath, soaring Sabbath, soulful Sabbath, sun-drenched Sabbath . . .

Wanted: Fewer "Happy Sabbaths"

An Adventist young adult confided to me, "I've heard 'Happy Sabbath' so many times that I've grown to loathe the *short a* sound." With all the riches of language at our disposal, why do we hang on to one prosaic, shallow word?

In less than an hour (and without a thesaurus), I rounded up 104 alternatives—enough for two years of Sabbaths. Add your own. Choose a dozen favorites and mercifully rotate them. Just substitute one of these words in place of "Happy" and follow with "Sabbath."

Feel the freshness.

Delicious	Halcyon	Tremendous	Heavenly
Godly	Truthful	Lavender-scented	New-earth
Excellent	Noble	Melodious	Remarkable
Sublime	Spirit-drenched	Authentic	Pleasing
Ebullient	Welcome	Numinous	Captivating
Splendiferous	Stirring	Soulful	Splendid
Superb	Shalom	Sensational	Exuberant
Restorative	Precious	Shimmering	Liberating
Energizing	Lovely	Radiant	Encouraging
Redemptive	Blessed	Glorious	Surprising
Magnanimous	Priceless	Exhilarating	Loving
Magnificent	Sensational	Timeless	Courageous
Marvelous	Fascinating	Scintillating	Sharing
Tasty	Prioritizing	Jesus-filled	Classy
Gracious	Pulchritudinous	Jubilee	Embracing
Serendipitous	Delightful	Clear-eyed	Certainly
Unwavering	Bright	Wonderful	Reviving
Generous	Bountiful	Satisfying	Lasting
Nurturing	Effervescent	Thankfully	Lively
Merciful	Amazing	Sumptuous	Abundant
Genuine	Fresh-squeezed	Dazzling	Luscious
Joyful	Extraordinary	Deepening	Thoughtful
Beautiful	Jubilant	Renewing	Artful
Savor	Luminous	Blissful	Nimble
Gorgeous	Honey-filled	Serene	Gentle
Peaceful	Peaceful	Guileless	Soaring ❑

The buildings stand empty, mute reminders of a useless past.

Norfolk Island's Magnificent Conduit

North of New Zealand and about a thousand miles east of Australia, Norfolk Island lies sprawled on its back in the South Pacific Ocean. Though only five miles long and three miles wide, the island features fertile glens and valleys beneath towering cliffs of gray lava rock.

Australia began as a penal colony, a far-off land where British prisoners were shipped out of sight and mind. The worst were transferred to Norfolk Island. Surrounded by shark-infested waters, it seemed a suitable spot for incorrigible convicts.

Because the gray cliffs provided an abundance of material, all of the buildings on the island were fashioned out of stone, all handcrafted by the prisoners. Therefore, any British prisoners who were formerly stonemasons were sent to Norfolk Island. English judges kept a sharp lookout for masons. Some were sentenced to Norfolk Island for life for offenses as small as the theft of a rabbit.

As a result, the architecture on the island is remarkable. Author James Michener visited the island in 1943 and admired "hundreds of superb pieces of construction. There were walls as beautiful as a palace at Versailles, old houses straight from the drawing boards of England, towers, blockhouses, salt works, chimneys, barns ... all built of gray lava rock, all superb and perfect."* Then Michener chanced upon the prison officers' bathhouse:

> The bath was a superb thing, walled with matched rock, patiently built in the perfection of men who had endless time. But it was not the bath which captivated [me]. It was the conduit by which the water of a little stream was diverted into the bath. This tunnel was six feet high. It was dug completely through the base of a small hill about 300 feet long. It was paved with beautiful stone. It was arched like the most graceful esplanade ever built. Down the roof of the 300-foot conduit were keystones of perfect design. And all this was buried under a hill of dirt *where no man would ever see.*
>
> I studied it in horror. I thought of the endless hours and pain that went into its building, the needless perfectionism, the human misery, when a pipe would have done as well.

---

*From *Tales of the South Pacific.*

Following the last of many mutinies, all of the prisoners were taken away. The island served no more as a prison colony.

What became of the magnificent buildings? Michener describes the buildings nearly a hundred years later: "They moaned beneath the Norfolk pines when winds whipped in at night, for they were empty. They were dead and empty ruins. They were not rotting by the sea, for they were stronger than when they were built. But they were dead and desolate."

The buildings stand empty, mute reminders of a useless past. The past was not useless due to a lack of materials or leadership. There was no lack of time or talent. But the marvelous efforts had been wasted.

Could we as Christians learn a lesson from Norfolk Island? How can we avoid being busy with impressive, dedicated, but ultimately useless routines of effort?

Two years after the prisoners were taken away, the deserted island was given to a band of settlers who arrived from another island four thousand miles to the east. These people knew of the island's history, yet they had a work to do.

The people chose not to live in any of the prison buildings, believing them to be "built by blood." Instead, they fashioned their own homes out of wood, and added one more building—a chapel. From Norfolk, these people set out across the seas to minister to nearby islands. Some of the missionaries were martyred for their beliefs. But as a result, from this tiny dot of soil, all the Hebrides and Solomon Islands—some thirty islands—were brought into the healing body of Christ.

Who were these settlers? They were descendents of Fletcher Christian's crew of mutineers from the ship *Bounty*, from Pitcairn Island.

They had converted the isolated prison colony into an outpost for ministry. The previous useless routines disappeared. The mutiny of love transformed their neighbors. In the process, the islanders helped build their own monuments, who laugh and learn and breathe to this day.   ❑

Can a naughty first-grader teach us anything? You might be surprised.

"I'm Not Gonna Do It!"

Micah's hand defiantly swipes his paper to the floor.

"I'm not gonna do it!" he hollers. His blue eyes glare, daring, daring. By now it's an old ploy. The rest of the class barely notices.

Yolanda, Micah's first-grade teacher, ignores him. After handing out the dot-to-dot assignment and suggesting that they use a pencil before coloring in the shape, she strolls through the class broadcasting compliments like seed to a furrowed field.

"Good job, Dylan! I like the way you're doing that, Mallory. Hey, Hailey, nice going."

"I'm *not* gonna do it!" Micah scowls at the teacher. Even at his tender age, he's used to getting his way, and he's puzzled. *What is she doing? Why doesn't she stop me?*

Yolanda continues to encourage others in the class.

"I'm not gonna do it!" Micah repeats to an unresponsive audience, but his fury is fading. He stares at the paper on the floor. Reaching down, he lifts the paper and begins working the dots.

"I'm gonna do mine with crayon," he smirks.

Yolanda stops by his desk. "I'm glad you're doing your paper, Micah."

"I'm doing it with *crayon*."

Soon he calls the teacher over. "Can I have another piece of paper?" he says. "I messed up." Yolanda kneels beside his desk. "I messed up right here," he explains, pointing.

"Well, what would you do differently next time?"

"I'll use a pencil first."

"Why would you use a pencil?"

"So I can erase it if I make a mistake."

The next day, as he is handed a written assignment, Micah declares, "I'm not gonna do it!" and swipes the paper off his desk. This time he follows Yolanda around the room, leaning forward, stalking her, intoning, "I'm not gonna do it. . . . I'm not gonna do it. . . ."

Yolanda turns around and smiles. He returns to his desk.

"Will you help me?" he asks.

In Psalm 73, Asaph laments, "I was envious of the arrogant, when I saw the prosperity of the wicked. . . . The people turn and praise them; and find no fault in them. . . . 'Is there knowledge in the Most High?' "

"Be not silent, O God of my praise!" entreats David in Psalm 109, "for wicked and deceitful mouths are opened against me, speaking against me with lying tongues. They beset me with words of hate, and attack me without cause. In return for my love they accuse me, even as I make prayer for them."

I can relate to Asaph and David's complaints. I too see the miscreants swipe at kindness and scream vileness, then go on lying, stealing, swaggering, killing the life in the love. I wonder, *What is God doing? Why doesn't He stop them?*

Because He is the patient Master Teacher.

Because He wants to redeem them.

Because He loves them.

What about me? As a Christian, I connect dot-to-dots without a whiff of outward rebellion, never hollering, "I'm not gonna do it!"

But like the first son in Jesus' parable (in Matthew, chapter 21), the one who said he *would* and *didn't*, I pledge allegiance to the Father and do not go, do not obey, do not do what He wants, exactly. I really want it my way. Jesus says to me (to *me*), "The tax collectors and harlots go into the kingdom of God before you," and I gasp, puzzled, as the Micahs move to the front of the line.

God allows me my inner crayons. He mercifully allows me to indulge sloth, lust, egoism, deception. He loves me. God strolls around, keeping His eye on the sparrow and me, waiting, waiting.

The third day, Micah swipes his paper to the floor and snarls, "I'm not gonna do it!"

Some people never seem to learn. ❑

Editors often face outrageous deadlines. Once I had two minutes to compose an entire editorial. This product of desperation remains a favorite.

What's Greater Than God's Love?

(Nothing.) ❑

Few habits are as pernicious and prevalent. May God have mercy.

On the Rock, Not Under It

It's parent-teacher conferences again, but I'm on the other side of the desk. Especially for a teacher, this feels strange, filling each fifteen-minute block ("Blakes— 5:45") to meet our child's instructors. Doubly strange because Yolanda is also a teacher.

We both know the vicissitudes of our vocation. A grim, tight-lipped couple edging into the room can within three minutes relax and smile in agreement or reach white heat.* We understand that one negative encounter can spoil thirty-four conferences.

Tonight, we communicate our appreciation and support, ask questions, laugh a little, and leave for home. Tonight, our communication is pertinent and positive. We pray that it may always be so.

Human beings are consumed by criticism. In our politics, work, schools, and churches, the negative overwhelms the positive. There is a place for pointing out wrongs, but it's a tiny, well-lit, redemptive place. There is a time for proclaiming that the emperor has no clothes, but the time must be absolutely right. There is a call to speak the truth, but the truth must always be spoken in love. Dark criticism too often eclipses our gracious goodness and extinguishes hope.

Many letters to any editor, for example, find "appalling" fault, but I wonder, *Will these complainers write as readily when they appreciate something?* When I was editor of a magazine, eventually I responded to extremely critical letters with a standard closing: "Please feel free to write to us at any time, even if you find something you like."

Jesus is the Rock that the builders rejected. His church is built on this Rock. We can choose to stand and rest on it, soaking in the light, or we can roll the rock over to peek underneath at the weird assortment of grubs and crawlies that dwell in darkness. The latter is the allure of criticism.

Nothing splinters unity and pulverizes love like a critical spirit—one that expends enormous energy in finding faults, that would sooner curse the darkness than flip a light switch. A critical spirit has destroyed countless marriages—and children. Ellen White observed, "The very act of looking for evil in others develops evil in those who look." In his paean to love in 1 Corinthians, chapter 13, Paul

---

*Because everyone has been a student, naturally, everyone knows how to teach. Isn't it strange that most people naturally know how to see, yet few choose to shower optometrists with advice?

wrote, "Love does not insist on its own way; it is not irritable or resentful; *it does not rejoice at wrong,* but rejoices in the right."

Criticism is the runny-nosed bully who picks a fight with you every day. Criticism is the lingering stink of skunk. Criticism is the eternally circling vulture. Criticism is the constant drip from your kitchen faucet. Criticism is the soap in your eye. Criticism is the narrow rupture that lets fizz out of the pop can of life.

Anonymous criticism ("People are saying . . .") is especially cowardly, and worth not a nanosecond of our concern. My senior pastor was the "recipient" of indignant displeasure over lively music at a youth program in our church—*one* youth program out of more than seven hundred church services while he'd been here. He told me that eight people had called the church to express their displeasure, but when the secretary requested their names and asked whether they wanted to speak to a pastor about it, all eight declined.

"So you didn't receive any criticism on the event," I said.

"That's right!" he chuckled. "We didn't, did we?"*

The story is told of Abraham Lincoln receiving a letter while he was United States president. The letter contained one word: "FOOL!"

"That's odd," said Lincoln. "Often one will send a message without signing his name, but this person merely signed his name and didn't send a message."

If we do anything of lasting value, over time we will receive criticism. And, of course, we may succumb to the temptation of demonizing the critics. As Nietzsche warned, "Be careful when you fight a dragon, lest you become a dragon."

Beyond Nietzsche's words, Jesus of Nazareth, Light of the world, has a word for those who indulge in destructive criticism.

Stop.   ❑

Do you yearn to see God? Perhaps this parable may help.

Four Men Who Wanted to See God

Once there were four men who wanted to see God. The men lived day and night in a cold, dark room surrounded by thick, towering walls. On the eastern wall, just below the ceiling, appeared their one source of hope. It was a window.

Each day a golden shaft of sunlight lunged through this opening and inched down the western wall. Fascinated, the men watched the light as it moved. They

---

*I added, "Please direct any actual complaints to me. My son was on that platform, playing trombone. There's no place else I'd rather have him playing."

longed to see beyond the window to the true source of warmth; they hungered for a glimpse of the great God.

Though the opening was small—too small for a man to fit through—the four men often made heroic attempts to reach it. Each tried running and leaping against the wall, clawing desperately toward the tiny opening, but to no avail. The window was too high.

It became apparent then that the men would have to work together, so they developed a plan. Perhaps if they stood one on top of another, the person on top might be able to see through the window.

However, the question soon arose: Who will be on top? Who will see God? All realized this was the supreme desire of each of them.

And so they sat, wondering.

Presently Rafael stood. "I will support you," he said, and waited for the others.

After a few moments, José slowly pushed himself up. "I will be next," he volunteered. The remaining two sat unmoving, staring at their feet.

At last, with a sigh, Weldon rose. "I will be third," he offered. The three men looked down at Sam. He would be on top.

Rafael moved to the eastern wall. He spread his legs, crouched, and pressed his palms against the stones. José placed one foot on Rafael and boosted himself until he stood balancing on Rafael's shoulders. Next Weldon clambered over the straining Rafael and past the struggling José until he could stand, his head just below the window.

Sam wasted no time. He scrambled over Rafael and José and, with help from Weldon, was catapulted to the opening, where he thrust his head through . . . ten seconds . . . the men below trembled . . . twenty seconds . . . the column shook . . . twenty-eight seconds. . . .

The column collapsed. Arms and legs plummeted to a tangled heap, where the men lay moaning, eyes closed, chests heaving. Slowly they untangled themselves, rolled to their hands and knees, and with painful effort crawled apart to sit. Then the three men eagerly searched Sam's face and waited for the vision.

"I looked through the window," Sam began, "and I saw many things. I saw wispy clouds laced across a bright sky. I watched speckled birds soar and wheel. There were oaks and sycamores on grassy hills, and distant snow-capped mountains. I felt the wind slap, I heard the rustling of leaves, and I smelled smoke in the air.

"I saw many things," he said again, and then he paused, gazing at the window. "But I did not see God."

The men sat huddled in silence, their heads bowed. The air was heavy in the room. The ground seemed unusually hard and cold. Suddenly, Rafael spoke.

"I saw God."

The others jerked and stared.

"As I shouldered the weight, the tremendous weight," Rafael continued, "as I staggered and strained under it, my muscles on fire, my eyes stinging, my mind crying out, as I carried it all for as long as I could and then longer—I saw Him."

The others sat, marveling.

"I saw God, too." José's voice shattered the silence. "As I balanced between what was above and what was below, as I felt the soles pushing against my back and head, as I struggled and shifted to keep us steady, to keep us somehow pointed up—I saw Him."

The others sat, thinking.

"I also saw God." It was Weldon. His eyes gleamed.

"As I approached the opening—so near—I wanted to be there myself. But it was when I stretched out my arms—so far—and lifted a friend, I saw Him." ❑

Here's a contemporary look at the book of Jonah, the most powerful Old Testament statement on prejudice. *

Joe and the Low Rider

Characters:

Narrator	*Bus driver*	*TV reporter*
Joe	*Tires (4)*	*Mayor*
Ticket attendant	*Engine/radiator*	*Large plant*
Passengers (3)	*Low rider*	

NARRATOR

Now the word of the Lord came to Joe,

JOE looks straight up.

saying, "Arise, go to San Francisco, that great city, and preach against it. The next bus for San Francisco leaves at eight-fifteen. If you hustle, you can make it." So Joe went to the bus station, but there was something weird about him. For one thing, he packed a bathing suit, a towel, and some tanning lotion.

JOE puts on sunglasses, picks up suitcase, walks coolly to ticket counter.

---

*Created and performed originally at Redwood camp meeting in Northern California. When performing, please change particulars to fit your locale.

NARRATOR

Then he bought a one-way ticket to Miami Beach.

TICKET ATTENDANT gives JOE a ticket and points to the bus, which has quickly assembled. The bus consists of FOUR PEOPLE hunched over on their hands and knees acting as TIRES, and ONE PERSON on hands and knees acting as an ENGINE in front. FIVE CHAIRS have been placed "on the bus."

Seated in the chairs are the BUS DRIVER and FOUR PASSENGERS. A CURIOUS PASSENGER pretends to read an upside-down book; a GAMER plays a video game; a ROCKER rocks out to tunes on an iPod; and JOE snoozes behind his sunglasses.

NARRATOR

For a while, everything went fine.

Everyone (TIRES, ENGINE, DRIVER, PASSENGERS) synchronizes precisely TWO BUMPS. The TIRES are pawing the ground as though racing. The ENGINE vibrates with energy. The DRIVER suddenly turns the wheel to the LEFT. With astounding timing, TIRES AND ENGINE lean slightly left, DRIVER AND PASSENGERS lean hard right.

The DRIVER straightens the wheel and everyone straightens as before. Then the DRIVER turns the wheel to the RIGHT. TIRES AND ENGINE lean slightly right, DRIVER AND PASSENGERS lean hard left. And everyone straightens.

NARRATOR

Suddenly, the left front tire went flat.

LEFT FRONT TIRE goes flat. NARRATOR makes hissing sound. PASSENGERS AND DRIVER lean far forward for braking, then slump left slightly. DRIVER gets out, pumps up TIRE with appropriate sound effects from NARRATOR. DRIVER gets back in, starts bus. EVERYONE goes through earlier timing sequence but this time with RIGHT TURN; ONE BUMP; LEFT TURN.

NARRATOR

Then, the right front tire went flat.

RIGHT FRONT TIRE goes flat. Bus riders bend through braking and slump to the right. NARRATOR makes hissing sound. PASSENGERS (except sleeping JOE) start acting as though they're complaining. DRIVER gets out.

NARRATOR

The driver was amazed. Rarely did he have a flat tire, but here were two of them right in a row. The passengers began to think that the bus might be cursed.

DRIVER goes to right front tire, pumps it up with appropriate sounds from NARRATOR. PASSENGERS act as if they are talking with each other. JOE wakes up but doesn't partici-pate in discussion. DRIVER climbs back in, starts bus. EVERYONE does TWO BUMPS.

NARRATOR

Then, all FOUR tires blew at once, and the engine overheated!

FOUR TIRES go totally flat with hissing. ENGINE rises and cuts loose dramatically with volcanic steam.

NARRATOR

Then the passengers knew something was really weird. They de-cided to use a foolproof method to figure out who was responsi-ble for their bad fortune.

DRIVER puts head in hands. ALL FOUR PASSENGERS stand and begin playing "paper, rock, scissors." JOE plays "scissors"—all the others play "rock."

NARRATOR

Joe played another short cut and was crushed. The other passen-gers asked him what he was doing. Joe said he was running away from God. "Are you crazy?" they said. "You can't run away from God!" They hated to do it, but they realized that Joe had to leave the bus. So they threw him off.

Suitcase in hand, JOE is tossed off the bus. The DRIVER gets in a kick as JOE is on the way out.

NARRATOR

Immediately after Joe left, the tires inflated and the radiator cooled down.

Appropriate sounds and movements.

NARRATOR

The driver and passengers were converted on the spot. They prayed thanks to God for the miracle. Then they continued on their way.

DRIVER AND PASSENGERS go through one left turn, one right turn, as everyone but JOE exits the stage.

NARRATOR

Joe started hitchhiking, still trying to get to Miami Beach. Just then a low rider came crawling along.

LOW RIDER sits on floor, leans way back. Heavy bass music pounds and then fades until it's barely heard.

NARRATOR

"Hey, man, where you headed?" he said.
"Miami Beach," said Joe.
"Cool, man," said the low rider. "I'll take you part way, man."

JOE throws his suitcase behind him and slinks low into the "passenger" seat, leaning way back. The loud bass music comes up and then fades. LOW RIDER looks at Joe and bounces to the music.

NARRATOR

And the low rider swallowed up Joe. And Joe was in the belly of the low rider for three days.

Bass music swells. JOE is in agony. LOW RIDER is enjoying himself. Music fades to soft.

NARRATOR

And Joe prayed to the Lord God from the belly of the low rider, saying, "Please, please, God, deliver me from this bass-rumbling beast! Will I ever again look upon my church? Will I ever get my hearing back? I will do whatever You ask." At that moment the low rider vomited Joe onto dry land.

JOE tumbles out with his suitcase.

NARRATOR

"Where am I?" asked Joe.
"You're in San Francisco, man," said the low rider.
Joe said, "Three days and I'm only in San Francisco?"
"Yeah, man, I get HORRIBLE gas mileage."

LOW RIDER scoots off stage. JOE walks around with his suitcase.

NARRATOR

Joe walked all around San Francisco telling everyone about God's message. He visited all the places he could—he even took the trolley and the Alcatraz tour. A TV station got wind of Joe, because he hadn't bathed in three days.

REPORTER with live microphone approaches Joe (still with sunglasses and suitcase).

REPORTER

Sir, we've been hearing that you're traveling around the city warning people.

JOE

Could you speak up? I think my hearing was damaged when I was in the belly of a low rider.

REPORTER (LOUDLY)
WHAT ARE YOU DOING HERE?

JOE

I'M TELLING EVERYONE THAT GOD IS GOING TO DESTROY THIS CITY.

REPORTER

ARE YOU CRAZY?

JOE

IT *IS* A LITTLE HAZY TODAY, ISN'T IT?

MAYOR joins JOE and REPORTER on stage.

MAYOR

My heart has been touched by Joe's message. As mayor, I hereby decree that everyone in the city should repent.

REPORTER

Wow. There you have it! The mayor proclaims repentance. Live from channel eight news.

MAYOR and REPORTER leave. PLANT comes onstage and grows. JOE removes things from his suitcase. He leisurely spreads a towel and straightens it. He puts on a hat and applies lotion.

NARRATOR

Joe went outside the city to watch it be destroyed. Joe knew this would be spectacular, even better than a Super Bowl halftime show or the finals of *American Idol!* And God caused a large plant to grow up next to Joe to give him some shade.

JOE looks through binoculars and becomes perturbed.

NARRATOR
But incredibly, the people of the great city *did* repent, and God spared the city. Joe was so upset. He sulked.

JOE pulls his hat over his eyes.

NARRATOR
He really HATED San Francisco. He wanted all the San Franciscans to die. Then the large plant shriveled.

PLANT shrivels to the floor.

NARRATOR
Joe was REALLY upset now. He was hot and bothered—and out of tanning lotion, too.

JOE really sulks. He looks up, crosses his arms, sticks out his lower lip.

NARRATOR
And God said, "Joe, you know what your problem is? You're prejudiced. You care more about that plant, which you didn't do anything to grow, than you care about My children. That is so wrong. You knew I would spare everyone I could, didn't you—because you know I am a gracious God, and merciful, slow to anger and abounding in love for all people. Grow up, Joe. Get with the program! And while you're at it, let these people in the audience know about Me."

JOE looks into the audience, thinking. He stands up, facing them.

NARRATOR
And so he did. ❑

If you've ever asked yourself why you bother coming to Sabbath School, this is for you.

The Little Sabbath School That Could

Dear Something Else,
"How does a person even begin to thank you for what you have done for me? I can think of no reason why my misfortune would matter to anybody. Especially something as 'minor' as vandalism—it wasn't life-threatening or anything 'important.' To think anyone would *care* about that was so unbelievable."

"Dear friends,

"Thank you for coming to the rescue of this school in Pakistan. What joy you've brought to the school personnel."

"Something Else,

"That's what you guys really are—the *prayers,* food, visits, the *long card,* and phone calls kept us both going—knowing that you were behind us in spirit and in love. Don't know what we would do without our S.S. class. You're such an important part of our lives."

Twelve years ago, a Sabbath School was born. Conceived under the best family-planning conditions, it emerged from the womb with mission statements in each hand (1. "The kingdom of God does not consist in talk but in power"* and 2. "Christianity is always intensely practical."†) because too many Sabbath Schools are all talk and intensely impractical.

Our church bulletin describes this one-hour class as "pointing toward Christ, and propelled by five ministries. Prayer. Time. Money. Study. Social." In the beginning, about fifteen people showed up. Now, more than seventy attend.‡

Each class period is divided into three sections. The first section is for prayer. During prayer time, we become grounded as a true community.§ A roller coaster of laughter and praise and petition gets us started. We learn what's going on in each other's lives. (How many times do people show up to church with personal burdens and no way to share them?) We pray regarding requests and thanks that we've written on the board. Cards are handed around, signed, and mailed out to encourage those for whom we've prayed. Prayer time is the foundation for all the other ministries.

Time, social, and money ministries take up the next section. An ongoing time ministry is the monthly operation—buying food, cooking, serving, cleaning up—of a soup kitchen downtown. Other time ministries help people move, clean out a burned house, or build a new bedroom for a boy with leukemia. Social ministries may be a Friday night campfire, a picnic potgoodluck, or a game night at the Lincoln Racquet Club.

---

*1 Corinthians, chapter 4.

†Ellen White, *Messages to Young People,* p. 200.

‡See the book *Reinvent Your Sabbath School* for more information. It's a quick read—about seventy-five pages. The book shows how to start a ministry-driven Sabbath School class at any level, from earliteens to seniors. You may order through an Adventist Book Center by calling 1-800-765-6955 (in the United States and Canada).

§I weary of hearing about a "sense of community." I want real community—not a sense of it, don't you?

Money ministry is perhaps the most cutting-edge ministry. While also supporting local Sabbath School expense, it operates under five premises* with now more than 470 projects completed, totaling more than $165,000—what we call "dollars of hope." (See sample projects at the end of this chapter.) It's astounded all of us. "I give more than I ever have before," says one member, "because I know it's going to something worthwhile. I see it every week."†

Every Christmas we hold a potgoodluck and a wrap party (with wrap music!) to help thirty to fifty needy children in our city. Using funds we collected in Sabbath School, members with the spiritual gift of shopping buy clothes, toys, blankets, school supplies, and anything else "Kathy—age 5" or "Jeremy—age 11" has asked for. We deliver the wrapped gifts to mothers, who receive them with tears streaming down their faces. We deliver to the F.I.R.S.T. Project—For Immigrants and Refugees Surviving Torture.

We help class members as well. Just one example: When a single mother didn't attend class one Sabbath, during prayer time someone announced that her car had died on Thursday, and she was in danger of losing her childcare business as a result. The class took up an instant offering and made pledges, the total reaching $875. The next day, a car was bought. On Monday, she had her business back. We are family. Miracle stories happen here.

Our study section focuses on the Bible using an AAA approach: ask, analyze, apply. Again, we're interested in spirituality that's intensely practical. We also drink in fun involvement with active learning. We are sorry when class ends.

I could go on, but Yolanda and I already did that when we wrote the book mentioned in the footnote that you should already have read by now and called the number. This new, ministry-driven approach provides a spark of courage and hope for readers who are like-minded. Adapt the ideas yourself.

Anyway, I understand that all this action has made Sabbath School inspiring and "unmissable" for members from Florida to Washington, from Norway to Australia.

I know it has for me.

1. $350 to a center for abused women
4. $40 to a young couple for Thanksgiving

---

*(1) Money ministry is a participatory process—it's the members' money, not the leaders'. (2) Acts 2—we give first priority to the needs presented by our class members. (3) Projects from outside the class need to have a class sponsor to be considered seriously. (4) Limited, short-term financial help is what we offer to anyone in need. (5) We prefer to pray for God's leading before giving.

†Some projects may require a few weeks' worth of offerings to complete. It's amazing how the total grows when we all work together.

10. $150 for electric and heat bills and grocery certificates for a local family

12. $80 to a Union College student for two coats and a pair of slacks

15. $194 for toys to a Romanian orphanage

34. $220 to an international student traveling home after eleven years

35. $300 to victims of a Grand Forks, North Dakota flood

46. $150 to a Union College student needing dental help

53. $1,200 to build six $200 churches in Peru

57. $500 to send five Union College students to eXcite98

59. $120 to buy sweat suits for people burned out of their home in Lincoln

70. $150 to a class member who needed temporary rent assistance

130. $125 to remodel a kitchen for a woman with cancer

132. $450 to buy fresh fruit through the winter for Native American students

133. $2,385 to bring a Uganda wife/mother and her children to the United States

141. $700 for carpet for a family in which the husband was injured in a farm-ing accident ❏

How should Christians respond to the complex issue of homosexuality? Sigh and shake our heads? Mouth a few platitudes and quickly switch the subject? If some opinion polls could decide for us, we might manage to avoid the issue altogether. Or perhaps, we can do more.

The following article was written fourteen years ago, but not much has changed since.

Redeeming Our Sad Gay Situation

Awareness
Scene 1

At the time of our encounter, Jack and I didn't know each other well. I lived in a cozy water tower apartment in San Luis Obispo, California, and he lived somewhere across town. Despite our lack of familiarity, we were enjoying a relaxed, meandering conversation. He lounged in my one overstuffed chair. I perched on the edge of my bed.

I had begun my fifth year at a public university, and our talk reflected a world still reeling from Vietnam and Patty Hearst and Watergate. Suddenly, Jack fixed me with a look that communicated a deeper level of intensity.

"You know," he said, "I'm gay."

I was stunned. *What was that he'd just said?* My thoughts catapulted, and an unnamed terror jolted through me.

"Well," I finally managed with a tinge of defiance, "I'm not."

The memory of Jack's revelation still evokes confusing emotions. Was I angry or afraid? Why did I feel somehow betrayed?

Scene 2

Beginning in 1981, a church-sponsored treatment center called Quest Learning Center, located in Reading, Pennsylvania, was promoted as the Seventh-day Adventist Church's chief response to homosexuality. In 1985, Quest's director, Colin Cook, appeared on the *Phil Donahue Show* in connection with Homosexuals Anonymous, a support ministry related to Quest. The response was overwhelming. Over the next seventeen hours, more than thirteen hundred calls requesting information poured in to Andrews University's Adventist Information Ministry (AIM).* Our church seemed to be on its way toward dealing with "the problem."

However, tangible results—meaning documented cases of "cured" homosexuals—still weren't appearing. An article in the March 15, 1986, *Columbia Union Visitor* cautioned, "The church needs considerable patience and sensitivity in its ministry to homosexuals, as well as in judging the results of the Quest program."† Two months later, Cook, an ex-gay, issued a correction to a quote of his from that same issue. He denied that "seeing a handsome man can present a temptation to him" and announced, " 'I do not experience this kind of temptation today.' "‡

A year later, Quest Learning Center was closed. During interviews with Ronald Lawson, a professor of sociology from Queens College of the City University of New York, clients of Quest revealed matters that led to its closing.§ Colin Cook later acknowledged in print that he had "indulged in very inappropriate physical intimacy with some of [his] counselees."** The ministry of Quest Learning Center ended on a tragic note.

One evidence of the true largeness of a person or an institution is the ability to admit, "I made a mistake. I'm sorry. Here's what I'm going to do, as far as I'm able, to make up for it." And so I waited for my church to issue a proclamation or an apology or *something* that began, "Though we acted in good faith, we could have made a mistake by suggesting that Quest was *the* answer to homosexuals' problems.

---

*Eugene Hamlin, "SDA Says Homosexuals Can Have Freedom," *Adventist Review*, Feb. 6, 1986, and Ron Graybill, "Freedom From Homosexuality—Goal of Quest Learning Center," *Columbia Union Visitor*, March 15, 1986.

†Graybill.

‡*Columbia Union Visitor*, May 15, 1986.

§Ronald Lawson to Neal Wilson, Oct. 23, 1986.

**J. Robert Spangler and Colin Cook, "Homosexual Recovery—Six Years Later," *Ministry*, September 1987.

We need to do more for this group of church members. For the future, here are some tangible ways we're going to help homosexuals." I waited and waited.

I'm still waiting.*

Scene 3

It's spring, and amid budding cherry trees, I'm attending a conference titled "Adventists and AIDS: Our Stories, Our Response" at Sligo Church in Takoma Park, Maryland. I consider myself fairly aware of the AIDS epidemic and its related anguish. What I'm not prepared for at this conference is the pain and helplessness that pour from the homosexual community in attendance. These aren't angry, profane protesters—these are hurt-filled, humble people. Most have been wounded by fellow church members.

One young homosexual describes his childhood, when from his first thoughts he knew he was different: He was attracted to males only. Then he points out the absurdity of believing that anyone would *choose* such an orientation. "Why would I *choose* to be excluded?" he demands. "Why would I *choose* to have my family be ashamed of me? Why would I *choose* to be subjected to constant persecution? Tell me this," he asks a stunned audience, "when, exactly, did you *choose* to be heterosexual?"

I couldn't say. Could you?

An older homosexual man recounts how three Seventh-day Adventist churches denied him membership despite his having been celibate for fifteen years. With tears in his voice, he asks the audience, "How long do I have to be celibate before I can become a member again?"

Scene 4

I'm in St. Louis, Missouri, at the annual meeting of Adventist Editors International. The AEI members are interviewing Robert Folkenberg, General Conference president of the Seventh-day Adventist Church. He has just expressed his view that he would appreciate knowing about especially sensitive and controversial articles before they are printed so that he might provide some broader input. It appears to me that this could be a good time to seek that input.

"All right," I say politely, "*Insight* is going to be tackling the topic of homosexuality sometime in the future. What input do you have for us?" The room is quiet.

Elder Folkenberg states his opinion and then responds to questions for clarification. For my final question, I ask, "How should the church treat people who are homosexual but who do not practice their homosexuality?"

He pauses to reflect, then says, "I cannot imagine God condemning someone for overcoming a sinful tendency."

---

*See epilogue.

Scene 5

A letter arrives for me at the *Insight* office. It's written by a Seventh-day Adventist mother of a homosexual. The following excerpts reveal her agonized journey.

I never thought of myself as the crusader type, but I guess that is what I've become in the past three and a half years since I found out about my son.

Not too long ago I talked to the senior pastor here and offered to lead a homosexual support group in the church if he thought there was a need. He said he could think offhand of at least a dozen families who knew about their kids' being homosexual, and several others who didn't. However, when a discreet announcement was put in the church bulletin, apparently nobody else felt brave enough to respond.

Because I still felt a need to talk, I attended a P-FLAG [Parents and Friends of Lesbians and Gays] meeting. I don't agree with everything they teach, but there have been a few—very few—people that I have felt comfortable talking to over the past few years. I still feel that I've touched only the tip of the iceberg of my feelings.

I think probably the great majority of our members are as ignorant, misinformed, and prejudiced as I was before I found out about my son. I thought gays were perverted weirdos who chose to live that way. My immediate reactions were disgust and refusal to think about it when the subject came up.

The really sad thing is that my son grew up feeling the same way, so when he realized he was that kind of monster, he had a terrible self-concept. He wanted so badly to be normal, to get married and have children, and he prayed for years that God would change him. When that didn't happen, he gave up on God.

What I would like so much to see is, first, that our church members understand what homosexuality really is and the difference between the condition and the behavior.

My second wish is that our children, while they are young, understand that being a homosexual is not a sin—it's a handicap that God can help them live with. They need parents and church members with whom they can be open; they need sympathy, understanding, and love. Other children who are not homosexual need to understand these things too, because often in the early years they are the ones who cause homosexual children the most pain.

Well, I've gotten carried away, as usual, when I get on this subject. But if I can help save our younger generation of homosexual children from the trauma and despair many older ones have suffered, it's certainly worth it.

Understanding

Homos. Gays. Lesbians. Queers. Dykes. Butches. Fags. Fruits. Pansies. These words roll off the tongues of some people with ease, contempt, and loathing. And fear. For others who are homosexual or who know a loved one who is, the words stab and scar with unimaginable force.

Some people's fear emanates principally from the mystery of human sexuality—a confusing, tumultuous, electrifying drive that can leave us breathless with wonder or plagued by guilt. Simply, we aren't quite sure of ourselves about this *sex* thing. The apostle Paul could have summed up eons of sexual tension with his admission in Romans, chapter 7, "I do not understand my own actions. For I do not do what I want, but I do everything I hate."

In researching this piece, I've read hundreds of pages of articles, reports, surveys, anecdotes, and testimonials on the subject of homosexuality. I've received input, some of it unsolicited, from dozens of heterosexuals and homosexuals. Upon hearing that I'm tackling the subject, people have commented, "I wouldn't touch that one." And "Good luck! You'll need it!" I'm not certain they aren't right in their concern. I am convinced that I will receive criticism from both extremes of the debate, those who believe I'm not giving enough "hope for change" and those who believe I'm giving too much. *C'est la vie.*

It's time to reason together. It's time for awareness and understanding on the subject of homosexuality, and it's time, especially, for healing.

The following are starting points for understanding homosexuality—twelve understandings before healing can begin.

1. There's a difference between being a homosexual and practicing homosexuality. Understanding this difference is crucial in determining how Christians ought to respond to homosexuals. As Letha Dawson Scanzoni writes in *The Other Side*, homosexuals belong to "that minority of persons who find themselves romantically attracted, through no conscious decision of their own, to someone of the same sex. Their *orientation* is homosexual. To speak of a homosexual orientation is to speak of a way of *being* and *feeling*—whether or not those feelings are ever translated into sexual acts."*

Other words used to describe this orientation are "inclination," "inversion," "desires," and "outlook." All of these are apart from actions or behavior. "It's like telling me I can't have green eyes," one homosexual says. "The color of my eyes is simply a natural part of me. Oh, I could cover them up for a while, wear blue or brown contacts, but that wouldn't change the reality. My eyes *are* green, and my sexual orientation *is* gay."

---

*Letha Dawson Scanzoni, "Can Homosexuals Change?" *The Other Side*, special undated issue; "Christians and Homosexuality—A Discussion of Biblical and Ethical Issues," copyright 1990.

The repeated theme one hears from homosexuals is this: "From my earliest memories, I always knew I was different." Their secret crushes and sexual arousals focused on persons of the same sex, and they often felt confused and trapped by their feelings.

I talked with Larry, a homosexual who told me that to him, the thought of sex between a male and a female is just as disgusting as the thought to me of sex between two males. That perspective astounded me. I'd never considered it before. Maybe you hadn't either.

2. *Virtually nobody* chooses *to be homosexual.* People may choose to do an all-or-nothing approach—bisexual or asexual—and may choose to engage in or not engage in homosexual acts, but sexual orientation as defined earlier is generally not a matter of choice. In this respect, the term *sexual preference* is a misnomer.

The exact causes of homosexuality are unknown. Many single-cause theories abound, but in general, homosexuality is "likely to be the result of an interaction of several different factors, including genetic, hormonal, and environmental factors."[*]

Much media attention has focused on the findings of Dr. Simon LeVay, a neuroscientist at the Salk Institute of La Jolla, California.[†] Dr. LeVay examined the brains of forty-one cadavers, nineteen of which belonged to homosexual men. He found that a cluster of neurons in the hypothalamus, which is believed to govern sexual activity, is on average smaller in homosexual men than in heterosexual men.[‡]

For centuries, the "nature versus nurture" debate on the cause of homosexuality has fueled fires in science and society, and at first glance, this discovery would appear to point to a genetic origin for homosexuality. But LeVay's work will do little to douse the flames until other questions are answered. As just one example, does the size of the cluster determine homosexuality, or does homosexuality determine its size? Nobody knows. Even LeVay admits his study leaves key questions unanswered.[§] William Byrne, resident of psychiatry at Columbia University's College of Physicians and Surgeons, comments, "If you look at any one piece of that evidence, it is inconclusive. It's like trying to add up a hundred zeros so you can get one." Richard Nakamura of the National Institute of Mental Health echoes the majority of scientific opinion by concluding, "it will take a

---

[*]Tineke Bodde, "Why Is My Child Gay?" a booklet published by the Federation of Parents and Friends of Lesbians and Gays, Inc.

[†]See, for examples, David Gelman et al., "Born or Bred?" *Newsweek*, Feb. 24, 1992.

[‡]Curt Suplee, "Brain May Determine Sexuality," *Washington Post*, Aug. 30, 1991. Note: This cluster is the size of a grain of sand.

[§]Denise Grady, "The Brains of Gay Men," *Discover*, January 1992.

much larger effort to be convinced that there is a link between this structure and homosexuality."*

Why is the origin of homosexuality such a charged topic? At the heart of the controversy is this question: Is homosexuality a changeable condition or not? If the root causes are strictly genetic, the chances for change are comparable to changing a leopard's spots. If the environmental context caused the condition, then changing the "environment"—even if it's the paneling of a mind—is a process that can effect change.

However, subscribing to an either/or approach can create overdeveloped conclusions. The genetics theory may lead some to believe that fate, or God's will, mandated the homosexual orientation. In turn, one could interpret this to mean that nothing substantive can—or should—be done about it. *Christianity Today* featured an article headlined "Born Gay?" with the subhead "How politics have skewed the debate over the biological causes of homosexuality."

The environmental theory can leave parents of homosexuals heaving great sighs of remorse. *Maybe I was a dominant or binding mother. Maybe I was a harsh or distant father. Maybe I didn't buy the right breakfast cereal.* The guilt index can rocket through the roof.

Moreover, homosexuals themselves may grapple with oppressive guilt over their part in their sexual orientation. In that sense, however, nature versus nurture becomes a moot question. Whether a person is born with the orientation, or it develops because of his or her upbringing, or it's a complex combination of both (which is most likely), it is *not* a matter of choice. A child chooses neither how she is born nor how he is raised. We shouldn't hold a person responsible for her or his sexual *orientation* any more than we hold a person responsible for skin color (nature) or how a preschooler is dressed (nurture). Whatever one's orientation, it happens early, prior to the age of accountability. Blaming the homosexual for his or her sexual orientation is both wrong-spirited and wrong.

3. The number or proportion of homosexuals is widely disputed. The *Washington Times* says, "[Ten] percent of American men are homosexual and 5 percent of women are lesbian."† *USA Today* refers to "25 million gay men and lesbians" based on a U.S. population of 250 million.‡ The American Psychological Association claims that homosexuality is "an orientation found consistently in about 10 percent of the male population and approximately 5 percent of the female population."§

---

*Joe Dallas, "Born Gay?" *Christianity Today*, June 22, 1992.

†Nov. 19, 1991.

‡Nov. 13, 1991.

§Cited by Family Research Institute as reported in Joseph P. Gudel, "Homosexuality and Fiction," *Christian Research Journal*, Summer 1992.

People often cite the famous figure "10 percent" when they estimate the number of homosexuals in the United States. Where did this figure originate?

The figure comes from a study conducted in the 1940s. In 1948, Dr. Alfred Kinsey and others published *Sexual Behavior in the Human Male*, in which they gave the 10-percent figure based on their findings. What is not generally acknowledged, however, is that their study was seriously flawed.

- Approximately 25 percent of the fifty-three hundred individuals in the study were prison inmates who by nature of their confinement couldn't have heterosexual sexual relations. Moreover, 44 percent of these inmates had had homosexual experiences while in prison.[*]
- Kinsey admitted that "several hundred male prostitutes" were used in his sample.[†]
- Because people responded to an ad to take part in the study, a "volunteer bias" was evident. "Research has shown that those responding to a study as intimate as the one Kinsey was doing would *not* be representative of the general population. In fact, the widely renowned psychologist Abraham Maslow pointed this out to Kinsey before his findings were published, but he refused to listen."[‡]

In addition, contrary to what is often reported, the study did *not* contend that 10 percent of the U.S. population was homosexual. Rather, Kinsey's conclusion was that "10 percent of White American males were 'more or less' exclusively homosexual for at least three years between the ages of 16 and 65. The statistic for females was 5 percent. The actual percentage of those thought to be *exclusively* homosexual for their entire lives was only 4 percent of men and 2 or 3 percent of women."[§] This was all based on his allegedly representative sample of the population.

Other studies have been conducted with different results. One study carried out between 1984 and 1987 by David Forman, senior staff scientist at the Radcliffe Infirmary (Oxford, England), found that only 1.7 percent of men in the sample

---

[*]"The Ten Percent Solution, Part II," *Peninsula*, October/November 1991. Also see Judith A. Reisman and Edward W. Eichol, *Kinsey, Sex, and Fraud* (Lafayette, La.: Huntington House Publishers, 1990), 23. In Gudel.

[†]Alfred Kinsey et al., *Sexual Behavior in the Human Male* (Philadelphia: Saunders Company, 1948), 216. In Gudel.

[‡]See Abraham Maslow and James M. Sakoda, "Volunteer Error in the Kinsey Study," *Journal of Abnormal and Social Psychology*, April 1952. In Gudel.

[§]See June M. Reinisch, dir., *The Kinsey Institute New Report on Sex* (New York: St. Martin's Press, 1990), 140.

had ever had homosexual intercourse.* And a 1989 study done at the University of Chicago resulted in a figure of "less than 1 percent exclusively homosexual."[†]

What is "exclusively homosexual"? Kinsey developed the "Kinsey Scale of Heterosexuality and Homosexuality," a scale that runs from zero to six. Category 0 includes all people who are exclusively *heterosexual* in experience and attraction. Category 6 represents those who are exclusively *homosexual* in experience and attraction. The remaining categories represent differing degrees between these two exclusive orientations.[‡]

In one sense, knowing the most accurate figures possible matters a great deal. Understanding how many people are likely to experience a homosexual orientation makes us better able to respond to groups and to individuals. In another sense, the numbers don't matter—whether homosexuals number thirty million or three million. As with any human beings, they all need and deserve our attention.

4. Many gays are not gay about their sexual orientation. I wrestled with terminology while writing this article. Should I use the term *gays* or *GLBT* (gay, lesbian, bisexual, transgender) to refer to both male and female homosexuals? And should I call heterosexuals *straight?* No, I decided, too much is implied there. A heterosexual can be crooked in a thousand ways.

Actually, many gays aren't gay in the sense of carefree happiness; they can in many cases be characterized as frustrated, angry, alienated, and depressed by their situation. (Of course, heterosexual people can be frustrated, angry, alienated, and depressed, too.)

Strict literalness may not be called for—most Blacks aren't black and Whites are not white. Still, the term *gay* in itself appears as a self-enclosed irony, an entombed oxymoron. Tim Stafford writes, "Over 15 years ago I started a column on love and sex for *Campus Life*, a Christian youth magazine. Among the letters I received was a steady stream from young people who felt sexually attracted to their own gender. Nobody could express more fear and despair. They wanted to be Christians yet feared they were damned."[§]

Homosexual men are six times more likely to have attempted suicide than heterosexual men. Studies indicate that at least 25 percent of homosexual men and women are alcoholics (the national average is 7 percent).** These statistics may say as much about heterosexuals as they do about homosexuals. Sick people in the "straight" community have long been bent on guaranteeing that life for homosexuals be a living hell.

---

*Reisman and Eichol, 194. In Gudel.

[†]Ibid., 195. In Gudel.

[‡]Bodde, 2.

[§]Tim Stafford, "Coming Out," *Christianity Today*, Aug. 18, 1989.

**Sy Rogers and Alan Medinger, "Can Homosexuals Change?" *Exodus Standard*, Winter-Spring 1991. See also Paul Cameron, William L. Playfair, and Stephen Wellum, "The Homosexual Lifespan," *Family Research Institute*, Feb. 14, 1992.

The religious community hasn't always helped in the understanding and heal-ing process, either. Pastors, ignorant as to the nature of homosexuality, write off their homosexual parishioners as basically bad people, destined to be eternally lost.* Is it any great wonder that homosexuals lose hope and turn to suicide?

5. *"Gay bashing" is never acceptable, especially for Christians.* From *Newsweek*:

> "Anti-gay harassment and violence increased 31 percent last year in five major U.S. cities."
> "Drive-by slurs and egg-tossings have given way with more frequency to nail-studded baseball bats and switchblades."
> "Gay bashing has overtaken opposition to abortion as the best way to rally the religious right."[†]

A Seventh-day Adventist university newspaper published an article that reported the responses of twelve students who were asked, "How should we as Adventists deal with homosexuality?" The responses astonished me. From four of these stu-dents emerged: "They should not be a part of our church"; "Send them to Canada"; "Castrate them"; and "Shoot them."

What do such responses say about us? What do they say about our God?

When we speak of gay bashing, we must define what it is and what it is not. Gay bashing is more than simply disagreeing with "gay rights" for the not-so-simple reason that the term can refer to anything on a spectrum from granting equal access to job opportunities to making homosexual marriages legal. We may be both for and against gay rights. And merely disagreeing with an issue doesn't constitute *bashing*. Bashing is attacking in a hostile, virulent way.

As *Newsweek* reports, most people are "torn between a basic impulse to be tol-erant and visceral discomfort with gay culture."[‡] The Christian community espe-cially is torn, because we want to do what's right, to be loving and compassionate, and we want to do what's right in the eyes of our loving, compassionate God. This same God communicated both "You shall not lie with a male as a woman; it is an abomination" (Leviticus, chapter 18) and "Neither do I condemn you; go, and do not sin again" (John, chapter 8).

It's the classic challenge of "reject the sin, not the sinner." We reject promiscu-ity. We reject immorality in any form. We do not reject homosexuals. Separating the sinner from the sin is difficult, but we must do it. And we must continue bat-tling against sin because (this is important) ultimately it hurts people.

---

*See Elvin Benton, "Adventists Face Homosexuality," *Spectrum* 12, no. 3 (1982); 34.
†Sept. 14, 1992.
‡Turque.

Christians should be at the forefront in protecting the rights of minorities, whether they are orphans and widows (see James, chapter 1), or the homeless, aged, uneducated, unborn, unattractive. The issue is really *human* rights, not gay rights. We are here to protect basic human rights for everyone.

What rights should we as Christians guarantee for homosexuals? " 'The right to have a job without losing it and the right to walk down the street without getting beaten up' would be a good start, says Gregory King of the Human Rights Campaign Fund."*

The right to be treated as a child of God is another.

6. Many fears about homosexuality are irrational. Through accurate information, particularly through understanding two facts, homophobia (an irrational fear or hatred of homosexuals) can be cured:

A. If you aren't sure whether or not you are a homosexual, the far greater odds are that you're not. Don't let the prospect petrify you. True homosexuals *know* they are different, as shown in the earlier portion of this article. (E.g., they have secret crushes on persons of their own sex.)

Sometimes people can have a homosexual experience and agonize about their sexuality as a result. Dr. G. Keith Olson, a Christian marriage and family counselor and the author of *Counseling Teenagers*, wrote, "Many young people experiment with sex in a variety of ways, often homosexual. . . . One experimental event during puberty certainly doesn't mean you're gay. . . . Panic about being gay . . . has nothing to do with whether a person really is a homosexual."†

Moreover, an absence of sexual attraction for the opposite sex doesn't make you a homosexual. You may simply not have strong sexual desires. Perhaps, as does happen, only one person can "light your fire." Consider yourself blessed if that person becomes your partner in marriage.

B. Homosexuals are not by nature necessarily promiscuous or child molesters. Homosexuals can be trusted around children when one uses the same caution one takes with all heterosexuals, especially males. And like heterosexuals, homosexuals are not attracted indiscriminately to every person of their sex.

Some statistics show that high percentages of homosexual males have had multiple sexual partners, but this may say more about the nature of males than about the nature of homosexuality. By comparison, many professional athletes are promiscuous, but they are that way based on lifestyle choices—they are not that way *by nature*. No responsible homosexual (yes, they do exist) advocates promiscuity or attempts to change anyone's orientation to homosexuality.

7. Few homosexuals are parading militants. What the mass media portrays isn't

---

*Turque.

†From G. Keith Olson, "I Think I'm Gay!" *Group Members Only,* January 1986.

typical of homosexuals either. Consider one complaint as it appeared in an advice column:

> Like most gays, I'm thoroughly disgusted with the way we are por-
> trayed in Hollywood and the media. To be fair, however, a large part of
> the blame must be placed on the shoulders of a small minority of the ho-
> mosexual community. I refer to the effeminate, limp-wristed, nasal-voiced
> queens who jump in front of cameras and make a spectacle of them-
> selves.
>
> Those weirdos do not represent me or any of my gay friends. . . . Small
> wonder average people are reluctant to give gays equal rights. They don't
> want men who wear wigs, dresses, and high heels teaching their kids and
> fighting in their country's armies. And who can blame them?
>
> Stable people, gay and straight, do not flaunt their sexuality and pri-
> vate lives. So please, "girls,". . . let the rest of us be judged for who we are
> and not by the distorted image you portray. You deny all of us the op-
> portunity to be accepted as decent, constructive members of the commu-
> nity—which we are.*

Homosexuals are found in all walks of life. Many are respected teachers, doctors, farmers, lawyers, nurses, mechanics, secretaries, and city planners. Many are
or have been married. To equate all homosexuals with a few militant or obnoxious
ACT UP people is as wrong as portraying all Americans as arrogant or tossing all
evangelical Christians into the "religious right."

8. *Changing one's homosexual orientation is apparently difficult and rare.* This
understanding should in no way undermine hope for realistic changes. The realm
of homosexual "change ministries" is riddled with claims and counterclaims. Exodus International and other ex-gay ministries believe the homosexual can be altered. They quote psychiatrists and researchers to support their assertions, such as
Dr. Edmund Bergler in his book *Homosexuality: Disease or a Way of Life?:* "The
homosexual's real enemy is . . . his ignorance of the possibility that he can be
helped."[†]

On the other hand, critics charge that change ministries set up homosexuals for
failure and despair. Michael Bussee helped organize the first Exodus conference,

---

*From Ann Landers, Oct. 12, 1992: "According to statistics from the Kinsey Institute, only 15
percent of gay men fit the effeminate stereotype and only 5 percent of lesbians fit the masculine
stereotype." (Interview with Jeannine Gramick, "Can Gays and Lesbians Come Out to Be Faithful
Catholics?" *U.S. Catholic,* August 1992 [no specific source from the Kinsey Institute is cited].)
[†]*Ibid.*

but four years later he left his wife and daughter to live with another ex-gay. Bussee says the term *ex-gay* is deceptive. "It conjures up in people's minds the idea that a person has actually gone from gay to straight, and they have stopped having gay feelings." He suggests this creates "false hopes."*

Detractors of the ex-gay movement contend that far more ex-ex-gays than ex-gays exist, that it's only a matter of time before homosexuals abandon their efforts to change their homosexuality. If so many people have been cured, they ask, where are they? Why aren't they queuing up by the thousands to trumpet their testimonies?

In a superb article in *Christianity Today*, Tim Stafford asked leaders of Exodus why they didn't talk more about "cure rate" statistics. He said he could feel the discomfort level rise. "But then someone asked what the general 'cure rate' for the church was. How many Christians really overcome the patterns they have grown up with—patterns of pride, or fear, or arrogance?"† Like other Christians, perhaps ex-gays are blending into churches and are reticent to disclose their pasts.

Few in homosexual change ministries claim that curing homosexual orientation is the norm. Even using the term *cured*—as though finding relief from a cold—is not encouraged. Instead, the words often mentioned are *process, growth, becoming, healing, discipling,* and *gradual.* Colin Cook remarked, "It may surprise many people to know that change of orientation was never a major issue at Quest, but rather a releasing from life dominance. It was the pro-gays who introduced the controversy of orientation change."‡

Perhaps there is a profound difference between curing and healing. Healing is often a fresh pathway, an altered trajectory, not an instant deliverance. For people with a homosexual orientation, it isn't a matter of "just control yourself" until you're "heterosexualized."

Think of it this way: How long would it take for you to "just control yourself" before you became "homosexualized"? Going the other way probably isn't much easier.

9. Homosexuals can be genuine, model Christians. A model Christian exhibits the fruit of the Spirit, as listed in Galatians, chapter 5: "love, joy, peace, patience, kindness, goodness, faithfulness, gentleness, self-control; against such there is no law." Then comes this verse, "Those who belong to Christ Jesus have crucified the flesh with its passions and desires."

Can these texts describe a homosexual? Can they describe a heterosexual? God doesn't save people in varying ways. "God shows his love for us in that while we were yet sinners Christ died for us" (Romans, chapter 5). We are *all* sinners. Christ died for *all* of us. We are *all* saved through Christ.

---

*"Former EXIT Counselors Debunk Exodus," *Exodus Standard*, Winter-Spring 1991.
†Stafford.
‡Spangler and Cook.

Robert Folkenberg remarked, "I cannot imagine God condemning someone for overcoming a sinful tendency." The crux lies in the overcoming, or as Paul put it, the crucifying. We can battle against gossip or envy or impurity or cowardice or laziness or love of money all our lives and still be model Christians, because we are overcoming and *because we point people constantly to Jesus.* Similarly, homosexuals may battle against their orientation all their lives and be model Christians the entire way.

"Ah," we say, "but if they are Christians, they must give up their homosexual lifestyle."

When we say that, what do we really mean? A homosexual writes, "I find that the words 'gay culture' are often used as a shorthand way to conjure up negative images of our lives. My experience of gay culture includes, among other things: poetry, music, literature, theater, sports, humor, and politics. My understanding of heterosexual culture includes, among other things: domestic violence, abortion, rape, and sexual harassment. My point is, to look at only one side is mean-spirited and inaccurate."

If by "homosexual lifestyle" we mean "having sex with persons of their own sex," that's one thing. But there's more to a lifestyle than sex. Not everything a homosexual person does is immoral. My sexual orientation does not make everything I do either right or wrong. We should take care never to communicate Christian disapproval of a lifestyle strictly based on taste or personality preference.

As I see it right now, God didn't create homosexuality as He didn't create loneliness or dyslexia. But God loves homosexuals just as they are now. His grace already covers them. And He expects them, as He expects everyone, to grow in His grace and to follow His leading. We should not ask for more. Or for less.

10. Being a homosexual is not a sin. Our church doesn't regard the *condition* of homosexuality to be a sin for which one must give an accounting to God. The *Seventh-day Adventist Church Manual,* under the section "Social Relationships," states, "Homosexual practices and lesbian practices are among the obvious perversions of God's original plan." The book *Seventh-day Adventists Believe . . .* continues the thought: "Scripture condemns homosexual practices in strongly negative terms (Gen. 19:3–10; cf. Jude 7, 8; Lev. 18:22; 20:13; Rom. 1:26–28; 1 Tim. 1:8–10). Practices of this type produce a serious distortion of the image of God in men and women" (page 303). Note the explicit references to "practices."

I searched through the *Index to the Writings of Ellen G. White* for her words on homosexuality. Amazingly, with hundreds of references on other topics, including roughly 150 entries on criticism, I couldn't find even one specific counsel on homosexuality. Isn't that interesting? I found nine entries in the *Index* under "perversity," including

- "God pities men struggling in blindness of perversity."*
- "Children inherit perversity from parents."† (The context refers to "traits of character.")
- "Christ bears with the erring through all their perversity."‡
- "God refuses to be wearied out with the world's perversity."§

The church's distinction between condition and practices underscores our first understanding, that of the difference between *being* a homosexual and *practicing* homosexuality. A person is not a contemptible pervert for being a homosexual any more than we are all perverted and retarded compared to the Creator's original design. Ellen White's counsels on perversity apply to all of us, whatever our sexual orientation.

Some have said that being a homosexual is a sin because it is "unnatural." And people use the line "God created Adam and Eve, not Adam and Steve" to highlight a crucial point—namely, homosexuality isn't how God intended the two genders to coexist. Then they imply that what is natural is good, and what is not natural is not good. (After all, aren't we supposed to eat *natural* foods?)

Yet homosexuals claim they have felt "natural" sexual feelings toward the same sex all their lives. Furthermore, if claims for a biological origin of homosexuality turn out to be true, some would argue this proves the condition *is* natural.

However, *natural* doesn't necessarily mean good. As Richard Lovelace wrote in his book *Homosexuality and the Church,* "An appeal to nature proves nothing in a fallen world." By the same token, unnatural doesn't necessarily mean bad. Adoption agencies, eyeglasses, pasta, airplanes, and mobile phones weren't in God's original creation either.

The danger here for the homosexual is that hearing "You're not normal" translates to "You're a freak"—and then depression descends. Instead, we need to communicate that we're all born with natural sinful tendencies. Every human being is naturally unnatural for one reason or another, and we must battle different *natural* tendencies that would rip us from the Father and rip up those we should love. "I find it to be a law that when I want to do right, evil lies close at hand. For I delight in the law of God, in my inmost self, but I see in my members another law at war with the law of my mind and making me captive to the law of sin which dwells in my members" (Romans, chapter 7).

At this point in my search for answers, I cannot condone homosexual sexual activity. In my limited understanding, homosexual sexual activity stands apart

---

Prophets and Kings, page 435.
†*The Adventist Home,* page 174.
‡*Education,* page 294.
§*Counsels to Parents and Teachers,* page 416.

from God's will. Yet there's a difference between those who fight against homo-sexual tendencies and those who experiment with or revel in them. Caving in to temptation is a sin. Being tempted isn't.

Sexual acts are charged with meaning because they involve our very beings. "Shun immorality. Every other sin which a man commits is outside the body; but the immoral man sins against his own body" (1 Corinthians, chapter 6). Like an electric current, sexuality can be life-enhancing or life-destroying.

11. There is no scriptural support for practicing homosexuality. As Seventh-day Adventists, we believe the Bible to be God's thoughts communicated in human language. Read any of the biblical texts that mention homosexual acts: Not one says homosexuality is in God's plan for humanity. The sexual relations that the Bible obviously condones are all heterosexual sexual relations (see Genesis, chapter 2; Song of Solomon; Ephesians, chapter 5). Other texts condemn homosexual sexual acts. (See specifically Leviticus, chapters 18:22; 20:13; Romans, chapter 1:24–27. Other passages that may do so as well include 1 Corinthians, chapter 6:9–11; 1 Timothy, chapter 1:8–11; and Jude 7.)

We should note that some theologians find these last texts to be obscure, and they say that the Leviticus and Romans texts refer to the *abuse* of homosexuality— to homosexual promiscuity, rape, or prostitution and not to consensual homosex-ual sexual relations. They point out that biblical condemnations against similar heterosexual acts are even more plentiful, and they conclude that "a simplistic English reading of the few scriptural references to homosexual acts [does] not suf-fice to determine the Lord's will for homosexual persons today."* These scholars also do not (without resorting to strained speculations) find in the Bible license or praise for or even one word of counsel on homosexual relationships.

The Biblical Research Institute of the General Conference of Seventh-day Adventists commissioned Ron Springett, professor of religion at what was then Southern College, to write a book on homosexuality. Published in 1988, *Homosexual-ity in History and the Scriptures* provides a thorough treatment of historical and biblical perspectives on homosexuality.† In the book, Dr. Springett examines "the claims made in much of the 'gay' literature" and looks at other texts "used by overzealous Christians bent on finding condemnation of homosexuality throughout Scripture."‡

Dr. Springett sums up his conclusion in the preface: "The church must accept the individual of homosexual orientation who needs help and support and [who] struggles against same-sex tendencies. But those who insist on and promote the active homosexual lifestyle as normal, natural, or even superior to heterosexual

---

*Benton.

†Ronald M. Springett, *Homosexuality in History and the Scriptures* (Biblical Research Institute).

‡Springett, preface.

relations by that very act disregard and undermine the sole authority upon which the church's very existence and mission is based, namely, the Scriptures."

12. The problem won't just go away. Whether people suffer silently with it, ignore it, or rage against it, the question of homosexuality remains. In some Christian denominations, the issue has reached epic proportions.

Rebecca Ruth Richards was a minister in the United Methodist Church until 1990, when she surrendered her credentials because of her homosexuality. In June of that year, she was granted an opportunity to address the Annual Conference Executive Session. She said in part, "I have come here today to tell you my story. But I do not speak for myself alone. . . . There are countless other lesbian and gay sisters and brothers who in previous years drifted silently away. And there are many others, whose stories cannot be told, whose courageous faithfulness in ministry and refusal to be driven away from their call to serve causes them untold pain and isolation. . . .

"It is long since time that these stories have a name, that we put a face to the pain and suffering that is happening all around us. It is time for the church to feel in its collective gut the hemorrhage that has been going on for far too long."*

The text of her comments continues under a banner that reads, "Homosexuality: A Difficult Issue for United Methodists." That was more than thirty years ago—1975. For United Methodists, the issue remains divisive today.

It's been a difficult issue for Seventh-day Adventists, too. The issue doesn't just "go away" because we want it to—because people don't just "go away." Even if they leave our congregations, even if they wander through waterless climes or grope for a mythical success ladder, people are still here on this planet, still needing the fellowship of the Spirit, still longing for unconditional love, still connected by invisible threads to Christ's body.

Healing

Healing is called for. Radical fringes of homosexuality have enraged people. Reactionary fringes of heterosexuality have hurt people. Those not on the fringes are left enraged, hurt, and torn.

Where does that leave us?

Though ultimately incomplete, comparisons to other conditions in life can enable us to find healing approaches.

Analogy A. Although the homosexual community dislikes the analogy,[†] alcoholism exhibits some resemblance to homosexuality in that it remains a lifelong characteristic, apart from behavior.

---

*Rebecca Ruth Richards, "Telling My Story . . . ," *Baltimore Conference Connection*, Jan. 31, 1991.

[†]They do not see homosexuality as a sickness, which is how alcoholism is often seen.

Moreover, science may have discovered some genetic similarities. "In the fall of 1991 [around the same time as LeVay's results were published], researchers at the City of Hope Medical Center found a certain gene to be present in 77 percent of the nonalcoholics also studied. This presented significant evidence for a genetic predisposition toward alcoholism."[*]

As many understand it, a true alcoholic is never *cured.* The predisposition is always intact; the temptation remains. But through programs such as Alcoholics Anonymous, alcoholics by the millions have been healed.

Analogy B. Some view homosexuality as a type of handicap. While people are born with or develop physical handicaps, homosexuals have a sexual handicap, although many contend that more may be involved. Dr. Elizabeth Moberly leads a school of thought that believes "it is misleading to assume that the homosexual condition is essentially sexual, and to evaluate it as such. The homosexual condition—although often an occasion for sexual expression—is in itself a state of unfulfilled developmental needs."[†]

Being handicapped is not a sin, as Jesus showed magnificently in John, chapter 9. Jesus doesn't cure all disabilities today. He does heal today—mentally, emotionally, and spiritually—even when a physical cure isn't evident.

Q: So how do I treat a handicapped person?

A: As a person. And realize that the expression "a deaf person" is worse than "a person who is deaf." Why focus on only one trait? How would you like to be referred to only by your most *unusual* trait?

An alternative perspective considers homosexuality neither as a sickness such as alcoholism nor as a handicap such as blindness but as an eccentricity such as left-handedness. The left-handed comparison assumes that either sexual behavior—heterosexual or homosexual—can be all right.

Analogy C. The sexual condition of homosexuals can be compared to that of singles. Whether divorced, widowed, or never married, Christian singles are to remain celibate, abstaining from sexual intercourse.

For many in the Christian community, the big debate resides here. Paul referred to celibacy as a gift: "I wish that all were as I myself am. But each has his own special gift from God, one of one kind and one of another. To the unmarried and the widows I say that it is well for them to remain single as I do" (1 Corinthians, chapter 7). Has God given the gift of celibacy to all homosexuals?

It may sound smug and self-serving for me, a joyously married heterosexual, to state that homosexuals should stay celibate, but we advocate precisely the same

---

[*]Dallas.

[†]Elizabeth Moberly, "New Perspectives on Homosexuality," *Journal of the Royal Society of Health*, December 1985. In Springett.

state for singles. As is the case with singles, this is different from advocating a life of loneliness or aloneness. And not all singles have a *choice* in becoming happily married. (We should avoid using heterosexual relationships—even marriage—as a "cure" for homosexuality, anyway. Such an approach leads to fractured lives.)

Christian homosexuals say that the nub of the problem is not promiscuity—we're all in the same boat up to marriage. Chastity is required of all singles. The nub to them—using their phrasing—is this: Is it right for homosexuals to enter into a loving, committed relationship (read "marriage") with a person of the same sex?

There is, of course, a sense of completion and bonding in human sexual intercourse that is not found elsewhere, and God intended it so. Yet Americans especially tend to overestimate the importance of sexual activity. Marlene Dietrich put it this way: "With Americans sex is an obsession. With the rest of the world, it is a fact." This obsession is in part a result of Americans' worship of the entertainment industry.

More to the point, as long as "straight" people buy and spread the message that we cannot *really* live without sexual gratification, then homosexuals are going to feel that it is an inherent human right. As Tim Stafford comments, this is an argument that "makes some sense in our modern therapeutic society, but none at all in biblical thinking: the claim that desires—particularly sexual desires—have a fundamental claim on us, and that those who cannot fulfill their desires must be unfulfilled."*

Stafford also points out that "the Big Lie of the sexual freedom revolution is that you have to follow your sexual preference (whatever it is), that you have no choice. If I fall in love with someone, it's inevitable we'll end up in bed. . . . But this is sheer nonsense. . . . One difference between human beings and animals is that we can control our sexuality; it doesn't have to control us."† Perhaps this is part of what Paul meant when he wrote, "I have learned, in whatever state I am, to be content" (Philippians, chapter 4).

In the end, true and total healing comes from God's unconditional love and forgiveness toward you and me, His fallen, failing children. It also involves radiating God's unconditional love and Spirit of forgiveness to others. "If we live by the Spirit, let us also walk by the Spirit. Let us have no self-conceit, no provoking of one another, no envy of one another. Brethren, if a man is overtaken in any trespass, you who are spiritual should restore him in a spirit of gentleness. Look to yourself, lest you too be tempted. Bear one another's burdens, and so fulfill the law of Christ" (Galatians, chapter 5).

---

*Stafford.
†Tim Stafford, "Love, Sex, and the Whole Person," *Campus Life*, September 1984.

Conclusion

The Seventh-day Adventist Church can reach out in practical, new ways to help homosexuals. Task forces, seminars, communiqués, brochures, and streamlined referral services to responsible support ministries are a start.* Churches compound the problem of homosexuality when they provide nowhere to go and no one to talk to. Churches and church members ideally should be the first place homosexuals want to go to, not the last.

A mother laments,

> When the clergy condemns a homosexual person to hell and eternal damnation, we, the congregation, echo "Amen." When the clergy says, "a homosexual person is sick, perverted, and a danger to our children," we again echo, "Amen." I deeply regret my lack of knowledge concerning gay and lesbian people. . . .
>
> I did not know that each time I echoed, "Amen" to the eternal damnation, [and to] referring to our son Bobby as sick, perverted, and a danger to our children, that his spirit was broken until he could no longer rise above it all. Bobby ended his life at age 20.
>
> There are children like Bobby sitting in our congregations. Unknown to you, they will be listening to your "Amens" as they silently cry out to God in their hearts. Your fear and ignorance of the word 'gay' will soon silence their cries. Before you echo "Amen" in your home or place of worship, think and remember . . . a child is listening.

Cruel and uneducated comments also demoralize the parents of homosexuals. They already feel enough pain without our adding to it. Many of us have become conceited, not realizing that "homosexual sins are not a special category meriting our hatred and disgust."†

The good news is that we can do our part in relieving the pain and in promoting the healing process. We must distinguish between the state of being a homosexual and being a sexually active homosexual, between the orientation and the practice. We must understand that acceptance does not mean agreement. And we must not allow the world's irrational fears to dominate us. "Do not be conformed to this world but be transformed by the renewal of your mind, that you may prove what is the will of God, what is good and acceptable and perfect" (Romans, chapter 12).

---

*Dr. Springett emphasized that his work was a preliminary study and said that "if the church is to gain a clear picture of homosexuals within its organization and how to relate to them, much consideration remains to be done" beyond his book.

†Stanton Jones, "Homosexuality According to Science," *Christianity Today*, Aug. 18, 1989.

When we are thus transformed, we know that the will of God is to defend and hearten people who are on the fringes. In characterizing the fringes of society, we may at once think of the poor, the handicapped, the elderly. Let us enlarge our vision to include the singles, the emotionally addicted, the homosexuals.

I didn't want to write this piece. For a long time I put it off. I don't intend to become *the* spokesperson for homosexuals; for me this is not an all-consuming platform. I'm telling you this because (probably like you) I wasn't naturally drawn to this topic, but I heard too many desperate, heartbreaking cries in the wilderness of our church to ignore them.

It is our duty—mine and yours—to alleviate suffering and to generate awareness, spawn understanding, and foster healing where we can, even when we are not "naturally drawn" to do so. To encourage, uphold, and point to our all-sufficient King when others are fearful is also more than our Christian duty—it is our joy.

Homosexuals can be members in good and regular standing of any Seventh-day Adventist church. They can hold church offices: If an alcoholic who doesn't drink alcohol can hold any church office, a homosexual who doesn't practice homosexuality can hold any church office.

Did we go too far? Please consider this: Susceptibility is not a valid reason for exclusion. Imagine what would happen if all of us who are susceptible to the sin of pride—the first sin, the worst sin—were excluded from the ordained ministry. How many pastors would be out of their profession? Many people succumb to the sin of pride when discussing homosexuality. Or when discussing pride, for that matter.

My fervent hope and prayer is that our church accept people with homosexual tendencies into our midst, that we will be known truly as Christ's disciples: "By this all men will know that you are my disciples, if you have love for one another" (John, chapter 13). May God rain His mercy on us.

Finally, if Jesus hung around with prostitutes, lepers, and tax collectors, would He hang around with homosexuals? With lesbians, gays, and queers?

You know the answer as well as I do. Yes, He would.

And yes, He does.

Addendum
Redeeming Our Sad Gay Situation

Overcoming Prejudices Against Homosexuals

You may be battling homophobic prejudices or you may know someone who is—or should be. These four directions will help.

Educate yourself about homosexuality. A good place to start is with the twelve points in the "understanding" section of the preceding article. Then try actually listening to a PWHT (person with homosexual tendencies) for his or her perspective.

Don't cave in to homophobia. Stand with as much courage and integrity against gay bashing as you would against any irrational fear that leads people to hurt other people.

Thrive as a living temple for God's Holy Spirit. "The acts of the sinful nature are obvious: sexual immorality, impurity, and debauchery; idolatry and witchcraft; *hatred, discord, jealousy, fits of rage,* selfish ambition, dissensions, factions and envy; drunkenness, orgies, and the like. I warn you, as I did before, that those who live like this will not inherit the kingdom of God.

"But the fruit of the Spirit is love, joy, peace, patience, kindness, goodness, faithfulness, gentleness and self-control. Against such things there is no law. Those who belong to Christ Jesus have crucified the sinful nature with its passions and desires. Since we live by the Spirit, let us keep in step with the Spirit. *Let us not become conceited, provoking and envying each other*" (Galatians, chapter 5, NIV; emphasis added).

Demonstrate compassion—Jesus' chief attribute. Recognize that we're all sinners, all in desperate need of forgiveness, all engaged in an uphill struggle. Remember the unforgiving servant of Matthew, chapter 18.

Look to the Cross, and show compassion.

Look to the empty tomb, and shower hope.

If You Know You Are Homosexual . . .

If you are homosexual, please don't give up hope. Do your research and contact an organization you can trust.* They'll put you in touch with people who can help you.

For immediate help, one approach to healing is found in refocusing on a new identity in Christ. For example, people who have a tendency to tell lies must develop a new sense of identity, one that frees them from feeling helpless or hopeless. They must not think, *I am a liar.* Instead, they can say, "I do have tendencies to deceive. But I am in Christ, and Christ is in me, the hope of glory" (see Colossians, chapter 1). This allows for a change in identity. Saul became Paul even though he was still the "chief of sinners."

We are *Christians* before we are anything else—male, female, Brown, Black, White, fat, skinny, blind, seeing, scared, or fearless. And Christ loves us unconditionally—meaning *no matter what our condition is.* Even if we slip up, we never slip out of His love. That's how God is.

Now that you have this new identity, even though you have these tendencies, you recognize that you are first a Christian. You must believe, *I am not just "a*

---

*Although I'm certainly not an expert in this area, one organization that has been recommended (in 2007) is peoplecanchange.com.

homosexual." I am a person with homosexual tendencies. Most important, I am a Christian; I am accepted through Christ; I am "dead to sin" but "alive to God in Christ Jesus" (Romans, chapter 6); I am God's child. This allows for a change in identity.

God has *not* cursed you. If anyone is cursed, it is Jesus, God's Son: "Christ redeemed us from the curse of the law, having become a curse for us" (Galatians, chapter 3). "Surely he has borne our griefs and carried our sorrows; yet we esteemed him stricken, smitten by God, and afflicted. But he was wounded for our transgressions, he was bruised for our iniquities; upon him was the chastisement that made us whole, and with his stripes we are healed" (Isaiah, chapter 53).

Glorious, liberating news! Let it inform and sustain your every breath.

To change any undesired behavior—whether promiscuity or gossip or whatever—it must be crowded out with good. We can't eliminate unwanted behavior by concentrating on it. If we stare into an oncoming car's bright lights, we tend to either turn into them or steer away, creating more problems. Instead, we need to focus our eyes on the road. Instead of focusing on ridding ourselves of sin, we need to focus on Jesus and fill our life with God's Spirit, with unselfish, freeing acts of service.

"Let not sin therefore reign in your mortal bodies, to make you obey their passions. Do not yield your members to sin as instruments of wickedness, but yield yourselves to God as men who have been brought from death to life, and your members to God as instruments of righteousness. For sin will have not dominion over you, since you are not under law but under grace" (Romans, chapter 6).

Epilogue

In the fourteen years since this article and its sidebars were written, I've done a lot of thinking about this difficult issue. It's still difficult. Last week I asked a good friend, one who believes civil marriages between homosexuals should be honored, if he thought the Adventist Church should endorse marriage between homosexuals. My friend stood thinking, silent, internally wrestling and weighing, for about twenty seconds. Then he said, "No, too much would be jeopardized."

The headline on page 3C of the July 8, 2006, Lincoln *Journal Star* read, "Like Episcopalians, Presbyterians are mired in tumult over gay issues."* Here are the opening two paragraphs: "The Episcopal Church's split over homosexuality is getting worldwide attention, but a denomination of roughly equal numbers and stature in the United States—the Presbyterian Church (U.S.A.)—is similarly torn up by the issue.

"And as with the Episcopalians, compromises have left both liberal and conservative activists unsatisfied."

---

*An Associated Press article by Richard N. Ostling.

On page 4A in the August 6, 2006, *Journal Star*, the headline announced, "Gay origins debate hounds scientists, religious groups."* The Born Different ad campaign and Focus on the Family, both from Colorado Springs, are jousting over the origin of homosexuality. R. Elizabeth Cornwell, a psychology professor and researcher at the University of Colorado at Colorado Springs, contends few scientists argue that there's "proof" people are born gay. " 'Studies have found that gay people are more likely to share some physical traits, from brain topography to hearing acuity, and other factors such as hormones play a role,' [Cornwell] said.

" 'The religious right has been very, very successful at creating controversy where there is none,' she said. 'The scientists who study in this area, it's not a question that there's a biological component, it's just how that biological component is working.' "

Focus vice president and psychologist in residence Bill Maier agreed that biological factors may contribute to "certain types of personality temperaments." He asserted, "These unique temperaments then interact with social, familial and environmental factors, leading (in some cases) to same-sex attraction. This is quite different from claiming that homosexuals are 'born gay.' "

The stakes in determining the outcome of this question are apparent to all. As Meier put it, "Americans are fair-minded people. And they think, 'Well, if an individual had no choice in the matter and was born this way, then certainly we should not try to obstruct them in their goals of same-sex marriage and parenting.' "

Three months after this article appeared, Ted Haggard, former president of the National Association of Evangelicals (NAE, which represents thirty million evangelical Christians) admitted that he was "guilty of sexual immorality. . . . I am a deceiver and a liar. There's a part of my life that is so repulsive and dark that I have been warring against it for all of my adult life."

He had resigned the week before as NAE president—in which role he had famously and repeatedly condemned homosexuality—after a man claimed to have had drug-fueled homosexual trysts with him. Haggard, a married man with five children, was also pastor of the fourteen-thousand-member New Life Church in Colorado Springs, which fired him the day after he acknowledged that some of the allegations were true.

The revelations came one month after Florida Congressman Mark Foley, who had pushed legislation to protect youth from "exploitation by adults using the Internet," was revealed to be an Internet sexual predator.

≈

I've been thinking about another comparison to homosexuality. Polygamy (marrying more than one spouse) provides this analogy. Advocates for bans on same-sex

---

*By Perry Swanson, from the *Gazette*.

marriages point to polygamy as a possibility on the slippery slope of tolerance. "If you permit homosexuality, would you also allow polygamy?" they inquire.

Polygamy does form an interesting example on many fronts. First, the Bible doesn't literally prohibit it, and some Bible heroes, most notably Abraham and Jacob, practiced it. Today, the Adventist Church actually takes a compassionate stance on polygamy. In the past, once a male with many wives became a Seventh-day Adventist, he was enjoined to divorce all of his wives save one. In many cultures, this led to alienation, untold heartache, and even death for the former wives. The Adventist Church modified its stance to allow polygamists who wished to become members to keep their wives but to have sexual relations with only one.

So, though the Bible doesn't specifically prohibit this practice, we do—and we don't.

Recently, a former student who had talked with me about his feelings wrote this hopeful letter. I received permission to include it here.

> For as long as I can remember I have always longed for real guy friends, but I didn't know how to get them. I wanted to share in the normal affection between guys, but felt awkward and nervous. In a group of guys I would still feel completely alone. I have had dark times of despair as well as high times of clarity and peace. God has led me on an incredible journey of growth and healing.
>
> My senior year of high school was a purging of years of bottled-up emotion as I began working with a therapist over the phone. Out of my brokenness I talked freely, and the walls that had been built around my heart slowly began to crack. At this time God spoke to my desperation and promised to bring me through this. It was like taking a deep breath after being held under water.
>
> I shared my journey with my immediate family. They were shocked but supportive. The disclosed truth opened avenues to more healing. No more lying. That felt like another breath of air.
>
> With college came a fresh start. I had learned much about myself through the work with my counselor, and I was better prepared to create healthy relationships with other guys. It took time, but God led amazingly godly men into my life. I now lived in connection. The gasping subsided into deep breathing. Sharing my journey with friends reminded me of God's faithfulness.
>
> God began the work of revealing to me who I was as a man. My identity in Him was forged through trials. He was no longer a mere theology but an intimate ally. He was making me into the man He had promised,

one with a new identity. It was a powerful realization for me when I understood that the intimacy I desired with men was not sexual. My longing for that connection had been sexualized out of desperation.

Our society has created a crippling polarity between *gay* and *homophobia*. Everything is sexualized until there is no longer a concept of brotherhood. Men are isolated out of fear that others may think they are gay. The Bible condemns sex between men. But the Bible also showcases the godly and extremely intimate friendship between David and Jonathan, who were both straight (see 2 Samuel, chapter 1:26).

As God continues to lead me, I choose to live in the identity He has given me as His man, and to dwell in the intimate brotherhood of godly men. It's not about changing who you are. It's about seeing yourself for who you really are.

≈

An official Adventist conference on homosexuality was held January 12–15, 2006, in Ontario, California. Titled "Christian Attitudes Toward Homosexuality: Seventh-day Adventist Perspectives," the conference was attended by about sixty selected delegates, including church leaders from the General Conference, six colleges, and several publications. Papers were read, updated research was shared, and an open, questioning, redemptive spirit was evident.

Topics by the thirteen presenters included "Homosexuality and Seventh-day Adventist Families," "Psychiatry, Anti-Homosexual Bias, and Challenges for Gay and Lesbian Youth," "Interaction and Angst: The Social Experiences of Gay and Lesbian Seventh-day Adventists," "Learning to Spin the Coin of Truth," and "The Caring, Welcoming Church? The Seventh-day Adventist Church and Its Homosexual Members." The papers, along with solicited responses, are scheduled to be published as a book.

Each day the conference started with an autobiography. On one day, a former pastor and the son of a division president told of his "gradual sickening awakening to the fact that [he] simply wasn't the same as others," his "private hell" as a married man, and the painful but restorative consequences of honesty.

My friend Willie Oliver, North American Division family ministries director, told of one of five initiatives voted by his department for the next quinquennium: "In collaboration with other NAD entities, sensitize and educate our membership on gay/lesbian issues for the purposes of fostering a non-hostile environment for gays and lesbians in the church in order to be biblically redemptive in our approach to this community and these issues."

The long-awaited time to address the issues surrounding homosexuals is here. May the Holy Spirit guide the Seventh-day Adventist Church as we learn to treat every person with awareness, understanding, and healing. ❏

Genesis Two

In the beginning God created.

And God said, "Let there be creativity.

Let it fill this spinning blue marble until it drips over and
soars noiselessly through the universe.

Let it flow roaring up chimneys to form puddles of clouds.
Let it spread glowing and snapping down molten mind fissures.
Let it draw on the right side of the brain

until it pauses,
pulsing,
tugging and lunging for expression."

And there was creativity.
And it was good.

But His children cried,
"Master of creation,
Creator God,

with all Your creating we are yet incomplete.

We need one thing more:

Create in us a new heart.

Create love from loathing,
hope from horror,
peace from pain.

Let our breathing You be our inspiration.
Let our asking You supply forgiveness.
Let our beholding You beckon birth.

Flame and flood our mindbodies with

Your pure Spirit of openness."

And God walked up to a wooden palette and
stepped into a picture
textured with splinters and thorns,
smeared with red,
laced with shadows
and an unending light.
And He said, "It is finished."

And there was a new creation.   ❏

---

*One thing I do, forgetting what lies behind and straining forward to what lies ahead,
I plod toward the goal for the prize of the upward call of God in Christ Jesus.*
—Philippians, chapter 3*

Plodding With the Prize

I used to run, sort of. Trudging, shuffling, dawdling, some would call it. Plodding, my friends called it. My former friends. They were right, of course.

My running hero—the person after whom I've patterned my racing life—is the guy who in 490 B.C. dashed from the Plain of Marathon twenty-two miles to Athens, delivered his irony-clad message ("We win!"), collapsed, and died.† From him I learned never to run long distances, especially in Greece.

Others haven't learned this lesson. Plodders know these people: the runners.

Runners run a mile to "warm up" *before* the race. Plodders park as close to the starting line as possible. Runners check their watches every half mile. Plodders follow my mother's advice: "Start slowly and then ease off." Runners breathe through their noses. Plodders take it any way we can get it. Runners lose their toenails. Plodders can't lose a pound.

Some of my friends who once seemed sane have run marathons. One of them, now a college president, decided one week before the race deadline to run his first

---

*All Scriptures in this chapter are from the Plodders' Revised Version (PRV). No copyright date. (We were too late.)

†Most people believe his name was Pheidippides. You will note that this is not in the "top ten most popular baby names" most years.

marathon. Before that, he'd followed Bob Hope's rigorous exercise regimen: "Sit in the bathtub, pull the plug, and fight against the current."*

Eventually, my friend finished the 26.2 miles with a limp and a time to do a plodder proud—more than six and a half hours—and enough sermon illustrations to play out the next millennium.

The most execrable example of a running fiend was my friend Mavis Lindgren. You've probably heard her sordid story. At sixty-two, she could barely walk around the block. At seventy, she ran her first marathon. In the twenty years after, she ran seventy-four marathons. Pathetic. Well, she was in my house, and I discovered her secret.

It was in December, and she asked me if she could use our mini-trampoline to "warm up." I was as gracious as a plodder could be in the presence of such an animal. Mavis weighed in at ninety-four pounds, and that's after a happy meal of legumes and tofu.

Mavis began bouncing. Bouncing. Bouncing. She showed me her special "kick," in which she thrust her legs out in various acrobatic positions. Yes, yes, very amusing for an eightysomething. She continued bouncing. Thirty minutes. Forty-five minutes. One hour. Bouncing. Bouncing. No abatement. No straining grimace. No visible perspiration.

No perspiration? Odd, I thought as I watched the incessant activity. *I wonder . . .* In a flash, I sped behind her, opened her back, and saw it. An enormous Duracell battery. She *was* a running machine! I knew this would come as a great shock particularly to her daughter, Karen, who was also in the house. Perhaps Karen started out as AAA herself . . .

I snapped out of my reverie. "So, Mavis, how's it going?"

"Fine." *Kick, kick.* "Just fine."

"Great," I winced. "Say, could you turn out the lights before you go to bed?" Another wince. "You *are* going to bed, aren't you?"

After my Greek hero, Mavis taught me all I needed to know about serious running. That is, if you are going to start running marathons, wait until you're seventy. Marvelous Mavis knew the Plodding Principle: It doesn't really matter how long we take to get there as long as we get there.

"There" is ultimately the upward call of God in Christ Jesus. The call, the goal, and the prize are all one attribute: *godly love.* With love, there is no finish line. Unlike racing, we don't have to wait to receive a prize at the end. We carry the prize with us all the way. As Oswald Chambers pointed out, "What men call the process, God calls the end."

We become healthy *so that* we can love better. If any exercise—anything—doesn't help me to love better, it is worthless. Love is the goal of a healthy lifestyle.

---

*This differs tremendously from swimming.

It doesn't matter how "healthy" we think we are if we're not a loving person.

Plodder Paul noted, "If I tread level 14 on the StairMaster for two hours, but have not love, I am a couch vegetable or a 'before' photo model. And if I work the Ab-ductor until my abs resemble the Alps, and lift weights until my arms thicken like young trees, and if I power-walk until I've crisscrossed the continent twenty times, but have not love, I have gained nothing" (see 1 Corinthians, chapter 13).

So the next time you hear something about health (or money or religion or anything else), ask yourself, "Will this make me more loving?"

Sure, it's great to be able to pinch your side and find just a little fat.

But can you pinch your soul and find the same?

My wife has generously [and graciously] allowed me to tell you ~~all the~~ [a few] details of our first encounter. She's ~~so~~ [too] good to me. Her only condition is that she be allowed to edit the final draft, but I'm sure that won't amount to much.

I Only Have Ice for You

Yolanda and I met on the only day it snowed in Ontario, California, in the past 100 years or ~~so~~ [more]. It was December ~~15~~ [20], a Friday afternoon, the last school day before Christmas vacation.

We were both seniors at Chaffey High School at the time. ~~I'm sure~~ [I'd hoped] Yolanda knew about me before we met because I was a varsity basketball player; she probably remembered my ~~muscular~~ [chicken] legs as they ~~dashed~~ [flew] down the court. [(gasp, pant)] In addition, she had dated one of my best friends.

[a throwback to] Social graces

That afternoon we were attending a school function when, somehow, ~~she~~ [I] was standing before ~~me~~ [her]. (I ~~think she~~ had obviously planned it that way.) Anyway, we spoke, smiled, wondered what to say next, and, to make a short story shorter, I ended [mercifully] up escorting her to the parking lot where her car waited, [hoping for a quick getaway.]

During our walk the snow provided a handy conversation piece, with such gems as "What is this white stuff?" [(You always had a way with words)] Then our talk got out of hand. Walking between parked cars, ~~Yolanda~~ [I] [(very punny)] suddenly and without provocation scooped

≈ 189 ≈

up a handful of Southern California snow, compressed it, and rifled it toward ~~my~~ *her* unsuspecting, innocent head. Not being one to shy from a challenge, no matter how unseemly, ~~I~~ *She* politely countered with a torrid and chilling volley. ~~She~~ *I* squealed and laughed. *After mashing a truckload of snow in her frozen face,* We raced around the parking lot in a wonderland of white, ducking and charging and bluffing and screaming between the silent cars. *and wonder we weren't arrested.*

It was a remarkable experience. One of a kind. *Unique, even.* Even if it had snowed in Ontario in 1856, or, whenever, no automobiles existed then for people to dart around in a flurry of *(a flinging flurry?)* freezing flinging. *(aw...)* Such a meeting was meant for us alone.

I suppose ~~you~~ could say things snowballed from there. Through no fault of ~~mine~~ *her own,* Yolanda had her tonsils taken out the next week in a place called Loma Linda. I brought her a rose to help her arise. For Christmas I presented her with a poster with *Joy* on it, and chocolates, *a large box of See's which I largely consumed.* We agreed to see each other more, *Since there was now more of me to see.*

And since that day, we've ~~always~~ agreed. *occasionally, and loved each other always.*

only a desperate person

♥   ❑

Every year I delivered the same speech on the first day of school.

The Sin That Drives Away

In the five years I taught grades seven through ten, my teaching style changed often. I adapted, learned, and grew to appreciate the nuances and benefits of a solid student-teacher relationship. However, one aspect of teaching never changed.

First day: Lay down The Law.

Any competent teacher will tell you it's a matter of classroom discipline, pupil contentment, and teacher self-preservation. Students are exceptionally eager, nervous, curious, and malleable the first day. Any pronouncement on that day is worth ten times what is mentioned any day afterward. The Law is different for every teacher, but whatever is The Law becomes nonnegotiable, unassailable, and sacrosanct. It may be presented with a smile and a soft voice, but The Law is seasoned with Tabasco sauce and strong as titanium.

In my classes, after a gracious greeting, a prayer, a joke or two, and getting to know each other better, I reviewed a few school and classroom rules. Then I laid down The Law. "Now, in the course of this year you may smoke or chew and spit tobacco. You may drink alcohol. You may brazenly break the dress code and swear like a salt-crusted sailor. You may cheat, steal, and lie.

"You may do those things, and obviously they will get you into trouble. But—please believe me here—those will not bring out my discipline and anger as fast or as far as something else will, for with those behaviors you are basically hurting yourself.

"Listen, now. In my class, and anywhere I am at this school, I will come down *hardest* if you are mean toward someone else. *Meanness will absolutely not be tolerated.* We will treat each other with kindness, dignity, and respect always. Do you understand?

"When you cross the doorway of this classroom, you enter a sanctuary. You are safe here. You can count on it."

≈

In our culture, love is flabby and flimsy. The notion is pathetically misplaced, mangled, mushed. We love our Hondas and our macaroni and cheese. We love our weekends and our Rockport shoes. We love celebrities. We love without principle, sacrifice, or nurture. The radio whimpers, "Baby, I love you, I need you—so let me mistreat you."

Yet despite the inane way we've treated it, love remains God's one defining characteristic. God is love. In contrast to Descartes, God declares, "I love, therefore I AM."

Is love *our* defining characteristic, or has the question itself become mushy? Is love a primary qualification for a church administrator? A pastor? A deacon? Or are we in danger of tossing it off along with The Caring Church motto? Maybe it's merely a polyester trend—it will pass. We'll move on to something else.

And we would lose our God.

≈

My wife teaches at an elementary public school of 650 students, grades one through five. Yolanda previously taught in Seventh-day Adventist schools in which the maximum enrollment (through grade five) was seventy. She wondered how this school would differ from her private school experience. Halfway through her first year, I asked her to describe the main difference.

"Even with all these hundreds of children," she said, "there are virtually no fights, no loud arguments." She spoke with wonder in her voice. "The students and teachers treat each other with respect and kindness. It's incredible."

"How do they do it?" I inquired.

Yolanda considered for a while. "The principal has us think about it continually," she concluded. "We teach respect every day through lots of activities. The teachers are reminded of it and trained to implement it in every meeting. Mutual kindness and acceptance are never taken for granted. We work hard at it."

Obviously, not every public school mirrors Yolanda's experience. However, could Adventist schools learn from this example? How hard are we working at developing a respectful culture? Is it top priority, or is this an illustration of the truth of Jesus' statement: "The children of this world are in their generation wiser than the children of light"?*

≈

Sometimes I hear people complain about "offensive" behavior. My response to those who try to offend or stun me through outlandish or frightful behavior is "I think you're a better person than that."

Inside, though, I'm thinking, *You can't offend me. Every moment I carry the nails from Christ's death in my pockets. I know what I am capable of, and that knowledge humbles me with every breath I draw. I can neither despise nor belittle you. Welcome to freedom. Enter the land of beginning again.*

≈

Any college recruiter or evangelist will tell you it's twenty times harder to bring in new people than to keep the people we have. That's why Adventists can afford to work five times as hard to *keep* people as to attract them, although the two are inextricably interwoven.

Tragically, we have lost hundreds of thousands of children to meanness—in our schools and in our churches. Dysfunctional pettiness and obstinacy have frozen and hardened children's hearts. You know it's true.

Ellen White wrote hundreds of pages on the urgency of loving. "We must be more tenderhearted," she contended. "God wants us to be pitiful and courteous. He wants us to educate ourselves to believe that our brethren love us and to believe that Christ loves us. Love begets love."

Perhaps our best evangelism would be to begin each school year and church year with an address declaring The Law against meanness and for love. Then we must continually work hard at affirmation and practical training, never taking it for granted.

We may be "good" Adventists: We may not smoke or drink or curse. We may not cheat or steal or lie. But if we are mean-spirited, we have gained nothing. Absolutely nothing. ❑

---

*Luke, chapter 16.

What are you "getting ready" for in the last days? Is it a hopeful picture?

Last Days Readiness

Just so you know up front, I'm not a last-days alarmist. I don't peruse survivalist "literature." I viewed Hal Lindsey's books as late great ways for him to scare up boatloads of income (which turned out to be right). When my son came home from academy with an extra-credit assignment to find in a newspaper ten signs of the end (wars and rumors, famines, earthquakes; people who are fierce, reckless, lovers of money, disobedient to parents, swollen with conceit), I suggested he would likely locate plenty of material—and added that he would also find ample signs in newspapers from eighty years ago.

Then *Newsweek* prophesied on its cover "The Crash of '99." *Fortune* preached financial cataclysm. *Esquire* billboarded "The Coming Economic Collapse," including a question hanging above a macabre photo of a shattered, cracked head and a stunned, staring eye: "What Did You Do After the Crash, Daddy?"

Esquire's Walter Russell Mead called it "the storm of the century," in which the Dow "could easily fall by two thirds—that's 6,000 points." In the United States,

> housing prices would plummet, leaving millions of highly leveraged home and apartment owners sitting on mortgages that are worth far more than their homes. Millions of people would lose their jobs, and tens of millions more would watch their wages drop as employers frantically tried to cut back their payrolls. Many cities would face bankruptcy as their tax revenues collapsed.
>
> All these things and more have already happened in many countries around the world. Thailand, Indonesia, Malaysia, South Korea, Japan, Vietnam, Russia, South Africa—stock markets in those countries have fallen by as much as 90 percent, unemployment rates are exploding, and countless people face the loss of their businesses, jobs, and homes. Even starvation.*

Elsewhere in *Esquire*, Jason Matusow, Microsoft's Year 2000 strategy manager, appraised the Y2K problem: "There is no one company or person who can [fix] it. Anybody who has spent significant time working on this will recognize that the problem is as serious as anyone has said it could be." *As anyone?* I wondered. Planes crashing, million-dollar phone bills, batty traffic signals, worthless banking cards?

---

*Of course, third-world countries have endured all these and worse for centuries.

Add to this biological weapons—anthrax, cholera, and plague—and a plethora of terrorist possibilities, including a few nuclear arsenals up for grabs. Moreover, the Leonid meteor storm could knock out hundreds of communications satellites; various environmental catastrophes loom; and an unflappable computer programmer told me he was pulling money out of his bank prior to January 1, 2000. I realized then that if concrete predicaments didn't get it done, the panic would.

I thought, *We're going down, people.*

Three nights later, the *reality* hit. I couldn't sleep. Most of the early morning hours I spent reading and praying. That night I shared my concerns at family worship. We discussed possible scenarios and our futures as individuals and as a family—about whether we could sell our house, how we might respond to chaos licking like dark flames around us. Afterward, we huddled in prayer. We were of good spirits because we reached a conclusion. Our only hope is in Jesus, the Light of the world. No change there.

At the time, Nike's ad campaign challenged, "What are you getting ready for?" Seventh-day Adventists, *what are we getting ready for?* Often people provide instructions on how to survive the time of the end. Are we content trying to *survive* until the Second Coming? Is that God's call for us?

John the Baptist certainly wasn't about surviving. Paul didn't preach survival. Peter, James, and John tried to merely survive when they deserted their Master. Jesus told parables describing the need for risky, trusting, absurdly joyous living beyond a survival mentality. Apparently, then, the kingdom of heaven is more than survival.

I've heard many times about "getting ready" for Christ's return, and I've always wondered what that means practically. The phrase "get ready" is not based in Scripture. "You . . . must *be ready*; for the Son of man is coming at an hour you do not expect" (Matthew, chapter 24). "Get ready" implies our doing enough good things to qualify for an exit visa—entirely the wrong message. I am first a human being, not a human doing; the difference is infinite. A fig tree produces figs because it is a fig tree, not to become one. Intrinsic, not extrinsic. Essence, not appearance. *Be*, not *get*.

Be ready—for death, for life, for adventure, for love, for freedom, for new birth. Be ready to join Jesus wherever He leads. Moreover, "we know that when he appears, we shall be like him, for we shall see him as he is" (1 John, chapter 3). *We shall be like Him*, entering life courageously. As Gandhi observed, "You must be the change you wish to see in the world."

So let the survivalists stockpile their Spam cans and their Smith & Wessons. Let God's people transition to new models of transforming grace of Christian community. Christianity has never been about isolationism, and never will be.

Watch the signs of the times become clearer. In the midst of an imminent collapse, Adventist homes open to the dispossessed and fearful. Adventist churches and schools become cities of refuge and outposts of mercy. Sanctuaries house the homeless. Playing fields plow up into gardens. As a world self-destructs, chapter 2 of Acts emerges before our wondering eyes.

We're going up, people.

Music, poetry, and testimony powerfully move us past lamentation to balm. Our choirs swell as "outsiders" join in, sensing a peace and joy that doesn't come from this world's merchandise. God blesses us in a thousand ways, whether or not we lose our savings or our lives. While other citizens quiver and kill, lie and steal, we remain true to our only King. Accepting, sharing, forgiving, merciful, and faithful to the End. Hallelujah!

This is our finest hour.

Light Carrying

Betrayed
bound
forsaken
rushed
accused questioned cursed slapped spat upon punched
taunted dragged ridiculed lashed humiliated condemned
You staggered
blindly under
the great weight
of splintered beam
slamming to
dust mingled
red with agony
and no one
to help.
O my Lord,
that I
could have
carried
Your cross.
Jesus, I
couldn't then.
I can now.

This post was read to loved ones assembled around the table one November.

A Thanksgiving Letter

As you are seated here at this time of giving thanks, I, your God, want you to know and feel a few messages from Me.

The first is that you are loved beyond measuring, loved with a boundless depth, to an everlasting end, by a faultless heart, loved without a particle of condemnation, loved with the fresh, invigorating breeze of My Spirit and the wellspring of liberating joy from My Son. Each of you is completely and spectacularly loved: My children (names of those present are mentioned individually).

As you give thanks to Me today for the gift of life surging through your wrists and temples, for the succulent tastes and vibrant colors spread before you, for the clear eyes of loved ones around this table, for the memories that warm you and hopes that sustain you, I want you to know that I also give thanks today for you.

You, each one of you, is the reason My joy remains, for you make My mornings vibrate with love, you are the reason I cause the sun and moon to rise and the cherry trees to bud and the mockingbirds to sing. You are the one I love supremely, with whom I long to share a forever friendship of Double Best Friends—deep, brave, and fun. My pulse of life races for you. I think about you all the time.

I know that the past year has brought sadness to each of you, and I want you to know that I have wept with you, that I never left your side, that you can always turn to Me whatever life pitches your way. Don't believe the lies. Look to My Son. Cling to Me. Listen to My Spirit whispering.

No matter what obstacle or pain or frustration you face, I am both walking with you and waiting on the other side with arms wide open. I am your only true reality, your only real hope. Remember that, My children.

Finally, as you enjoy the bountiful meal ahead, pay particular attention to Delores's delectable casserole and to Yolanda's mountainous apple pie. (Remember: I can move mountains.) Pay attention also to the peppermint ice cream (Andrea's and Natalie's favorite), and to the fact that while I created peppermint, it took My children to make peppermint ice cream.

Now eat with gratitude and in peace. Go in grace.

Love always,
Your God ❑

What is your dream? Is it God's dream for you?

All for Me

I beheld as in a dream my God. He stood, arm extended, to one side of a changing panorama.

I saw first a wide beach packed with crunchy sand. The surf roared and the gulls dipped and called and the sun baked. Heat waves shimmered on the lip of the horizon. No one else was on the beach; it beckoned only me.

Next appeared a flawless mountain lake ringed with waving wildflowers of every hue. Cool air pressed against me, pristine and invigorating. The azure water glistened and rippled. Towering snowy peaks stretched across the water's reflective surface. No others wandered there; the scene was meant for me.

A forest of giant coast redwoods sprang up. I bent my neck back to see pieces of blue sky. Shafts of slanting sunlight fell on ferns and bark to bathe the scene in golds and greens and browns. Young trees rose in a line from a fallen trunk. It was a magnificent, silent sanctuary, and I was the lone worshiper.

Amazed, I turned to my God and said, "All this—for me?"

He looked into my eyes, and He smiled and nodded.

The scene changed, and I beheld a great city with multitudes streaming down sidewalks. Some paced behind office windows or rode taxis and subways or slouched on front stoops. Others waited in long lines to eat or watch. All types of people were everywhere, crushing and rushing, and they were alone.

Then my family, friends, and acquaintances entered the picture. Neighbors, attendants, cashiers, mailpersons, all the people I can physically touch, appeared in a line. Some were first-name familiar; others I knew only by face. Quiet, bold, friendly, distant, sassy, inquisitive, different people. The line seemed to never end.

A desert village drifted into view with thousands crouched outside a wall. They shuffled forward with metal cups to be filled. Many leaned or laid on each other, their bellies distended, arms and legs like twigs, faces fly-covered, vacant, hopeless. Many more were walking into the village.

Amazed, I turned to my God and said, "All these—for me?"

He looked into my soul, and He pleaded and nodded.

At last a new series of images appeared. I watched the great events of my life roll past—the victories, the awards, the promotions. My baptism shone lustrous. Friendships were kindled; good habits sprouted in profusion. A hundred sources breathed encouragement. These were the sweet, glorious, high moments of living.

Then the picture darkened. The failures of my life broke like a thunderstorm. Guilt-stained, worthless acts. Cowardice. Selfishness. Deception and treachery, sordidness and hate. Wasted hours, days, months. The people I'd let down, the ache I'd caused. These were the despairing depths of life.

Finally, my hopes for the future flashed into view. My family arose noble and strong and giving. My church was to the world an example of compassion and integrity. The works of my hands bore fruit and became rooted in countless lives. My character steeled and softened in godly ways. My words were ever healing. Suddenly, the image flared and faded.

My God turned to me and said, "All this—for Me?"

Tears streamed down my face. I looked deeply into His eyes, and I smiled and nodded.   ❏

Loving Mercy

He knows the baseness of this man before Him. He knows what fiendish plot is brewing.

Jesus bends down to His knees, lifts one of Judas's filthy feet, bathes it thoroughly, the basin water darkening, and rubs the warm skin dry with the towel about His waist. Then the other foot. Gently, around the toes of His betrayer.

Wondrous love.

As Christ's followers, we are asked to love like this, purely and mercifully. Too often, love turns to lust. We love stories, but this love morphs to carnal curiosity as we leer at local and world tragedies on "details at eleven" news. We love people, but our love veers to lust when we view others as potential sales, networking contacts, and sexual objects. Do not use people and love things, Jesus cautions. Love people and use things.

Love is generous; lust is promiscuous. Love is a welcome, reviving rain; lust is a hurricane. Love is a glowing fire in the fireplace; lust is an unlit match looking for a place to strike. Love is a gardenia; lust is a weed. Love is a tender kiss; lust is Judas's kiss of death. Love is a sonnet; lust is a screech. Love is fresh sweet corn; lust is leftover fast-food grease. Love is the one antidote for lust's toxic bite.

In the profitable land of Technicolor lust, Hollywood rarely "gets it" on the subject of God. For example, in the film *Patch Adams*, Patch complains to God, "You rested on the seventh day. Maybe you should have spent that day on compassion." Of course, that *is* how God, through His Son, spent the Sabbath. Jesus went out of His way to work miracles of mercy on the seventh day. But Patch's complaint may be valid regarding the state of Adventist Sabbaths. Shouldn't we also spend that day working on compassion and kindness? In Matthew, chapter 12,

Jesus says of Sabbath keeping, "I will have mercy, and not sacrifice." How much of our Sabbaths are devoted to mercy?

The real question on mercy is how "soft" we ought to be. For example, where do tough love and discipline enter the picture? What if someone rips us off seventy-times-seven times (easier uttered than endured), taking advantage of our forgiveness or generosity? How should we feel about Charles Colson's innovative InnerChange program for restorative (not retributive) criminal justice?* On a larger scale, do we know how the world's most impoverished nations, those economically enslaved by interest payments, would use their debt relief? Will the extra new money be diverted to military buildups and out-of-country stashes for corrupt leaders?

What if God saved the world and the world didn't respond as He hoped? What if He granted us each day amazing blessings and we didn't always use them wisely? What if Jesus healed ten lepers and 90 percent didn't appreciate it? Would our crazy-loving God stop giving, saving, healing? God disciplines whom He loves (Hebrews, chapter 12), yet the wild wideness of His mercy is ever extended.

As when Jesus served Judas, our kindness may be trampled and betrayed. What can we say? The merciful shall live by faith.

We are asked to be judicious stewards, yet when we determine precisely who is eligible for our kindness, we become narrow, exclusive, prejudiced Jonahs, praying for molten fire to pour down on despicable enemies. We resent the pastor who ministered to Timothy McVeigh. Like Jonah, we're fearful that God is like that, keeping no record of wrongs, "a gracious God and merciful, slow to anger, and abounding in steadfast love." Deep down we fear He's too hard on us, too soft on *them*.

In the end, whenever we stop loving mercy, we mutate into the prodigal's older brother—plagued by hailstorms of bitterness, soured with curdled contempt, the basin of our benevolence darkening as under the feet of Judas. The word *prodigal* has nothing at all to do with returning. *Prodigal* literally means wasteful or reckless spending, one who misuses blessings. And how are prodigals turned around? In the case of the priest in *Les Miserables*, outlandish kindness leads Jean Valjean to repentance. Prodigals turn around—repent, convert, come back, realize that something is missing, discern the narrative arc to their lives—because of their contact with surprising kindness.

God seems to desire that we all be prodigals, spending our mercy with extravagant prodigality—like grateful Mary Magdalene, our cracked alabaster flasks of costly compassion filling the universe with a savor of life unto life, the eternal fragrance of our merciful God.

Even if mercy weren't required, don't you just love it? ❏

---

*For details, visit his InnerChange Web site.

Walk Humbly
With Your God

"He must increase,
but I must decrease."

—John the Baptist

Trilling can be thrilling. But what awaits us is even more fulfilling.

Notes From a Solo Songbird

Dan Lynn, Union College's marvelous choral director, is a good friend despite his never inviting me to sing the Unionaires' theme song, "I Want to Walk as a Child of the Light." He probably isn't aware that I come from a highly musical family. My mom was a choral director and is a superb pianist, and my father excelled at listening to her play. Moreover, my brother worked as a disk jockey for public radio, one sister skated to music in professional ice shows, and my other sister once liked Barry Manilow. Music, you see, flows lyrically in my veins.

I have sung one public solo. This premiere took place during the Christmas season at our church in California, where I was one of three unwise men to sing a stanza of "We Three Kings." I wore a regal crown and a regal robe that covered my regal wingtips. However, though I had performed in choirs, I felt out on a limb in this trio.

My two kingly comrades and I had sung the first stanza, and Evan, the guy with the best voice, had completed his second-stanza solo. The memory of my part still tastes as fresh as raspberries on the vine. I commenced singing.

"Frankincense to offer have I . . ."

Immediately following those soulful words, I noted a look very like shock smiting the faces of the listeners—people who once claimed to know me. My gracious wife told me later that their altered visages reflected astonishment that I could sing at all, but at the time, that prospect didn't surface for me. I saw only blank, ghastly, horror-stricken looks. Bravely and numbly, I pressed on.

"Incense owns a Deity nigh . . ."

Frankly, that line had never made a lot of sense to me, and by this time my head swam with fears and misgivings. *Why are they staring at me? Can incense really own a Deity? What am I doing here?*

All rehearsed words vanished from my thinly stocked mind. I didn't have a clue what came next. So, being the type of person that I am, I started *making up my own words.* My habit of creating absurd, rhyming ditties for our young sons now came in handy. But you know how you tend to say precisely what you're feeling?

"Ever reaching, thus besee-ee-ching . . ."

Though somewhat reaching and certainly beseeching, I would be finished with one more line. The expressions on the audience's faces hadn't changed, which could have been a good or a bad sign. However, my somersaulting brain, working feverishly to make a connection, had lost the original rhyme scheme. I actually needed to rhyme with "nigh," which would have been a piece of pie. As in:

"Now we look toward the sky."

Or, more appropriately: "O what a fool am I."

Instead, I was attempting to compose on the spot a tough rhyme with "beseeching." *Breaching? Leeching? Screeching?* I ended with this:

"We are all now . . . oh, I blew it."

This might have destroyed the atmosphere of "We Three Kings," but we kept on singing ("Oooh, OOOOOHHHH, star of wonder . . ."), and the horrified expressions in the audience never changed. I definitely took that as a bad sign.

Three morals emerge from this dirge.

1. Sing your song. Someone in your audience will make faces. Are you overly concerned with what others might be thinking and thus losing your place in life? Though you feel as graceless as a hippopotamus setting up dominoes, be your own person. Sing your own psalm. God knows it's worth hearing.

2. You can't always "wing it." Deep preparation pays.

3. Even when you blow it, life goes on. Chapter 15 of Revelation describes a new song, the glorious song of Moses and the Lamb, that no one in the universe can sing but we, the faulty, frail, and finite. The singers of that song haven't been unduly swayed by others; they have deeply prepared so that they can literally wing it, and they understand that even though they have on occasion blown it, eternal life goes on.

The surprisingly good news about this new song is that we will somehow know the words, we will know the tune, and—befitting each of our life-songs—we won't be singing solo.   ❏

Have you ever been absolutely astounded by an answered prayer? So have I.

Closed Doors

To begin with, I don't know how prayer works. I don't understand how God honors our personal freedom and yet accomplishes His designs, or why some obviously good answers don't occur while some obviously infantile requests seem to gain a positive response. So when I share the upcoming story, it's not with the idea that I have God all figured out.

I do know this: Somehow, prayer enables God and ennobles me.

Generally, I don't share the miraculous in my life. I think Jesus cautioned people not to broadcast His miracles because they give a misleading impression of what He's really about—bringing grace to normal living. He said, "Don't tell any-one about this" because He didn't want to sensationalize what it means to trust Him.* People talked anyway, until He "could no longer openly enter a town" (Mark, chapter 1).

Frankly, most of my perceived yes answers to prayer don't seem worthy of shar-ing because they happen every day—yet their *everydayness* makes them mean more to me. Thank You, Father, for those. Thank You also for this one.

≈

Standing outside the armory, I panicked. Too soon, 225 people would begin arriv-ing for our community stress seminar, *and they had no place to go*. Talk about stress.

Our 140-member church had rallied to spend uncounted hours producing and mailing eleven thousand brochures to households in San Luis Obispo, California. We had come up with twenty-six leaders—including friends who were not mem-bers of our congregation—to handle discussion groups. Our registration numbers had encouraged even the most skeptical: 175 of the 225 registered weren't mem-bers of any Adventist church.

I had arranged with city hall (after numerous routings) to open the armory for us by 5:45 P.M. that opening Tuesday night, leaving plenty of time for our 7:15 start. Having toured the facility before, I knew the three outside doors leading to the foyer and the three doors opening to the auditorium would need to be unlocked, so I double-checked. Yes, I was brusquely assured, it would be taken care of.

At 5:45, I pulled up in my Honda Civic Wagon—which was crammed with transparencies, two overhead projectors, music stands, leader and participant book-lets, and cups for juice—looking like a one-man mobile stress-reduction clinic. I had anticipated meeting a custodian, at least. My anxiety and dread rose when I spied no one there to meet me.

Odd, I thought. *Perhaps they left the doors open for me.*

I tried the three large outside doors. All were locked. Suddenly, like a quarter-back hearing footsteps, I knew that I was in deep, deep trouble. From experience, I had learned that city hall closed at 5:30, and no one would check the answering machine until morning. (No crises, please.) More discomfiting was the fact that I didn't have a clue whom to call. No name. No home phone number. *Nada*.

I was throwing a party for 225 people in about an hour, and we couldn't get into the house.

It's at times like this that one learns the power of panic. I paced like a crazed man around the armory, yanking and hammering every door and window I could find. No. No! *No!*

---

*Showcasing God's miracles can make others wonder why God didn't do the miracles they wanted, leading to disappointment, bitterness, and, in the end, a diminution of faith.

Despair crashed through me. *What could I do? Should we hold it in the church? Should I break a window? Should I run screaming into the street? Should I read some stress materials myself?*

What I did resonates clearly in my memory. I prayed. Not that I hadn't been praying all through the process, from the conception of the seminar to the most recent door whacking, but I was near tears with fear and frustration when I stood on the east side of the armory and prayed these words out loud: "God, this is Your seminar, not mine. These are Your children showing up here in a few minutes. I give this all to You. If You want it to happen, You are going to have to do it. I'm out of ideas. Thank You, in Jesus' name."

At that *instant,* I noticed some stairs leading down the side of the armory. Walking toward them, I saw a door at the bottom of the stairwell. I walked down those stairs, breathed another prayer, and squeezed the handle.

The door opened.

I walked into a hallway that led to the foyer and threw open the three outside doors as though they were life itself. From my car, I brought in a load of supplies. Then I tried to open a door to the auditorium.

It was locked.

I tried another.

Locked.

I thought, *Two hundred and twenty-five people are going to feel a weensy bit crowded in this foyer.*

With heart poundings measurable on the Richter scale, I squeezed the final handle—the only way in—and breathed another prayer. *God, please.*

The door opened.

Exultant, I walked through the door, letting it close behind me, and then I propped open the other two doors. When I returned from another trip to my car, I reached to open the closed door—the door that had provided entrance into the auditorium.

The door was locked.

Chills sprinted up and down my arms and coiled at the base of my neck. I nearly collapsed with grateful weeping on the spot.

Now, I have to confess that I'm not easily swayed by "stories." I should have been raised in Missouri—the "Show Me" state. The disciple Thomas could have been my patron saint. I'm well aware that the primary purpose of prayer is communication. Yet God has astounded me so many times in answer to my prayers that I am . . . speechless. Miracles of forgiveness and vision and energy and patience and humility and hope have flooded my life until I must, as an intelligent being, believe.

I could have rationalized the open door in the stairwell. (*Somebody must have left it unlocked.*) But the door to the auditorium was different.

Why did God allow me to go through all of that panicked anxiety? Why didn't a helpful (or surly) janitor appear? It occurs to me that I wouldn't be telling any of this, replete with renewed tears and chills in my writing, if He had done it any other way.

God has opened doors for me all of my life. I just have to keep showing up and squeezing those handles.   ❏

He said "There was a man who had two sons . . ."—Luke, chapter 15

The Other Son

It began to gnaw at him, their irksome fretting over his departed brother. His brother the ingrate, the playboy, the traitor.

All day and far into the dreary night his father and mother pined. Whispering and sighing over the other son, they set an empty place at the table, filled the silver goblets with red wine, broke the crusty, warm bread, and gazed out the window toward a country far beyond the waving golden fields. Fields plowed by *his* straining back and watered by *his* sweat.

Still he worked on, though obeying his father brought no gladness whatsoever. How could it? He was forever resentful, wondering, *What is he doing right now? What forbidden pleasure, what indulgence is he tasting? What is he getting away with?*

He brooded. He made sure that everyone knew this was *his* house, these were *his* things, and *his* tastes prevailed. When the hired workers or even his sisters appeared to be enjoying themselves, he grew stern and indignant. "This is work, not play," he grumbled. "Play is the devil's tool, the enemy's seed—sowing license and disobedience. As if you didn't know." He shamed them to silence.

Then he would set his aching teeth and plunge ahead, not looking up, not savoring the space granted nor celebrating the assurance of his inheritance. He slept through Sabbaths and holidays. He walked stiffly away from problems. He followed prudent health principles, burying himself under his work and his numbness to arrive at death safely.

Eventually, by innuendoes and malicious motives, though appearing to desire only what the father wanted, he spread blame and disharmony throughout the household. He questioned his father's choices and blasted high spirits wherever he found them. After all, if he couldn't be at peace, nobody should be.

"Doesn't it seem we should have more workers?" he asked innocently. "Why is so much money spent on those festivals and the contributions to the poor?

Wouldn't it be better to put money toward more seed for the fields?" All the while he inwardly questioned, *Will my brother really get what he deserves? Will I?*

Feeding on overripe fears, he scratched out a patch of identity, his rancor cutting like a scythe through slender grasses. Though lonely to the core, he carried grudges and accepted only those who gritted out their lives as he did. He embraced the frozen past until it clung to him.

Now, years later, he was in the field in the cool twilight, and as he drew near his father's house he heard music and shouts of laughter and dancing. He called one of the servants to ask what was going on.

"Your brother has arrived," explained the servant. "Your father has killed the fatted calf because your brother is safe."

My brother? That disloyal, irreverent scoundrel? He spun on his heel and stomped away. The noisy celebration receded in the distance. Soon he heard footsteps and whirled to see his father running, robes flapping and sandals slapping dust.

"Come, join us!" said his father breathlessly. "Your brother has returned!"

"*Join* you? No, no. You go on with your merrymaking; it's what you've always wanted anyway!" he shouted. "I could have left, too. The years I've served you, working hard, never disobeying—but did I get a fatted calf? Go ahead! Spend it *all* on him!"

"You know that everything I have is yours." The father placed two strong, weathered hands on his elder son's shoulders. "I would be so happy," he said hoarsely, his eyes filling, "if both my sons who have left would come home this day."

The elder son stared incredulously. What was his father saying? He'd been there all along. He had worked there all his life. *He* had never left.

Had he? ❑

Tempted to complain about how tough you have it? Check this out first.

If You Had Only a Left-Eye Blink

Last week I bought and read a book, marked down from $20 to $3.98, titled *The Diving Bell and the Butterfly* by Jean-Dominique Bauby. I can't get the book out of my mind.

Bauby was a forty-three-year-old editor-in-chief of French *Elle* when he incurred a massive stroke that affected his brain stem. He described "swimming up from the mists of coma" twenty days afterward and emerging to a maddening condition called locked-in syndrome, wherein the victim is virtually paralyzed from head to toe, his mind fully intact, imprisoned inside his own body.

In Bauby's case, blinking his left eyelid was his only means of communication. He awoke from his coma to find a doctor sewing the right eyelid shut with a needle and thread "like he was darning a sock." Bauby feared his other eye, his one avenue for contact, would also be closed off. "I have known gentler awakenings," he quipped.

His right ear was deaf, and his left ear amplified and distorted any sounds farther than ten feet away. Moreover, his head "weighs a ton, and something like an invisible diving bell holds my whole body prisoner." On many occasions, however, his mind "takes flight like a butterfly."

His crafted words tumble in my head like polished rocks. In his own head, he churned over the book's every word ten times, learning the text by heart before he let it out.* His transcriber recited the alphabet one letter at a time until Bauby blinked. The letters were arranged in the order of frequency of their use in the French language: E S A R I N T U L O M D P C F B V H G J Q Z Y X K W.

Bauby reveled in simple pleasures and modest requests. "I would be the happiest of men," he announced, "if I could just swallow the overflow of saliva that endlessly floods my mouth." Ever fashion conscious, he turned down a "hideous jogging suit" provided by the hospital for clothes he was accustomed to, proclaiming, "If I must drool, I may as well drool on cashmere."

He recalled how on the final day before his former life was snuffed out, "I mechanically carried out all those simple acts that today seem miraculous to me: shaving, dressing, downing a hot chocolate."

"How can I describe," he lamented, "waking for the last time, heedless, perhaps a little grumpy, beside the lithe, warm body of a tall, dark-haired woman?" When his ten-year-old son sat beside him, he said, "I, his father, have lost the simple right to ruffle his bristly hair, clasp his downy neck."

"I can weep quite discreetly," he confided. "People think my eye is watering."

Some of the hospital staff enraged him, particularly "those who wrenched my arm while putting me in my wheelchair, or left me all night long with the TV on, or let me lie in a painful position despite my protests," yet he forgave them.

Somehow, he maintained his sense of perspective and humor. "I've lost sixty-six pounds in just twenty weeks," he said. "When I began a diet a week before my stroke, I never dreamed of such a dramatic result."

He received remarkable letters, which were spread before him in "a hushed and holy ceremony."

> Some of them are serious in tone, discussing the meaning of life, invoking the supremacy of the soul, the mystery of every existence. And by a curious reversal, the people who focus most closely on these fundamental

---

*He died two days after the book was published.

questions tend to be the people I had known only superficially. Their small talk had masked hidden depths. Had I been blind and deaf, or does it take the harsh light of disaster to show a person's true nature?

Other letters simply relate the small events that punctuate the passage of time: roses picked at dusk, the laziness of a rainy Sunday, a child crying himself to sleep. Capturing the moment, these small slices of life, these small gusts of happiness, move me more deeply than all the rest.

I read his words and wonder, *What am I doing with this enormous life of mine?* ❏

Forget "conservatives" and "liberals." Where would you place yourself?

Are We Guardians or Seekers of Truth?

Of the many fundamental divisions in the Seventh-day Adventist Church (or any church), perhaps none is as practically meaningful as the difference between Guardians of Truth and Seekers of Truth.

Guardians serve God and fear Him. Seekers serve God and enjoy Him.

Guardians talk of historic truths. Seekers live out present truth.

Guardians emphasize performance. Seekers emphasize participation.

Guardians consider early Adventists guardians. Seekers consider early Adventists seekers.

Guardians interpret literally. Seekers recognize irony, audience, symbolism, and context.

Guardians believe the church is an organization. Seekers believe the church is a force.

Guardians defend the truth. Seekers feed on it.

Lamentably, modern society too often undervalues truth. As I've said, if we are not committed to Truth as true north, spin doctors do their damnably effective work, and our spiritual compasses spin. These doctors appear in the form of friends, parents, teachers, pastors, administrators, commentators, entertainers, and a thousand other insistent voices. Paul Tillich observed, "The passion for truth is silenced by answers which have the weight of undisputed authority."

The essence of Guardians of Truth (GOT) is the oft-heard maxim, "We have the truth." They treat truth and its offspring as a quantifiable, objective package to be tightly gripped with both hands. *There, we have it.* Guardians propel in me the unnerving feeling that their efforts to ensure orthodoxy on campuses and church boards will lead to truth squads, legalism, creedalism, and members fleeing. Buying into their philosophy, we become hard, dated, and narrow enough to fit easily upon the shelf on aisle seven.

By its very nature, truth cannot be possessed. If that were possible, it could be sold or bartered or placed cautiously in a napkin or a safe-deposit box. We won't find truth on the commodities market. We can't visit a manufactured truth port-folio. Jesus said, "I am the way, the truth, and the life" (John, chapter 14), and, "Abide in me, and I in you" (John, chapter 15). We can't own the truth any more than we can own Jesus. The truth owns us. We abide in truth. The truth inhabits us. The truth immerses us.

Guardians believe everyone should learn from us. Seekers believe we can learn from everyone.

Guardians approach church as a citadel. Seekers approach church as a hospital.

Guardians talk. Seekers talk, too. They also listen.

Remembering the Great Disappointment, Guardians don't want to get it wrong again. Remembering Calvary, Seekers don't want to disappoint Jesus.

Guardians warn of a future time of trouble. Seekers warn of anything that is based in fear.

Guardians often point to icebergs. Seekers often point to galaxies.

Guardians cover their ears for purity. Seekers dance for joy (though not very well).

Truth is air rushing and water surging through our very lungs and vessels. We can experience air and water, but we cannot *have* them. We gulp them in and still seek them. In the long run, we all must breathe unborrowed air—six times a minute inhaling oxygenated, fresh nourishment. And living water cannot be bottled.

Seekers of Truth could be SOT ("They are drunk with new wine," from Acts, chapter 2) but are perhaps best characterized as SOUGHT (Seekers Of Undeniably Good, Healthful Truth). The parables of the lost sheep, the lost coin, and the lost son involve Seekers. Jesus' parable of the talents exalts creative Seeker risk-taking.* Seeker stories abound in the New Testament: Nicodemus, the woman at the well, the blind man of John chapter 9, the centurion and his servant, Zacchaeus, Peter on the water, Paul in prison, Mary's anointing, and scores more.

---

*See Matthew, chapter 25.

This distinction goes beyond political conservatives and liberals, for one discovers conservatives who are at heart Seekers and liberals who are in practice Guardians. On a philosophical level, the division reflects the current worldwide debate over the relative merits of safety versus freedom—evidenced in the United States of America's Patriot Act—with eye-opening repercussions.

Guardians defer to tradition. Seekers refer to an untraditional Carpenter.

Guardians stand for the status quo. Seekers stand for those on the margins ("guarding the edges").

Guardians are immovable. Seekers are irrepressible.

To GOT, God is imminent. To SOUGHT, God is immanent.

Guardians seek conformity, affirmation, and predictability. Seekers guard hope, compassion, and vitality.

GOT assess effective evangelism as information transmission. SOUGHT assess effective evangelism as nonmanipulative dialogue.

For Guardians, the gospel is validation. For Seekers, the gospel is freedom.

Admittedly, whether the construct is guardians and seekers, sheep and goats, wise and foolish, or sacred and secular, binary thinking runs risks. Nuances become hidden. The potential for misapplication escalates. Note: The intent of this catalogue of twenty-eight is to enlighten and even inspire.

Both GOT and SOUGHT camps harbor committed Christians. Both carry accumulated penchants, motivations, and aptitudes. And depending on the issue or circumstance, we can all find ourselves out of our usual camp and deep in the other one. Still, we see differences emerge in myriad ways.

For GOT, the life of a Christian is mainly sin management. For SOUGHT, the life of a Christian is mainly inclusive friendships.

Guardians confuse tastes with morals. Seekers confuse saints with forgiven sinners.

Guardians define who is worthy to belong. Seekers refuse to allow others to define them outside the church.

Guardians prescribe and proscribe. Seekers say "whosoever will."

Guardians are quick to count decisions. Seekers aim at creating disciples.

To Guardians, it's all about salvation. To Seekers, it's all about love.

Guardians see life in terms of "us" and "them." Knowing we're all in this together, Seekers don't view even Guardians as "them."

Of course, epigrammatic generalizations can lead to arrogance, polarization, and hostility. At times, Seekers need to have icebergs pointed out and historic truths recalled. Balance is mandatory.

However, after thirty years as a Christian, I find myself asking of my fellow believers which fundamental question we live by: "Got Jesus on aisle seven?" or "Sought Jesus with all our heart, mind, soul, and strength?" In the end, our choice of question will determine our church's direction.

Anne Mellor muses that Mary Shelley's *Frankenstein* is "a book about what happens when a man tries to have a baby without a woman." What title would describe a denomination's attempts to have a redemptive existence without a Seeker vision?

All disciples of Jesus need to fashion a salutary life-view that is based in reality, both seen and unseen. Within that reality, we cannot own gifts of truth or life— they arrive from Another and return to Another. This is the humbling Truth that sets us free. ❏

What if they really did find Noah's ark?

Noah's Ark Discovered!

When I arrived home from work that day, I had no idea what would be in store for me. Carrying my briefcase, I picked up the newspaper in the driveway, ran up the steps, and unlocked the front door. "Hello!" I hollered.

No response.

I assumed Yolanda must be out shopping for groceries, so I settled into my comfortable reading chair, turned on the lamp, and cracked open the paper.

I generally enjoy our newspaper. It isn't too sensational. Certainly not the sort of tabloid that blares "I Gave Birth to an Alien's Baby!" and you discover the author is married to a man named George Alien. Or the article on "Keira Knightley's Midnight Madness!" turns out to be the time she stubbed her little toe on the nightstand. It wasn't like that at all.

Glancing over the first two sections, I read a few items. The latest medical finding was that soap doesn't kill germs. Congress was working with a federal deficit of $934,000,000,000,000,000,000,000,000,000. Tehran had been reduced to rubble. And near a toxic waste-disposal site, the lawns were trapping birds. Nothing especially noteworthy.

But just before the entertainment section, which featured an ad for the box-office hit *Scary Movie XVIII*, I found the following news release:

Ark Find Spurs Planning

ANKARA, TURKEY (API)—Speaking at a packed press conference, Blaine Feinswald today showed previously unpublished photographs of the legendary Noah's ark. The photos depicted an immense, ship-like structure with Feinswald and his team gathered around it.

"We have proof positive," Feinswald declared, "that this is Noah's ark. The radioactive dating we've done places the wood right at the time of the Flood. There is no question now."

The search team brought back videotapes, samples of the wood, and other specimens for scientific inspection. Any final verdict on the claims, however, may not be made for years, and when it is made, it is certain to be disputed.

"It's fantastic!" exclaimed Ashley Barber, the team's archaeologist. "I've never seen anything like it."

Morris Waynant, of the National Museum of Natural History in Washington, D.C., disagrees. "Not surprisingly, here's another of the miracle claims of the Religious Right. We'll go look at it, but we've known about big boats for thousands of years. Frankly, I'd rather know for certain how the East Asians sailed to the Americas."

No matter how valid Feinswald's claims turn out to be, interest in the find is growing. A McDonald's official, who requested anonymity, said his company is already developing plans. "We're going to be giving away millions of ark T-shirts, and there'll be a forty-day contest with a grand prize of visiting the McDonald's Ark Park to be built at the base of Mount Ararat. We'll also have ark specials. You'll be able to buy a double cheeseburger or two orders of chicken McNuggets and get a discount. You know, the animals came into the ark by twos."

In addition, such corporations as Disney Productions, Coca-Cola, Halliburton, Exxon Mobil, and also the Arkansas State Senate have expressed interest in the discovery and are *Please turn to ARK, C9*

Just then, I heard the sputter of our Mercury Villager van in the driveway. I know the sound well because the car has 873,000 miles on it. Soon, Yolanda entered the house carrying a bag of groceries.

"Hello!" she hollered.

I met her in the kitchen and gave her a kiss. "How did it go?"

"Pretty well," she replied. "I found some bargains and spent only $358."

"That *is* good. The bag is almost full."

"Yep. So, what's new?"

"I just read in the newspaper that someone discovered Noah's ark."

"Really?" She placed a $45.98 quart of soy milk in the refrigerator. "What's the general reaction?"

"Nothing much. Most people don't believe it, or they're saying, in effect, 'So what?' "

"That figures," Yolanda said.

I looked at her curiously. "Why do you say that?"

"Because," she answered, putting away the grapes, "when it comes to religion, most people wouldn't believe even if someone rose from the dead." ❏

This convocation address was presented to students at Union College.

A Whole New World

On this first day of college, I think back to my own college beginnings, which took place somewhere between the dawn of the horseless carriage and the emergence of Britney Spears. I arrived from Chaffey High School in Ontario, California—a high school of four thousand students (larger than any Adventist university in North America), to Cal Poly San Luis Obispo, a university of seventeen thousand students. At registration, I stood in one of six *long* lines and peered up at a huge wooden board as the classes I had planned to take closed one by one.

That registration took me five-and-a-half hours to complete. I suppose I might have made it through quicker if I'd had an advisor, but he was nowhere to be found. After that, I didn't use an advisor for the rest of my college experience, which I managed to cram into six years. This was actually pretty fast, considering that I didn't go to school much the first four years—I was too busy playing NCAA basketball.

Times have changed. Registration is now just a few keystrokes, along with more candy and pizza than one could possibly eat. In the decades since my college years, I've thought a lot about education—specifically, about encountering an academic climate that can energize and stretch you.

College is more than thirteenth or fourteenth grade, a continuation of high school life. This is a new world of freedom and responsibility, a world that will energize and stretch us only if we understand—and put into practice—some key academic values. Believe me, these values will enable you to flourish here at Union College.

First, we value *cooperation over competition*. Ninety-nine percent of life is cooperation. Literally millions of people have cooperated to make you who you are today, from your shoes from Taiwan to your watch from Germany to your banana from Brazil. Somebody had to take the oil out of the ground in Saudi Arabia to make the gasoline that powered the truck that drove over the smooth roads to bring the machinery that created the screws that hold together the church pews on which you're sitting.

Even competition is mostly cooperation. Opponents agree on the rules and the times and the referees, and the best team—the one with the players who best *coop-*

erate with one another—wins. Here's the essence of what's wrong with competition: Somebody has to lose for me to win. But cooperation is ninety-nine times better than that. Cooperation says everyone can win when we all work together. Cooperation keeps us from becoming savages.

Second, we value *active learning over passive.* You will learn more if you involve yourself in the process, because as humans, we tend to believe what we do even more than we do what we believe. That's why we can't continue to do something if we believe that it's wrong. Instead, we rationalize it: *It's all right this time,* or *They deserved it.* That's also why you can hear eight hundred sermons on the value of helping others, but you don't *really* believe it until you go on a short-term mission trip.

Active learning also requires you to extend your language. Because ideas can't be separated from language, the limits of your language are the limits of your world. (This includes the languages of music, numbers, and visual arts.) So get involved in activities, in open microphone night and college bowl. Attend your classmates' recitals. Participate. Go beyond what's expected. Jesus said, "If someone asks you to go one mile, go two." He was talking about taking control of your life and your own education. Read other books than the ones required. (It's possible. Really!) Do it on your own. Explore the world of ideas.

Next, we value *community over celebrity.* Since our society is infatuated with celebrity, this is certainly a countercultural value. We have television channels and magazines dedicated entirely to entertainment figures. We have celebrities' birthdays scrolling across the bottom of CNN News. We have *American Idol.* But this is not an academic value.

I remember a professor at Cal Poly saying to our class, "You won't receive a passing grade for doing nothing, because I love humanity more than I love you." He was speaking of uplifting the common good, of reaching toward cooperation and community, of looking out for people on the margins of life who can't look out for themselves—the handicapped, the elderly, the unborn, the poor. That's a product of the highest education. Celebrity is a fad; community is a virtue.

We value *questioning over groupthink.* Thoreau suggested that in a world of fugitives, the person taking the opposite position will appear to be running away. At Union College, we like people who think for themselves, people who will stand for the right though the heavens fall. This involves asking questions.

A couple years ago, I had a class that was told, minutes before class was to begin, that the class had been cancelled. Unfortunately, the messenger had gone to the wrong room. Imagine my glee when I walked into an empty room a few minutes later. As you can imagine, our next class was about asking questions. Asking more questions could have prevented the eight-hundred-thousand-person holocaust in Rwanda ("Is Rwanda just the same as Somalia, or are we treating all of Africa the same, as if it's a country and not a continent?"). Asking questions could have changed the rush to war across history. Throughout the Bible, God's best friends ask questions. Not just the questions of "How much can we get away with?" or "How long does this have to be?" but "Why is this happening?" "How can we do better?" and "What would happen if . . . ?" Questioning often requires discernment and courage, two valuable traits.

We value *objectivity over bias*. I don't believe people are truly educated until they can hold their opinions away from themselves, so that when someone challenges or attacks their opinions and ideas, they don't feel attacked personally. This inability to look objectively at ideas leads to defensiveness, stonewalling, and narrow-mindedness, which are unfortunately becoming more common in our society.

To be educated is to read things objectively and to listen to people you don't agree with. Yesterday, I had a long conversation with a young man who came into my office with a very firm opinion, but he was willing to listen and to consider other possibilities, and he changed his perspective. I call that education. It's the education Jesus asks of us.

Objectivity calls for honesty. Couple that with the courage of questioning, and we have "integrity"—a combination of honesty and courage.

We value *accuracy over carelessness*. Because the key to life is communication, how we communicate matters. Words matter. For example, does "making love" really mean making love or does it mean making sex? There is a difference, and not recognizing the difference often results in traumatic consequences.

Quoting information from the Internet is a dangerous practice also. Anybody can put anything on the Internet—and they do. My mother used to tell me, "Don't put money into your mouth, because you don't know where it's been." The same holds true for the Internet. Just because you "read somewhere" or "heard somewhere" a piece of information doesn't make it true.

Once, as an experiment, our Rhetoric and Persuasion class made up a rumor about the pope getting together with certain Protestants to create a credit card that only a few people could use. (We thought this was a good one.) We spread this rumor around campus. Three weeks later, I asked in chapel, "How many of you have heard about this?" About fifty people raised their hands, including grinning members of our class. "Well," I said, "it's a lie. We made it up." Then I spoke of the need for verification. I imagine the story is still wobbling around some Adventist circles.

This quest for accuracy doesn't mean we don't believe anything. It means we don't believe everything—we test the spirits. And we communicate accurately what we know.

We value *eternal perspective over transitory view*. Our college's mission statement says we seek to develop "an eternal perspective." But what does this mean? I'm glad you asked. Let's take a look.

An eternal perspective means that *entering life is greater than withdrawing from reality*. Reality is where God lives. God wants us to *enter life*. Have you noticed how many people use their money to withdraw from life behind gated communities and headphones and tinted windows? The eternal perspective enters life, just as Jesus entered and enters our life. I'm glad He did and does, aren't you?

It means *diversity is greater than uniformity*. This goes beyond *tolerating* differences to *celebrating* differences. I like you *because* you're different. God is a diversity junkie—no two people, snowflakes, or leaves on a tree are alike. This of course leads to the great truth that you're unique, just like everybody else. We should prize our distinctions.

An eternal perspective means *holistic balance is greater than unhealthy focus*. Our minds, bodies, and emotions are intertwined, so each one affects the others. Take care of your bodies and your emotions. Be a well-balanced person. Listen to Dr. Nancy Petta when she teaches Concepts of Wellness.

This leads to the truth that *lifelong learning is greater than cramming*. How many of you have ever crammed for a test and forgotten much of it five minutes after it was done? Raise your hands. . . . Come on, faculty, hands up! Mark Twain wrote, "I never let schooling get in the way of an education." By "schooling," he meant, for example, the pursuit of grades. Grades can get in the way of an education. Learn for life.

An eternal perspective means *imagination is greater than imitation*. As Albert Einstein said, "Imagination is better than knowledge." (But then, what did he know?) God really doesn't want clones or robots or mere reflectors of others' thoughts. He wants you to go beyond "What Would Jesus Do?" to create your own discipleship, to work out (not work *for*) your own salvation. Then it becomes yours.

It means *joy of service is greater than accumulation*. Einstein also wrote, "Not everything that can be counted counts, and not everything that counts can be counted." Too many people climb the ladder of success to find when they reach the top that the ladder is propped against the wrong wall. A recent survey showed that 38 percent of college students wouldn't go to college if it didn't further their career. That's not an eternal, godly perspective. Accumulating money, awards, and things won't bring lasting peace and joy.

Finally, *truth and beauty are greater than mediocrity*. Excellence is an eternal value, and true beauty is eternal. Now, this also involves having fun, because we were made for fun. You know that, don't you? If we leave out the fun in the fundamentals, all we have left is "da mentals."

Consider the beauty of the lilies of the field, and consider what graduate school you might attend based on many factors. For instance, note the elegant beret that President Smith is wearing. Some people might say it looks like a crushed muffin, but I wouldn't. Note that the tassel doesn't slap him mercilessly in the side of the face, as is the case with a mortarboard. This is the result of higher education!

You might also choose your postgraduate school based on the color of the robe. Does it highlight your natural color? Note the royal blue in Dr. Roeske's gown. As he stands for us, look at those magnificent stripes. Would you turn around, Dr. Roeske?*

Thank you. Yes, a whole new world awaits you. Not just here, but on the new earth, for we will spend eternity on this world made new—a real place. You'll appreciate and need all the academic values on the new earth: cooperation, active learning, community, questioning, objectivity, accuracy. And see the *eternal perspectives.* All of them will be forever used and useful. You see, we are educating you for eternity.

The good news is, forever begins now. It begins because we look constantly into the face of Jesus. It begins because of the greatest value of all. *Love is greater than anything else.* Nothing else ultimately matters or lasts. That's why *Union makes better lovers. (See 1 Corinthians 13.)* Wouldn't that make a great bumper sticker?

Enjoy the journey, friends. Savor the moment. Relish the reality of being valued and loved. You are here. Now, go with God. ❏

"Blessed are those who are persecuted for righteousness' sake, for theirs is the kingdom of heaven. Blessed are you when men revile you and persecute you and utter all kinds of evil against you falsely on my account. Rejoice and be glad, for your reward is great in heaven, for so men persecuted the prophets who were before you."—Matthew, chapter 5

Just a Stone's Throw

It strikes during the sermon. Leaning forward, I mutter to Yolanda, "I need to go home." Halfway there, I change my mind. We head for a nearby twenty-four-hour health clinic instead.

Something is stabbing me. Impaling me. Skewering me. Groaning, I whip off my belt. My ragged breathing comes in gasps. Presently, Yolanda pulls the car into the space nearest the clinic. The parking lot is virtually empty. By now, my face and shirt are drenched. I can't move even to open the door.

Then, unbelievably, I hear Yolanda whisper, "Shoot. Handicapped." She backs out and powers past five empty spaces to park again.

What? Look at me! This *is handicapped!* Fortunately, I'm incapable of articulation. The coils of persecution wrap around me.

Yolanda helps me stagger inside. A smiling receptionist croons, "How may we help you?" and I writhe, moaning, on my back in the middle of the floor. Are others

---

*Uplifting lyrics from *Aladdin's* "A Whole New World" were primed to play at this time.

present? I neither know nor care. But through the thick, blaring fog of pain, I catch "There are two patients ahead of you." The coils constrict.

A nervous nurse ushers us to an antiseptic room to take my pulse.* Relaxed, cheerful banter drifts from an adjacent room. Persecution's fangs fill me with venom. I hear people chatting, chuckling, exchanging medical pleasantries—perhaps another amusing anecdote that they care to share. I want to strangle them.

"We're leaving," Yolanda informs the nurse after ten minutes. "We're going to the emergency room."

As we lurch down the hall, the doctor materializes, empathy creasing his face. "What seems to be the trouble?"

"Aaaaaaaaaaahhhhhhhhhhhhhhhhh!" I reply.

Yolanda translates: "He's in a lot of pain."

"Where," the good doctor inquires, "does it hurt?"

"Ooooooooohhhhhhhhhhhhhhhhhh!" I reply.

"His lower back," offers Yolanda. "He thinks it's a kidney stone."

"Does it feel like a hot knife twisting into you?"

I nod vigorously, snorting like a stallion.

His expression is benign, almost beatific. *Odd for one to be so calm in the presence of imminent death.* "Well," he surmises finally, "you should go to the emergency room." *What a profound concept!* Through mists of agony, I hear echoing behind us his jovial, "No charge!" Persecution's leering grin.

Thus begins The Ride From Hell. Each start, stop, turn, bump, or nudge fires me to greater frenzy, and as the infernal boulder rumbles farther down the fleshy duct my delirious shrieks ascend. I pray. I beg. I babble. I whimper. The world blurs. Yolanda drives like a woman possessed.

Around twenty-three days later, we arrive at the hospital. Somebody scrapes me up and launches my wheelchair toward a holding area, where I promptly tumble to the floor in a fetal position, groaning. My nurse, Sheila, arrives, takes one look, and flatly announces, "Kidney stone." Somehow this comforts me.

What comforts me more, however, is the morphine she administers through my IV line. Instantly I become a drug convert. *Just . . . say . . . yes. . . .*

≈

C. S. Lewis remarked, "Everyone feels benevolent if nothing happens to be annoying him at the moment." But what if something goes way beyond annoyance? Other than masochists, who on earth feels "blessed" when they are being persecuted?

During my kidney stone ordeal, I felt persecuted. Do we truly comprehend what persecution is? Often I sense that we—savvy technology masters of the marvelous new millennium—don't. We misconstrue Jesus' beatitude in five ways.

---

*690.

1. Inconvenience is not persecution. One of my favorite cartoons* depicts four frames under the title, "How Christians have coped through the ages:

"New Testament Christian: 'Lord, give me the courage to face this accusing mob.'

"Reformation-era Christian: 'Lord, help me declare your truth despite the cost.'

"Twentieth century persecuted East European: 'Lord, may we persevere faithfully under these burdens.'

"Modern American Christian: 'Lord, the Audi's been running rough lately. . . .'"

God has a message in the midst of our inconvenience. He bends low and cups His magnificent hands to our ear. Then He gently whispers, "Grow up and deal with it."

2. Genuine hardship is usually not persecution. I was not persecuted by the kidney stone. In itself, pain doesn't signify oppressive and persistent harassment. In addition, the only ones Jesus mentioned as deserving a blessing are those who receive persecution *on His account.* My being persecuted by my sons for laughing at odd times in public does not, apparently, qualify.

In a related vein and despite my country's penchant, victims, per se, are not heroes. While the tragedies of September 11 memorialized the victims, not all of them were heroes. Heroism mandates a heroic response. Moreover, not everyone who suffers is a victim. The driver applying makeup while chatting on her mobile phone who crashes into a parked truck and breaks both her wrists is not a victim.

On the other hand, the firefighters who raced up the tumbling stairways of the World Trade Center may have been "just doing their jobs," but they are heroes nonetheless. The same is true for the mothers and fathers working three jobs to help pay for their children's education. They may not be persecuted, but their loving sacrifice establishes them as heroes.

3. The persecuted may also be persecutors. Stephen, the first official Christian martyr, died under the concussive impact of stones thrown by members of a persecuted sect.† We're all just a stone's throw from being persecutors. The stones we heft may be words heavy with hate, hard looks, flinty hearts hurled from glass temples.

Persecution often turns on a moment. Many schoolyard bullies are pounded mercilessly at home. Each insane Middle East bombing is likely an errant response

---

*By a cartoonist named Dahl.

†John the Baptist might properly qualify as the first Christian martyr, having died "for righteousness' sake" after giving testimony to Jesus. The infants slain by King Herod in association with Christ's birth were victims, not martyrs. Similarly, Lazarus died "so that you may believe" (John, chapter 11), but his death was not on his part a conscious decision toward righteousness.

to immeasurable tragedy. If we knew the background of our persecutors, we would sooner mouth with Jesus, "Forgive them, for they know not what they do."

4. *Many who are persecuted are not blessed.* The "blessing" that comes of actual persecution is not inevitable. Jesus says we are blessed when "all kinds of evil are uttered against you *falsely* on my account." If the evil surmising is true, we've apparently lost that blessing.

"I do not believe that sheer suffering teaches," writes Anne Morrow Lindbergh, who endured her unfair share. "If suffering alone taught, all the world would be wise, since everyone suffers. To suffering must be added mourning, understanding, patience, love, openness, and the willingness to remain vulnerable."

What must be added to persecution are Jesus and His beatitudes.

5. *This blessing is not a material blessing.* Scripture many times warns of the dangers of material prosperity (e.g., Deuteronomy, chapter 8; Proverb 30; Matthew, chapter 19; Revelation, chapter 3). As Jesus pointed out in His mountain sermon, if we trust Him totally and follow Him steadfastly, our material needs will be cared for.

Persecution is undeniably fearsome, yet under its serpentine stare God supplies peace. One of my favorite texts is, "No temptation has overtaken you that is not common to man. God is faithful, and he will not let you be tempted beyond your strength, but with the temptation will also provide the way of escape, that you may be able to endure it" (1 Corinthians, chapter 10).

What does it mean to be *blessed?* The blessed difference is peaceful love. "There is no fear in love, but perfect love casts out fear" (1 John, chapter 4). We endure persecution for the love that blooms within. We love even those who persecute us, as Jesus did and does. And we love to the extent that *we* will not persecute—neither individually, corporately, nor nationally. Rather, we defend others.

Of such is the kingdom of God.

As the morphine-induced tranquility floods my system, I am suddenly at peace with the world. Forgiveness and acceptance surge within my being.

An epiphany strikes me: I love everyone. Are not all people my brothers and sisters? The clinic doctor and his patients, the receptionist, the phantom handicapped parkers. I can hold nothing against another. God is in His heaven. The winged birds are singing. *Isn't life grand?*

All previous turbulence sails far behind. My rolling stone now gathers moss.* And though I have to acknowledge that I wrestled through my time of trouble resiliently, patiently, courageously—gracefully, perhaps—I am left with one question. Turning to my nurse, I reflect aloud on how such throbbing torment (surely

---

*This, too, shall pass.

few have endured such agony) could escalate from a thing so small and deeply hidden. *Simply amazing.*

Sheila shoots me a smile that I cannot readily decipher. It is a smile that has remained a mystery to all men, a smile that veils secrets I can never fathom, a smile that carries the cries of centuries.

"Yes," she says. "I hear it's a lot like labor pains."   ❏

And just as it is appointed for men to die once, and after that comes judgment, so Christ, having been offered once to bear the sins of many, will appear a second time, not to deal with sin but to save those who are eagerly waiting for him.—Hebrews, chapter 9

Why Jesus Comes Back

They were "doomed to a slow, suffocating death." In a small pool, a back eddy of Eagle Creek, young steelhead and salmon no bigger than minnows were trapped behind a sandbar. Jim Robertson had been fishing for early summer trout, but seeing the plight of the fish, he leaned his fly rod against a tree and set about to rescue them.

In "Pool of Death," he writes, "Already the water in their pool was becoming stale and accumulating a slight scum on the surface. *If I had a shovel,* I thought, *I could easily dig a channel through the sandbar.*" Instead, he used his hands. When a narrow channel eventually opened, the flowing water caused the sandy sides to slough off. He worked hard to open a generous channel and then "stood back to watch the fish flow out—but no fish flowed out." The fingerlings were schooling in the far side of the pool.

Jim tried chasing them toward the outlet to no avail. "Since there was no one else around, I puzzled aloud, 'Fish, can't you see that I'm only trying to save you?' But they could neither hear nor understand me. I thought about how an incarnation (inichthyation?) might help the situation. I could become one of them."

Finally, he resorted to catching them one at a time in his cupped hands and tossing them into the main stream. The smaller, slower ones were easiest to grab; the larger, faster ones eluded him. He was able to scoop up four or five dozen and release them into the living part of the stream. "The rest were too hard to catch. I had to leave them to their 'freedom.' "

Picking up his rod, he looked back and was stunned to see a rescued fish starting to work its way from the river back to the stagnant pool. "After shooing it downstream, I kicked in the sides of the channel to close it. I didn't want those I had freed going back, even if it meant permanently sealing in those that remained in the pool."

When I read Robertson's piece, I marveled at its insights into the Second Coming. The original Fisherman used His hands to save us. Though stuck in this stagnant pool, the stronger, faster "fish" still try to cling to their "freedom." At some point, the Rescuer must kick in the channel.

Adventists are clear about the fact of the return of Jesus. But *why* does Jesus come back? Here are two typical answers to that question, and one suggested by the fisherman's story.

1. Jesus returns when the gospel goes to the whole world. "This gospel of the kingdom will be preached throughout the whole world, as a testimony to all nations; and then the end will come."* However, this text raises more questions than it answers.

How does one practically measure "throughout the whole world"? Do radio waves carrying Jesus messages overhead qualify? Can we calculate based on "people groups entered"? What does it mean to "enter"? Has every people-group been entered when every language has a Scripture translation? Have we "finished the work" when a Christian church is within walking distance for all people on the planet?

Moreover, we run the risk of following the *post hoc, ergo propter hoc* fallacy— "after this, therefore because of this." Other signs of Christ's coming are false prophets, sun and moon darkened, and stars falling, but do we claim Jesus comes *because* of these?

The vital question is why. If Jesus requires that everyone experience an equal and adequate chance to "hear the gospel," that likely won't happen. Obviously, people are born every second—do we count them as well? Or maybe, depending on what the term "gospel" means, it's already happened. I'm getting confused. Time to move along.

2. Jesus returns when His character is "perfectly reproduced" in His children. Again, this raises numerous questions. How many children is enough? Half? All? And what sort of perfection is called for?† If we don't pass the character test, could we hold off Jesus forever?

Deuteronomy, chapter 9 provides enlightenment. The Israelites are crossing over into the Promised Land after forty years of wild wandering. What could they be thinking? Moses knows them well: "Do not say in your heart, after the LORD your God has thrust them out before you, 'It is because of my righteousness that the LORD has brought me in to possess this land'; whereas it is because of the wickedness of these nations that the LORD is driving them out before you. Not because of your righteousness or the uprightness of your heart are you going in to possess their land."

This is a precursor to entering heavenly Canaan. It's not because of *our* righteousness that Jesus comes back. The contemporary current against which we

---

*Matthew, chapter 24.
†See "The Perfect Crime" in this book.

struggle is filled with sloth, lust, egoism, and deception. First Peter, chapter 2 describes the "chosen people"—the elect—as those who "have received mercy." The conclusion of the song of Moses and the Lamb in Revelation, chapter 15 is "God, *You alone* are holy." This is the refrain of the redeemed.

Pauline is a former student who returned to visit me in my office. She was radiant with Christ's love—she was born again. I asked her what she had learned that changed her life. She leaned forward and intoned reverently, "It's not about us. When we think it's about us, we start to look at exteriors and judge people. It's all about Jesus."

3. Jesus will return when life here becomes so bad that He's losing more people than He's gaining. One huge message in the parable of the pool of death is this: God is interested in numbers. In Matthew, after detailing the tribulations of the end times, Jesus adds, "And if those days had not been shortened, no human being would be saved; but for the sake of the elect those days will be shortened." *Jesus will show up to save the most people possible* by kicking in the channel. I like that reason for His return.

When I've heard, "Jesus has waited to return so that He could save *us*," I've thought, *But there will always be more people to save.** Apparently, however, things will become so bad that even the remnant would turn back to the sand bar. How could this be?

At some point, the world's fragile economic structure will bend, sway, and topple. What currently passes for bedrock decency and manners between people will vanish.† I caught a glimpse of this when patience frayed and tempers flared during the 1970s gas shortages. (And today, whenever a flight is cancelled.) But even before the impending collapse, we can find hints of how God can't get through to us.

Years ago, I registered for the National Do Not Call Registry, a patently providential intervention that prevents telemarketers from reaching me on my telephone. My computer is not nearly as security conscious. I have deleted thousands of electronic offers for Swiss watches, sweepstakes winnings, mortgage deals at 2.8 percent, pharmacy discounts for Cialis, Nigerian money transfers, and all manner of bodily enhancements, none of which interests me. With this mudslide of information, I'm pretty sure I have deleted other things that I might actually like, but because of the state of spam marketing, I'm not interested in giving anyone a chance.

Maybe this is how it is just before Jesus comes back. The world cannot trust Christians or their gospel because some of the messages we send have been shallow, corrupt, and manipulative. Like others, Christians hate and lie and steal and poison the environment and kill and torture—or condone these practices—until the world deletes without thinking twice. In North America, my freedom has eroded because I'm drowning in information and instant messaging (today's great IM).

---

*Hector Belioz muses, "Time is a great teacher, but unfortunately it kills all its pupils."
†See "Last Days Readiness" and "Thank You, God, for Knotheads."

I've lost not the ability but the desire for input. As described in Aldous Huxley's *Brave New World*, in a trivial culture, truth is submerged in a sea of irrelevance.

Bombarded with news of tragedies from all over the globe, I can lose the ability to care—I might as well just plug in an iPod and tune out. The mutilations that result from leprosy (Hansen's disease) are literally the result of losing the ability to feel. Today's leprosy is a deadening of feeling, or as Jesus describes it, " 'because wickedness is multiplied, most men's love will grow cold.' "*

I think at that point, when we cannot trust and cannot feel, when we effectively close off godly influences as well as evil ones, we might start heading back to the pool. Everything around us looks murky, with the sides sloughing off. In the midst of murkiness, Jesus returns—not to deal with wickedness (which He did at the cross) but to rescue those who allow Him to scoop them up and hold them wriggling in His cupped, scarred hands.

≈

At the front of the Des Moines Seventh-day Adventist Church stands a narrow vertical stained-glass window of blues, reds, and purples with a swath of aquamarine swirling throughout. The window depicts three angels, but their typical aspect is changed. Here their heads are down, they're descending, not ascending—and they appear to be surrounded by trailing clouds of bubbles.

They are diving underwater. The three angels are willing to throw themselves into a foreign element, like pelicans crashing beneath waves or flying fish piercing air.

Jesus also descended from another dimension. Diving down, He "emptied himself, taking the form of a servant, being born in the likeness of men."† And, He promises, it will happen again.

He holds His breath and takes one last dive. ❑

They are all plain to him that understandeth.—Proverbs 8

Notes From a Non-Esdeeay

Recently, I happened upon a sort of journal. This journal had apparently been kept by a young man who attended an Adventist church for a few months. Then suddenly, without explanation, the young man stopped coming. The journal was found in a pew on Sabbath. Here's what it contained.

---

*Jesus still heals leprosy today.
†Philippians, chapter 2.

≈

I'm attempting to figure out the peculiar dialect spoken by members of this church. Some of the terms they use seem so strange, but I'm too shy or maybe embarrassed to ask what they mean. The members all take it for granted that I know, I guess. Anyway, here are a few samples and explanations, as nearly as I can figure them.

esdeeay—"Is he esdeeay?" This means, "Is he A-OK?" An esdeeay is someone who has learned the dialect.

vespers—"Are you going to vespers?" The meaning is uncertain, although it's apparently an ongoing process. Haven't figured out yet how anyone vespers. Everybody assumes I've vespered before.

sabbath—Confusing variant of Saturday, yet no one says Saturday. Esdeeays say Sabbath even when pointing to the calendar—which says Saturday. Yet they also celebrate Sabbath on Friday. Is "Sabbath evening" Friday or Saturday? You got me.

brothers and sisters—This church is one enormous family. Strangely, most siblings don't look a bit alike. Gregor Mendel would be astounded, I'm sure. Maybe he didn't give peas a chance.

dork us—"Let's give it to dork us." Apparently, a way of giving away something you don't want in order to receive something you do want. Somehow, this helps to keep people clothed and warm. Dorking is quite popular.

Alan Jeewite—"Have you read any Alan Jeewite?" Popular author. Important issue apparently is whether he made a profit or didn't make a profit.

P-U-C—"I'm going to P-U-C." Appears to be not a spelled-out declaration of imminent illness but an esdeeay college in northern California.

loamel—Meat substitute used in many foods. There's *loamel in the* steaks, *loamel in the* chili, *loamel in the* hot dogs (which someone named Big Frank likes). There's even *loamel in the* university.

church bored—As I look around, sometimes, yes.

going and gathering—"Are you going and gathering?" A method of going door-to-door around Christmastime to gather money from the community. This money is used to help the church reach Argole, wherever that is.

pathfinders—Young people who meet to find a path, I guess. They have to find it while keeping a level on their eyes and walking softly.

cradle roll—How esdeeays keep track of their babies. The roll is called "up yonder"—in the attic, perhaps. I see esdeeays carrying out crying babies for roll call quite often.

tie, then offerings—"The time has come to give our tie, then offerings." Apparently a generic idiom not to be taken literally. I have yet to see a tie in the offering plate.

haystacks—Lots of esdeeays claim to eat these. (With a pitchfork?)

jeesee—"Are you going to jeesee?" A large sightseeing event that takes place every five years. Tons of esdeeays traveled to jeesee St. Louis.

cold porters—Underclad people who carry books and bags to others' doors. I don't know why they can't give something to the church to get themselves dorked. It sure would beat being cold.

translation—I hear people talk about being *ready* for translation: "When Christ comes, we will be translated." The trouble is, I don't know if I can wait that long.

≈

The journal entries ended here, and no forwarding address for the fellow could be found. It's too bad he left. He seemed nice enough.   ❑

Definitely, I needed to get free—until I discovered I couldn't. But that changed, too.

Getting Away

Some snapshots stick in your brain. I remember my dad standing in front of the TV in the living room, cradling his head in his hands, covering his eyes and slowly rotating his torso. Mostly, I remember his moaning over and over, "My son . . . is a moron. My son . . . is a moron."

I had just informed Dad that I would be hitchhiking across the country with my friend Don, who was also a freshman in college. We were prepared, as we had read an entire sixty-five-page book on hitchhiking. We were practically experts. Though tossing confetti might have been over the top, Dad's commentary was not the send-off I had hoped for. I laughed it off. He didn't seem amused.

Anyway, I wanted to get away. Away, away. From coaches who screamed and swore. From pointless, droning classes. From insane living in an athletic dorm. From a mind-numbing, soul-shriveling summer job at a Sunkist factory. From suffocating smog. From life's assembly-line sameness. I *needed* to get away.

So we left on August 10 from Ontario, California. We traveled across to Washington, D.C., up to Montreal, and back. I dropped off Don at Kearney State College in Nebraska and returned home September 10.

Thirty-six years later, I can still recount each new-minted day of that trip. On the day I left Don in Kearney, I caught a fifteen-hundred-mile ride with a student from New York headed to Stanford. I forget his name, but I remember his dog, Azdak, which lay facing me across the top of the old front seat. Each time we stopped or started, Azdak skittered off and clambered up. I helped drive, and we slept in the car outside Elko, Nevada. Azdak got the top bunk.

I remember sleeping on the grass outside a corporation in Rockville, Maryland, awaking as suited businesspeople arrived for work. Feeling grit in my eyes after an afternoon of New York City. Folk dancing in a public square one evening in Montreal. Wondering where the falls were on a foggy, roaring Niagara night, and abruptly, unexpectedly, peering over the boiling, tumbling waters. Kind strangers of every stripe* going out of their normal paths to cart and deposit us where we wished.

Though Don and I traveled as safely as possible,† I'm not recommending hitchhiking for everyone. Dad's discomfort was justified. And I recall something else distinctly. Though I traveled eight thousand miles that month, I never really got away. Everywhere I went, I dragged along my greatest frustration, my deepest regret. Myself. My lack of focus, my impure thoughts, my laziness. I could never truly get away because, as the saying goes, wherever I went, there I was.

Years later, following my conversion to Christianity, I realized that *we can get away only as the Way gets in us.* We carry bracing freshness and beauty within. Freed from ourselves, we become ourselves. Dying daily, we live abundantly in the thrall of peace.

≈

Another snapshot. I remember squatting in the hospital corridor outside the room where Dad had just died. He had been dying for weeks—no, years—yet I was unprepared. The cancer had consumed his kidneys, and he had said No to dialysis. Our family—his wife of thirty-five years, two sons, two daughters, two grandchildren (our younger son Geoffrey not yet three months)—crowded around his bed and laughed and watched home movies and talked and watched him slowly die. I prayed with him. He croaked, "Take care of this family forever." This to his son, the moron.

For some reason we allowed him to be taken to the hospital at the very end. I sat beside my father—my honest, intelligent, giving, witty father—and listened to his rasping breaths until he breathed no more. I notified the nurse and crouched in the corridor as staff rushed by. I wanted to get away, and I knew I could not.

It wasn't the send-off I had hoped for. As a son, I had lost my father. I thought later of the Father who lost His Son.

Life knocks us down, kicks us with heavy boots, and laughs. The Son of man showed that true Christians get disappointed, gored, betrayed. We long to get away from all the boring pointlessness of life, to have this cup taken from us. But whether we go to British Columbia or Copenhagen or Cancun, we cannot fully escape. Hebrews, chapter 12 states, "It is for discipline that you have to endure."

I look forward to when we catch the ultimate ride with the Way. He reaches out His arm to open the door, beckons us in, smiles, and says, "Let's go." ❏

---

*Not all of them were Christian, either.
†During the day and together most of the way.

What I Would Add to Baptismal Certificates

Have you looked recently at the thirteen baptismal vows of the Seventh-day Adventist Church? They are a mouthful—particularly when compared to Peter's pithy response to the shining-faced Pentecostal converts who, aglow with godly zeal, wondered aloud, "What should we do now?"

"Repent, and be baptized," Peter cried, "in the name of Jesus Christ, for the forgiveness of your sins, and you shall receive the gift of the Holy Spirit." That's it. So to suggest that our list of thirteen lengthy pledges be *expanded* appears strange. It's like requesting that fifteen more verses of the national anthem be sung before the game may begin. *Puh-leeze.*

But I have watched newly baptized believers, each as sincere and impassioned as Peter's rapt audience, stray from the course, crestfallen and disillusioned. Their vessels of faith became lost or crippled, and they either abandoned ship or capsized like tiny *Titanics* to settle on a floor of fathomless depths. Could we have given them a better launch? A better map? Better instructions "in case of emergency"? Even the venerable Constitution of the United States, as brilliant as it was, added life-preserving amendments.

In that spirit, here are some proposed additional baptismal vows—adding up to twenty-eight, because the number now seems so . . . right.

Amendments to Baptismal Vows

14. I believe that the church is not principally a building or an organization. The church is people.

15. I will not be totally stunned and dejected when the church lets me down. I know that God is divine but His church is human. When I see flaws in my church, I will look to Jesus, who died for all of us while we were yet flawed.

16. I will learn from people who don't believe exactly the same way I do. No matter how much I know, I will remain teachable.

17. Because I have been covered and refreshed by God's grace, I will be gracious—accepting, giving, and forgiving—even to those who seem undeserving. I will strive always to be a living sanctuary—a safe place—for all.

18. Though I live in a world of decay, fear, deception, inflexibility, and cynicism, I will continue to prize beauty, courage, truth, creativity, and hope.

19. I will strive to develop godly friendships with people both inside and outside my church.

20. I will resist all efforts to make me believe that I can earn my own salvation—or that God cannot enable me to overcome sinful ways. In doing so, I will escape the twin pitfalls of pride and discouragement.

21. I will involve myself in risky, godly sharing. At times, I will move outside my comfort zone to spread the good news about Jesus. If necessary, I'll use words.

22. I believe that our Christian faith should enable us to be honest about our church's problems and to seek solutions together. Committing to God's church means that we grow under His canopy of grace, watching in awe as He works His will in the midst of our struggles, successes, and failures.

23. I believe that my body is the temple of God. Therefore, I will abstain from polluting His temple with gossip and negative talk.

24. I believe that the Bible, obedience, the Sabbath, health reform, and historic prophecies are wonderful, but these cannot save me. Only Jesus, God's Son, saves me.

25. I will do my balanced best to do justly and to love mercy.

26. Because I believe my church has been granted a distinctive, ennobling message, I will be grateful and humble.

27. I believe that baptism is not the end. Baptism is a beginning.

28. I will *never* let go of my Savior. Never, never, never.

Let's launch our new friends securely in the faith. Help them stay afloat on the ocean that opens before their eyes. Give them a vessel that lasts to the end, a bucket for the right type of bailing, and helpful directions for sailing against the current. ❏

One Sabbath I found myself in the wrong place at the right time.

"Reserved for Hearing Impaired"

Well, the church is full," I murmured to Yolanda. "Where can we sit?"
She craned her neck to study pews that were filled like Subway sandwiches. "I don't know," she whispered. "What do you think?"

We had lingered after our Sabbath School class to clean the room and talk briefly with friends, then had walked upstairs and pulled open a large door to find that the church service had begun.

From past painful experience, I knew that an apparent pew space doesn't necessarily mean seating is available. I have sauntered confidently down fourteen filled rows of the College View Church only to discover the desired opening "saved" under a litter of bulletins, purses, and hymnals, or else occupied by small children on their knees playing with Old Testament action figures. And I'm too self-conscious to have a deacon find us "perfectly good" seats, then beckon us grandly to a spot where I can casually shake hands with the speaker. (Do I hear an "Amen"?)

One scarcely populated pew appeared two sections to the right, so we entered another door. It wasn't until we started shuffling into the pew that we realized our error. A sign stated, "Reserved for Hearing Impaired."

The service has already started, I rationalized. *Surely no one else will show up now.* Feeling as though we were parking in a blue space, we scooted as far as possible down the line of headsets. As it happened, no one else did arrive. And as the service progressed, I began thinking more about where I was sitting.

Paul Tournier noted, "It is impossible to overemphasize the immense need humans have to be really listened to. Listen to all the conversations of our world, between nations as well as those between couples. They are, for the most part, dialogues of the deaf." Of all communication skills, *listening* is the one learned first, used most, and taught least. Few college graduates have a clue what the seven types of listening are.*

In a startling assertion, Jesus said, "Every one who is of the truth *hears my voice.*" Our conversations and prayers can move to three deepening levels: talking *about* God, talking *to* God, and the most prized level, talking *with* God. Finding our own style of prayer is as individualistic as finding a style of breathing. We cannot live for long by having others breathe for us; we must breathe, and we must pray, for ourselves.

Despite our personal styles, everyone engages in the same two breathing patterns—inhaling and exhaling. In the case of prayer, most of us are expert exhalers—expending at least 95 percent of our time letting God know exactly how things are "down here" and what we expect Him to do about it.

Inhaling is listening to God. We are typically impatient in this—as restless as a ten-year-old in a tie. Yet who of us would dare to portion only 5 percent of our breathing time to inhaling? Listening requires taking the time to wait on God, to clear away distractions, to remain focused and patient. As with most skills, listening also requires practice.

In his superb book *Prayer: Finding the Heart's True Home,* Richard Foster deftly poses the principle of prayer progression: "We do not take occasional joggers and put them in a marathon race, and we must not do that with prayer either." Foster

---

*Supporting, analyzing, advising, judging, prompting, questioning, and paraphrasing. (You knew that, didn't you?)

suggests, "In the beginning it is wise to strive for uneventful prayer experiences. Divine revelations and ecstasies can overwhelm us and distract us from the real work of prayer . . . 'to keep my soul tranquil and quiet like a child in its mother's arms' (Psalm 131, JB)."

Does *God* have an immense need to be really listened to? Does God become lonely and frustrated, as Jesus did, hoping and waiting for those who have ears to hear, but who seem as thick as waterless stew? Could I spend half my prayer time listening?

The longer I sat looking at the "hearing impaired" sign, the more I thought, *Every pew in every church could rightfully carry this sign.* And I felt that, just for this week, I was parked precisely where God wanted me to be. ❏

"There is none righteous, no, not one."—Romans, chapter 3, quoting Psalm 14

We have many lessons to learn, and many, many to unlearn. God and heaven alone are infallible.—Ellen White

---

The Perfect Crime

On my first attempt at water skiing, a couple guys took me out to Lake Perris in southern California. They were friends of a friend of Yolanda's, and though we had just met, they offered to teach me to ski. I knew practically nothing about the sport. Thus, I manifested no concern when whitecaps appeared on the late afternoon water. In addition, the guys figured that, as a college athlete, I could skip the basics and start on just one ski. I agreed, thinking, *How hard can it be to stand up?*

After listening to their quick instructions (because the water was growing choppier, they said), I took off. Sort of. I did have a problem or two for the first fifteen attempts. When I did get up, I didn't stay there for long. My balance, I discovered, is not world class.

At twenty-two tries, I was edging toward getting frustrated. The guys suggested we call it a day, but I was not about to give up. "Give me three more chances," I gasped, leaking water from my ears as billows pounded against the sides of the boat. They agreed, though one of them appeared to be developing elbow bursitis from raising the red flag.

This time, I decided, *I'm going to stay up no matter what.* The boat powered forward, and I rocked up and steadied and wobbled back and forth more and more *and more* before again tumbling face first. But this time I tried something different.

I held on to the rope. Dismissing the elementary laws of physics, I determined that by sheer grit I would *pull myself up.*

Feature, if you will, a sublime impression of a torpedo for about six seconds, my head producing massive plumes of water as the boat circles around, chasing its own tail. In one of my finer moments, I remember thinking, *No, I don't believe this is going to work.*

By the time the boat reached me, the guys were in high spirits. They appeared to have been stricken with apoplexy. Screaming utterances of ecstatic joy, one of them managed through hiccups and shrieks to choke out, "Maybe we should have mentioned that when you fall, *you need to let go!*" I was just pleased to provide such stellar entertainment. As I flopped into the boat, my eyelids felt as though they had been peeled back by a fire hose.

≈

I didn't learn to ski that day, though I learned a few important spiritual lessons on perfection and reality. The subject of *perfection* has been hotly contested. Rabbi Harold Kushner summed up centuries of wrangling with his book title *How Good Do We Have to Be?* So in addressing that question, let's first dispel some perfect myths.

Myth 1: If you or someone else did reach spiritual perfection, you would know it.

Reality: No way. As imperfect beings addicted to ourselves in an imperfect world, we are incapable of recognizing perfection. An inbred goldfish in a fishbowl can never know what an orca experiences in the ocean. What's incredible is that so much debate and dissension should generate over a bottom line no one can measure. The point is pointless.

Take a peek into one infinitesimal portion of our lives. Do you think you are a good automobile driver? Well, have you ever

- stopped over the crosswalk line?
- taken a shortcut through parking spaces in a parking lot?
- failed to signal at least one hundred feet before you turned?
- exceeded the speed limit by even one mile per hour?

If we have these imperfections in one tiny area, what do you think happens in an entire spectrum of life? Most spiritual giants recognize their insufficiency more *and more* the closer they get to God. As Francois Fenelon commented, "We see our malady only when our cure begins." Most of us are neither as good nor as bad as we imagine ourselves to be.

Myth 2: Spiritual perfection means the absence of mistakes.

Reality: If that is true, then the most purely perfect people in the world, the ones free of mistakes, are dead people. Mistakes are not sins. I believe that Jesus made mistakes. He stubbed His toe, rubbed in splinters, and stepped into mud puddles. He didn't spring from the womb prattling fluent Aramaic. What set Him apart as a perfect person was how He responded to His mistakes.

The Greek word for "perfect," *telos*, means mature, full-grown. One of my favorite Bible verses is found in Proverbs 24: "A righteous man falls seven times, and rises again; but the wicked are overthrown by calamity." Notice the one difference between the righteous and the wicked: The righteous fall, but they keep getting up. (It helps if we let go of the dragging rope.) To use another metaphor, though we sometimes drop the soap, we're still under the shower of God's grace. We simply have to pick up the soap.

In the new earth, it's entirely likely that we will make mistakes. What will set us apart is the way we relate to our mistakes and to those of others. We'll respond to them with Christlike patience, maturity, acceptance, and good-natured forgiveness—the same attributes that set us apart on this old earth.

Myth 3: God wants us to strive for sinless lives.

Reality: Sins are best crowded out, not tweezed out. God knows that when we focus on avoiding sins, we become sin-centered. Jesus told about an evil spirit that leaves a man, but upon returning finds the house "swept and put in order"—and empty. The evil spirit invites seven other spirits to join him there.* Our house, our mind, our life, must be filled with the furniture of God's Spirit—His sturdy, healing, pervasive thoughts and habits.

Even more frighteningly, in our quest for sinless perfection we inevitably become self-centered, caring more about our own "development" than about other people.† This was evidently the original sin.

God wants us to strive to know Him, to love Him, to love as He loves. This is the prevailing good that crowds out the bad.

Myth 4: God saves only perfect people.

Reality: "While we were still weak, at the right time Christ died for the ungodly" (Romans, chapter 5). That's us. God saves imperfect people.

Further, "If we say that we have no sin, we deceive ourselves, and the truth is not in us" (1 John, chapter 1). No one is good; God alone is holy. We simply cannot earn our way to eternal life and the new earth. God has been gracious enough to give them to us.

≈

Like most truths, perfection is a paradox.

We are already perfect: "By a single offering [Christ] has perfected for all time those who are sanctified" (Hebrews, chapter 10).

---

*See Luke, chapter 11.
†We call this navel-gazing habit "navel warfare."

We aren't perfect yet: "Not that I . . . am already perfect; but I press on to make it my own, because Christ Jesus has made me his own" (Philippians, chapter 3).

We look to the perfect One: "Let us run with perseverance the race that is set before us, looking to Jesus the pioneer and perfecter of our faith" (Hebrews, chapter 12).

Often we dialogue and debate over which should receive more emphasis: faith (what I believe) or works (what I do). Many times the analogy of two oars will be made; both oars—faith and works—are needed for our boat to make progress toward our destination.

But grace is more than either oar. Grace is more than both oars pulling together. *Grace is the boat itself.* Without grace, we're up a creek with no boat, and oars don't do much good when we're sitting on a sandy streambed.

There's nothing naïve about Jesus. He's rock-hard and street smart. He's not only in our face, He's in our DNA. This Jesus wants all of us, and He wants us to admit, "I have a problem." He desires His disciples to listen and act with imagination and resoluteness and candor.

Stephen Eastwood remarked, "God does the hard part. We get water, He gets nails." Furthermore, as Martin Luther attested, we carry those nails in our pockets. In his book *People of the Lie: The Hope for Healing Human Evil,* M. Scott Peck said he'd found that "the central defect of evil is not the sin but the refusal to acknowledge it." Consistent, destructive lying, or "hiddenness," characterizes evil. Evil people are masters of pretense and disguise, of "scapegoating," and are intolerant to criticism.

When Becky Pippert attended graduate studies at Harvard University, she noticed an odd circumstance. In her classes, students were totally open about their problems, but they had no real answers for them. Then Becky walked across the street to the church she attended. There people had all the answers but no one was open about their problems. She wondered how anyone could be whole without both sides of the equation.

We can learn a few things from Harvard and Yale and Stanford and Oxford and M.I.T. We can provide an atmosphere that deals more directly and imaginatively and redemptively with reality.

Where in the Adventist Church can we find think tanks to deal with authentic, tough questions? In our churches and in our schools. In the classrooms and in the libraries and in the dormitories. Spiritualizing seeks to avoid reality and cover up problems. If we are retreating from reality, setting up a pseudo existence, confusing innocence with naïveté and image with substance and bravado with valor, exchanging unvarnished truth for unwarranted faith, believing that spirituality lies primarily in what we don't do, we are deceived and are being led by the father of lies.

My friend Bret was preaching in a small church when he mentioned that believers shouldn't be overly concerned with "perfection." A man immediately rose from his pew, stomped up to the podium, and literally pushed Bret out of the way. "Turn to Matthew chapter five, verse forty-eight," he roared, flipping pages furiously. " 'Be ye therefore perfect, even as your Father which is in heaven is perfect'!"

Bret stood astonished for a moment before bedlam broke out. Eventually, though the interrupter continued to murmur comments from his seat, Brad was able to finish his sermon.

What makes this story so strikingly ironic is the context for Matthew's verse: *Unconditionally love your enemies.* Our Father brings His impartial love and daily blessings to the undeserving, and we should also. The parallel Luke passage translates the identical verse this way: "Be *merciful,* even as your Father is merciful." Matthew's "perfect" means "merciful."

Perfection is never the goal we strive for. Love is. *Grace and effort are not mutually exclusive.* The apostle Peter began his second letter by saying: "Make every effort to supplement your faith with virtue, and virtue with knowledge, and knowledge with self-control,* and self-control with steadfastness, and steadfastness with godliness, and godliness with brotherly affection, and brotherly affection with love." All efforts under the umbrella of grace.

What goal should we strive for? The good fight of faith is one of fighting to grow in trust. In my office, I have posted this aim: "When we seek to gain heaven through the merits of Christ, the soul makes progress."[†]

We cannot bless ourselves any more than we can kiss the top of our own head. We cannot pull ourselves up to perfection any more than I could, through main grit and willpower, pull myself up from under the water to a vertical skiing position.

We cannot.

We don't have to. ❏

---

*With which Peter struggled mightily.
[†]From Ellen White.

"There shall be a time of trouble, such as never has been since there was a nation till that time; but at that time your people shall be delivered, every one whose name shall be found written in the book."—Daniel, chapter 12

"Do not be anxious about your life, what you shall eat or what you shall drink, nor about your body, what you shall put on. . . . Which of you by being anxious can add one cubit to his span of life? . . . But seek first his kingdom and his righteousness, and all these things shall be yours as well. Therefore do not be anxious about tomorrow, for tomorrow will be anxious for itself. Let the day's own trouble be sufficient for the day."—Jesus, in Matthew, chapter 6

No Worries

The opposite of faith is not doubt but worry. We should doubt many things in this life.* Doubts may lead to greater faith in reality, which is where God lives. Doubt can be beneficial.

Worry, on the other hand, always drains, always disables, enfeebles, exhausts. Worry consumes us with crippling toxins. There is no good side to worry, no silver lining, never an adequate rationale. Worry is absence of trust.

This may come as a shock to "professional worriers." You probably know someone who qualifies. They worry about their allergies, they worry about their money, they worry about their children, they worry about their car, they worry about their cat, they worry about the Middle East, they worry about unlocked doors, they worry about the shoes they just bought, they worry about what they should eat, they worry about the pimple on their chin, they worry about what the neighbors might be thinking, they worry about celebrities' problems, they worry about fear-drenched local news reports, they worry that you don't worry enough.

Are they aware that worry is faithless living? Do they know the pain they cause their God? If your young child admitted, "I'm just not sure you can take care of me, and I worry all the time," wouldn't that break your heart? Wouldn't you try with all your might to reassure your child? God whispers through tears, "Please, for both our sakes, trust Me."

Valid concerns are different in that they motivate us to action. Here's the principal distinction between worry and valid concern: *Can you do something about it?* If you can, then do it. If you can't, pray about it and leave it in God's trustworthy hands. That's it.

In particular, Adventist worries and paranoia about the time of trouble are dreadfully wrong. Seriously, I can't think of one benefit derived as a church from

---

*For example, we should doubt offers of instant riches, college degrees earned in two weeks, promises of Internet love, and glowing prospects found in radioactive fields.

concentrating on it. Some people list the advantages of "preparedness," but all purported benefits pale before the specter (largely in the past, I hope) of Adventist children trembling in bed, imagining ever more hideous atrocities "worse than you can imagine."

We have squandered far too much energy fearing fear itself. Do we really, truly believe that perfect love casts out *all* fear? Consider how many Advent believers have worried about and prepared for the time of trouble—and died without seeing it. They spent their lives fearing it needlessly. Isn't that a tragedy?

Moreover, uncountable numbers of people have already endured their time of trouble. It will never get any worse for Rwanda than it was when ten thousand people a day—eight hundred thousand in all—were hacked to death by the machetes of their neighbors and former friends. It won't get any worse in Cambodia's killing fields. It won't get worse in regions of Kosovo and East Timor. But it also won't get any worse for millions, including children, who are scalded by the betrayal and bitterness of divorce. Nor will it get worse for victims of cancer or cystic fibrosis or chronic fatigue syndrome, for those who have lost a child, for millions of child prostitutes, for those who wither under an interminable blight of loneliness.

We need to stop talking about the time of trouble. Who among us, when going to visit a beloved, best friend whom we haven't seen in years, would talk about the travel? *You're going to see your friend.* Do you go on about long lines at the airport and the possibility of flight delays and the pretzel mix you will be served? No, you talk about what a joy it will be to embrace your friend. "Now when these things begin to take place, look up and raise your heads," the Bible says, "because your *redemption* is drawing near."

One worry cure is to live with an attitude of gratitude. Savor every precious second. Can we see a pinkening sunrise? Can we hear an oboe pour out its mournful call? Can we taste a succulent salad? Smell bread baking? Touch a baby's toes? Sit up and fog a mirror? *Thank You, God.* Don't worry; be grateful.

A young woman once asked me, "What would you study in the Bible to prepare for the time of the end?"

"I would study the Gospels," I replied. "Matthew, Mark, Luke, and John."

She looked puzzled. "And how," she inquired, "would that help, exactly?"

"So we can get through all the times of trouble in our life," I said. "We get to know Jesus, we fall in love with Him absolutely, because the best way to make it through any crisis is to rely on a living, loving, moment-by-moment friendship with God."

Jesus is the Prince of Peace. He brings a calm in the midst of our storms. He places a hand on our shoulder and says softly, "Peace, be still." He heals us of our worrisome infirmity.

One of many sayings I enjoy from Aussie friends is "No worries, mate!" Apparently, Jesus speaks Australian. ❑

"I'm Thinking of Leaving"

You might as well know this from the start: I think you could be a breathtaking, extraordinary Seventh-day Adventist.

No, not for the usual reasons. (At least not for the reasons I've often heard.) The reasons I have in mind are kind of . . . personal. So maybe we could personally dialogue. Go ahead, you first.

I really don't even know why I'm reading this.

Neither do I. Let's just concede that somehow God thinks the timing is right.

Are you saying you want me to read this bold print as if these are my thoughts? Is that the idea?

Yeah. It's kind of hard for me to climb inside your cranium any other way, so let these letters slip behind your eyeballs to the genuine you. Internalize what you're reading. Wrestle with the words. Agree. Disagree. Let them shudder and groan and breathe in you.

What if I don't want to?

Hey, it's your cranium. But if you're going to allow *anything* to make an impression on you, that's what you have to do.

Okay, first of all, what makes you think I'm not an Adventist already?

You might be—I don't know. But there are Adventists and there are Adventists.

Uh . . . profound. What does that mean?

Some Adventists stay in the church only because they're looking for the retirement package. They're not fully convinced of the rightness and attractiveness of being at home—of being in the church. They stick because of duty, fear, ego, dysfunction, habit, or fire insurance. There are those Adventists, and there are Adventists who are in the church for the right reasons.

Which are . . . ?

Above all, love and freedom.

Ha! I was hoping you'd mention those.

Go on.

You talk about love and freedom in the church? You obviously don't know the church near my home. You want to know what they care about?

Go on.

They care about rules and positions and appearances and the past. They don't really care about people who are desperate and hurting, and they don't tolerate people with different ideas. Where's the love and freedom there?

That reminds me of the story about the public sinner who was excommunicated and forbidden entry to the church, so he took his woes to God. "Lord," he said, "they won't let me in, because I'm a sinner."

"What are you complaining about?" said God. "They won't let Me in either."

Exactly my point.

Moreover, in *The Grace Awakening,* Charles Swindoll describes those among us whom he calls the freedom killers:

> More and more Christians are realizing that the man-made restrictions and legalistic regulations under which they have been living have not come from the God of grace, but have been enforced by people who do not want others to be free. . . .
>
> [Freedom killers] kill freedom, spontaneity, and creativity; they kill joy as well as productivity. They kill with their words and their pens and their looks. They kill with their attitudes far more often than with their behavior. There is hardly a church or Christian organization or Christian school or missionary group or media ministry where such danger does not lurk. . . .
>
> This day—this very moment—millions are living their lives in shame, fear, and intimidation who should be free, productive individuals. The tragedy is they think it is the way they should be. They have never known the truth that could set them free.

So you agree with me?

I admit that people in our churches are struggling with demonstrating love and allowing freedom. In fact, I admit to being one of the strugglers. And you're right—I don't know that church near your home. But I'll bet you don't know that church either.

Yes, I do. I've been there lots of times.

Do you know *why* the members act the ways they do? Do you know about the woman who lost four precious children through miscarriages, or the deacon whose boss treats him like garbage, or the couple teetering on the edge of a heartbreaking divorce? Do you know about the man who is worried sick about how to take care of his aging parents, or the woman who as a child was repeatedly abused, or the pastor who has too much to do and is pressured from every side to do more? When you think about it, can you say that you know them?

Well, not really, I guess. But that's one of the problems with the church: You never *truly* get to know anybody.

The answer to that problem, though, is in your own hands. You see problems boiling in the church, and you're tempted to let them stew in their own pot. You start packing when you see the politics heat up. But is that the loving, liberating path to take?

Your point?

A while back, I was reading about H. Norman Schwarzkopf, the general who directed Operation Desert Storm. I was impressed with him because he's the best type of general—a general who hates war. He also has an IQ of 170, likes listening to Luciano Pavarotti and Willie Nelson, is fluent in French and German, and enjoys the ballet and opera. (So much for military stereotypes.)

Schwarzkopf was recalling how after graduating with honors from West Point and entering active duty, he almost resigned. "I had an alcoholic commander," he explained. "I had an executive officer who was a coward. I saw terrible things going on around me and I said, 'Who needs it? When my three years are up I'm getting out!'

"But a very sage guy sat me down and said, 'Young man, you know, if all the guys who see these bad things happening [decide to] quit, then all the guys who don't think these things are so bad are going to be doing them later on. If you really think it's that bad, why don't you stick around until someday you get into a position to do something about it?' "

Of course, later he was in a position to do "something about it."

It's up to you to hang in there and fight for the right, just as your Savior did—and does.

Okay, but sometimes I'm not even sure what *is* "the right." I have some questions about what Adventists believe.

I started attending a Seventh-day Adventist church after graduating from a public high school and a public university, and, as you might imagine, what I heard in church and in private conversations with church members astonished me. What particularly astonished me was how Adventist beliefs make so much sense and are so consistently life-enhancing. However, I was also puzzled that Adventist beliefs aren't seen by all Adventists as promoting love and freedom.

Go on.

We could fill up this book with prophetic messages. For now, though, look at just two distinctive Adventist doctrines for love and freedom that swim against the current:

1. No eternal torment. One reason I hadn't become a Christian earlier was that I couldn't reconcile God frying people forever—out of "love"—while His virtuous children enjoyed eternal bliss. I was and am among the millions who continue to say, "Deliver me from a God—or a love—that would do that." No life-respecting, humane human would keep someone alive for even one week to torture him in flaming agony. The hideousness is incomprehensible.

That's why I'm curious when people from other Christian churches speak of God's love. Do they mean a love that would leave their loved ones screaming in pain forever? Then I want no part of that love. I think that's what Jesus referred to when He said, "The hour is coming when whoever kills you will think he is offering service to God. And they will do this because they have not known the Father, nor me" (John, chapter 16).

Thank God, He is as compassionate and fair as Adventists know Him to be.

2. *Honoring the Sabbath.* Despite being misrepresented constantly, God's Sabbath remains an awesome defender of freedom. Just look at three ways it sets us free.

a. *Freedom from the tyranny of the urgent.* On the morning of March 3, 1991, a United Airlines plane took off from Denver's Stapleton Airport. Minutes later, as the plane approached Colorado Springs, it rolled over, nosedived into the earth, and disintegrated in a massive fireball, killing all aboard.

That same morning I had also caught a flight. Out of Denver's Stapleton Airport. On a United Airlines plane. When I heard news of the tragedy, I began thinking about what might have been the last terrifying thoughts of those passengers. If you were plummeting to certain death, what would you be doing?

Besides screaming my head off?

Yeah.

I'd be praying to God and thinking about my family.

Most people would do the same, because we recognize that God and family are important matters. But too often we allow the urgent—like cars, phone calls, grades, jobs, clothes, food, deadlines—to squeeze us and control us while the important gets minimal attention. Urgent matters are seldom important, and important matters are seldom urgent. You wouldn't be thinking about your car on the way down in a plane.

You're right.

The Sabbath brings our attention back to the important areas in life—God and family. Sabbath time puts our lives on another plane, so to speak.

b. *Freedom from trying to earn God's love.* In our society, our worth is based on what we produce. Much production equals much worth; little production equals little worth.

But God says, "Put aside your striving on this day. Produce nothing of material benefit. Now note this: I love you *just as much* on this 'unproductive' day as when you're productive." That's the gift of God's grace. The freeing gift of His saving acceptance apart from our works is reinforced each week as we swim in the Sabbath.

c. *Freedom from mindless meanderings in misty religiosity.*

Excuse me?

What I'm referring to is a *current* trend toward believing the most preposterous, brainless things if we only affix a spiritual label to them. The conventional wisdom here is: If it can be conceived, it will happen. Perception is reality.

Some reincarnationists thus believe they can, without direction from any god-like personal casting agent, live multiple lives as a hairy yak, a rock, a star, or a hairy yakking rock star. Some evolutionists embrace scientific impossibilities such as nonlife developing completely on its own into billions of life forms of incredible complexity. Some religionists attempt to manipulate God. And some New Age believers claim to *be* God—as if making a good cup of coffee is equivalent to making the universe.

Religion should make sense, in keeping with natural laws of the universe. Spiritual beliefs ought to be subject to analysis and open for discussion. Defensible. Rational. Reasonable.

The Sabbath provides a testing ground for belief. We test our spiritual hypotheses on others during Sabbath School. We hold up concepts against time-tested truths in the Bible. We examine the evidence for our beliefs and acquire a sense of proportion on a Sabbath afternoon nature walk. Our minds are freed this day to focus on realities beyond ourselves.

Yet the most personal reason to be an Adventist is none of these. Another supersedes them all.

Which is . . . ?

To simply and deeply and unwaveringly fall in love with God. Look searchingly at Jesus—the clearest picture of God—and continue to fall in love with Him. Read and talk about Him. Think about Him from the time you get up until you lie down. Converse with Him in your thoughts. Ask Him for His guidance. Thank Him for His leading. Marvel at His creative goodness. Falling in love with God is simply the best reason to be an Adventist.

Once when I had strayed from God, I came across a verse and it shook me up. With tears in His voice, God told me His dream for me: "I thought how I would set you among my sons, and give you a pleasant land, a heritage most beauteous of all nations. And I thought you would call me your Father, and would not turn from following me" (Jeremiah, chapter 3).

The Father does long to give us an inheritance, now and forever. Our leaving would break His heart.

Yeah, I can see that.

Anything else you want to say about the church?

Something I should have mentioned earlier: Church services are *boring*. What difference does it make whether I go to church?

I like the answer C. S. Lewis gave to that concern:

> When I first became a Christian, about 14 years ago, I thought that I could do it on my own, by retiring to my rooms and reading theology, and I wouldn't go to the churches. . . . I disliked very much their hymns, which

I considered to be fifth-rate poems set to sixth-rate music. But as I went on I saw the great merit of it. I came up against different people of quite different outlooks and different education, and then gradually my conceit just began peeling off. I realized that the hymns (which were just sixth-rate music) were, nevertheless, being sung with devotion and benefit by an old saint in elastic-side boots in the opposite pew, and then you realize that you aren't fit to clean those boots. It gets you out of your solitary conceit.

This doesn't mean that attending church services is always pleasant. But the Adventists who remain faithful for love and freedom are a wonder to behold. As Ellen White observed, "Those who in everything make God first and last and best are the happiest people in the world."

One last thing: Suppose I had left and wanted to come back?
Well, would you?
All right, I'd come back—for my Father's sake. Even if nobody knew I'd left.
I was hoping you'd say that. ❏

I wouldn't give a fig for the kind of simplicity which exists on this side of complexity, but I would give the whole world for the simplicity that exists on the other side of complexity.
—*Oliver Wendell Holmes*

Do not be children in your thinking; be babes in evil, but in thinking be mature.
—*1 Corinthians, chapter 14*

Lethal Reasoning: Black or White

When I was in high school, I decided that there was one topic I'd never again discuss with anyone. Every time this subject was raised, so were voices. I had never heard anyone change his mind about it. Classroom discussions proved frustrating and fruitless. Any conversation about *abortion* generated more heat than light. And this was before *Roe v. Wade*!

But during those years and for decades afterward, I listened. I listened to pro-choice people and to pro-life advocates say you're either for or against abortion. And I reached a conclusion: Both sides are wrong. Abortion is a matter of life or death, but it's not a matter of black or white.

While I was editing a youth magazine,* I experienced a momentary lapse of

---

*Q: What do you get when you swallow your contact lens? A: Insight.

sanity and decided to tackle the topic of abortion. In that issue, we discussed all sides of the debate, pointing out that much of the controversy rests between black-or-white positions—"no contraceptives allowed" and "abortion is always accept-able." Considerations such as health of the mother, severe child malformation, rape or incest resulting in pregnancy, and adoption possibilities all fell into gray areas. I concluded that four points influenced me toward a pro-life position: degree of responsibility, opportunities for adoption, God did not abort our planet, and protecting those on the fringes of life.*

But I was blasted by some for my assertion that this issue was often a matter of grays. Critics claimed I was waffling. Compromising. Selling out to sin. Disregarding clear biblical counsel. Dishonoring my God. When I met with a primary critic (and became friends), we eventually discovered that we essentially agreed on our abortion stances. He remained angry about the "gray matter" comment though. That's when I reached another conclusion: Anyone on either side who doesn't acknowledge abortion to be a complicated issue doesn't understand it.

Black-or-white thinking won't admit a particle of truth in other points of view. Extremist thought embraces the either/or fallacy when other options exist. Simplistic reasoning finds no intermediary *better* or *worse*. This mind-set has created incalculable damage.

Carrying an all-or-nothing posture, we can turn a minor mess into a massive problem. We slip to a knee and, because of the misstep, jump off a bridge. *I broke my diet, so I might as well eat this entire apple pie, along with a quart of Chunky Monkey ice cream.*

I'm going to the theater anyway, so I'll watch a movie of irresponsible violence, damaging stereotyping, and dehumanizing sex.

I'm with someone I like a lot, so if we start heavy kissing, I might as well have sexual intercourse.

I got someone pregnant, so I'll tell her to get an abortion.

I yelled at my child, so I'm not going to church.

I'm not attending church, so forget about God.

Can you see the power of evil here? Black-or-white thinking induces muddled morals and bizarre behavior. Black-or-white extremists leap from one side to the other without ever landing in the saddle; middle ground for them is mid-air. They are living embodiments of the chaos theory. They won't allow a fleck of mustard to foul their lips at a potluck as they shovel through four helpings of lasagna. Eating their cooking may be like taking your colon to a car wash, but listening to their

---

*Also, discovering that the fine for destroying the egg (fetus) of a bald eagle is up to five thousand dollars and/or a year in jail.

diatribes makes you feel dirty. Wearing a wedding ring is sinful; wearing a scowl is somehow sanctified.

The end for people who cleave to this approach is often terribly sad. After their children have bolted from the church because they have connected the dots to create a joyless, arbitrary God, extremists often become more extreme, growing increasingly obsessive and judgmental—or else carelessly tossing off all constraints for a lifestyle of bitter debauchery.

I once knew an extremist pastor who argued *ad infinitum* his position on the nature of Christ. Years later, when he had changed over to the opposite position, he still was every bit as passionate about his rightness. Black-or-white thinking throws a speeding car into reverse. Black-or-white thinking strips our gears. Black-or-white thinking leads to Black and White churches.*

Simplistic reasoning results in faulty upper-room experiences, not as in the roaring, fiery upper room of Pentecost but as in two prior episodes. In the upper room at the Last Supper, the disciples presumed they were unbeatable, strong, secure. They were abysmally mistaken. In the upper room after the Crucifixion, they judged that they were weak, destitute, defeated. They were gloriously wrong.

Life happens. It happens on the edges of passion and peace, chaos and comedy, pretense and poetry. Much of life will remain a mystery. If God spelled out everything, we would lose our healthy capacity for analytic thought.

The closer we get to truth, the closer we get to paradox. Die to live, the first shall be last, your judge is your defense, freedom in obedience, a mother made by her child.† Swimming against the current doesn't always present a choice of polar opposites—hot or cold, good or evil. We live on the rim of warm sunlight and cool shadows on a twirling sphere, and which temperature we seek depends on whether it's summer or winter. Context matters.

In his book *Organizing Your Inner World,* Gordon MacDonald recalled, "Years ago my father wisely shared with me that one of the great tests of human character is found in making critical choices of selection and rejection amidst all of the opportunities that lurk in life's path. 'Your challenge,' he told me, 'will not be in separating out the good from the bad, but in grabbing the *best* out of all the possible good.' "

Frankly, however, I've had a problem with how to "do my best," because I don't exactly know what *best* means. Study and work eighteen hours a day? Focus primarily on excellent nutrition? Go to extremes in prayer or exercise or

---

*In truth, there are no Black or White Adventist churches. Every Seventh-day Adventist church welcomes people of all colors. Otherwise, despite the sign out front, it's not an Adventist church.

†Perhaps the best sample of paradoxical truth is found in Luci Shaw's classic poem, "Mary's Song."

friendships? I now aim to "do my balanced best"—and I counsel overwhelmed students to do the same. Many have found contentment with this new aim. Doing our balanced best is God's ideal; it relieves us from exhaustion, compulsive behavior, and despair. Like a rocking chair, we stay stable—in spite of life's ups and downs—when we remain balanced.

Yet the best stance isn't always in the middle. "Say you were standing with one foot in the oven and one foot in the ice bucket," quips Bobby Bragan. "According to the percentage people, you should be perfectly comfortable." Some matters, such as excusing torture or rape, are simply never acceptable.

Jesus says, "He who is not with Me is against Me." This radical call should never lead us to extremism, for a vital difference exists between radicals and extremists. "Radical" literally means "to the root," as in the case of radical surgeries. The opposite of radical isn't conservative—it's superficial. A true radical is like Jesus, always plunging to the damp, earth-clutching root of the matter.

Adventist extremists tend to become Sadventists, Badventists, Madventists, and Fadventists. Those Adventists who discover the simplicity on the other side of complexity are Radventists.   ❑

If you've ever been tremendously, astoundingly surprised, you'll relate to this.

I Didn't Know

Even before I began college, I knew quite a lot. For example, I knew college would be different from high school, and it was. I somehow knew Mark Twain's counsel, "Never let schooling get in the way of an education." I didn't. I also knew that my roommate and I would become friends.

When I opened the door, the first thing I noticed was his eyes. His eyes danced with amusement. "Hi, I'm Billy Jackson." He smiled, offering his broad hand.

Our room was cramped and stunningly inelegant. One bare window poised above an iron radiator that banged throughout the night. There was no carpeting, no sink, no desks. We decided that the room called for a personal, decorative touch, so we dragged our bunk beds from one side of the room to the other. Then, with a final flourish, we hung a sheet over the window. *Dorm chic.*

We were the only freshmen scholarships on our floor. The two-story athletic dormitory with the peeling stucco was officially Chase Hall, but students tagged it the Zoo for reasons we learned too well. Acid rock and marijuana assaulted our senses day and night. We encountered rooms set on fire, gunshots fired though closed doors, roommates beaten into unconsciousness. We heard and saw pranks that were disgusting and hurtful. We muttered when the water fountain was again torn from the wall.* From this fertilized soil sprang our friendship.

We spent that first year talking, eating, groaning, and laughing. When I couldn't find a hill to park on, we pushed my '61 Volkswagen to get it started. My "money saved for college" I transferred to a Taco Bell account. We wrestled, ran wind sprints, and traveled home together. And we endured the indignities of Zoo life together.

He was a six-foot, five-inch forward who could jump and run. I was a six-foot, two-inch guard who could pass and play defense. We knew that both of us would be stars at Cal Poly San Luis Obispo, and we were half right. Billy became the university's all-time scoring leader.

Off the court, Billy was cheerful and easygoing. In basketball games, he performed with sullen intensity. Quick and powerful, he could single-handedly change a game's complexion. He would streak for a fast-break lay-up, score on a fade-away jumper, and tip in a shot. More than once, however, he also dealt elbows, delivered curses, and drew technicals.

Billy held one tangible dream—to play in the NBA—and he had an excellent chance.† Then word got out that apparently our coach had branded Billy "uncoachable." He never received an offer. After the last season, we went our own ways. Billy played pro ball in Mexico, winning league MVP honors. (I knew he would.) I started attending classes and began student teaching. We kept in touch about once a year.

Then a curious thing happened. I was converted.

After becoming a Christian, I prayed every night for my family and my friends, including Billy. He was invited to my wedding, but he never showed up.

Three years passed before I talked with Billy again. One night he called me. His speech was slurred, and he said he might come by sometime. He wasn't working much, he was playing ball, and he had seven girlfriends. Eventually I told him I had become a Christian.

He seemed surprised. "You did?" he said. "I never knew that. What religion are you?"

"Seventh-day Adventist."

"You're a cabbagehead? Hey, that means I can't bring in my brew when I come over. I can't go anywhere without my brew!"

---

*This is only what I can mention here. Believe me, it was bad.
†I don't say this lightly. Almost no one who plays college basketball makes the NBA.

I told him he would be welcome with or without his brew. He laughed. He said he'd come by to see me. He didn't. I kept praying for him, knowing he was in trouble and hoping he would just stay alive.

Two years passed. Out of nowhere, Billy called and left a phone message.

"Billy's married," Yolanda told me. "And he's a Christian."

I called him instantly. "Billy! What's this I hear?"

"Yeah, it's true," he said. "I'll send you some wedding pictures."

We visited him the next summer. His wife, Rita, was beautiful and demure. They attended church four times a week. He sang in a men's quartet. Trophies covered one side of the front room. I kept looking at him, his long arms spread across the back of the couch.

"Hey," I said finally, "how is your life now compared with before?"

"Like a mountain to a molehill," he said. "Like a mountain to a molehill." His eyes danced with amusement.

I sat in his living room and studied the carpet. *Could it happen to Billy? He was the one person I never really thought . . .*

Wow, I concluded with amazement, *God can save ANYONE.*

I should have known that.   ❑

I'd rather learn from one bird how to sing than teach ten thousand stars how not to dance.—e. e. cummings

---

A Time to Mourn, a Time to Grand March

My friend Steve Case told me about meeting some extremely nutrition-conscious Adventists who, while working at a mission project on a Caribbean island, refused to drink coconut milk offered to them.* Their reason was simple: "We don't drink milk." That settled it.

Of course, people who avoid drinking milk do so because it emanates from an animal, but this premise didn't stir them. Milk is milk, after all. The prohibition could therefore extend to mother's milk, milk of magnesia, and, supernaturally unhealthy, the Milky Way galaxy.

Words will fool us. Our resulting confusion may be amusing, but we act foolishly when we neglect to make timely distinctions. The wise Solomon wrote in

---

*Coconut "milk" is the whitish juice inside the coconut.

Ecclesiastes, chapter 3, "For everything there is a season . . . a time to weep, and a time to laugh; a time to mourn, and a time to dance."

It's Solomon's "dance" that's the sticking point because, as you may have heard, "Adventists don't dance."* Yet turn on music and watch an infant move instinctively to the rhythm. It's cute when little children dance because it's so harmless, so innocent, so *natural.* So, naturally, we shouldn't be surprised that *every people group on earth* in some fashion associates music with movement.

Our prohibition against "dancing" is too sweeping. I'm writing to those readers who sense that Hebrew dancing, for example, or river dancing, or square dancing, isn't inherently evil but aren't certain what precisely the church should say about it. Frankly, I'm weary of hearing how we are so susceptible and immature and ignorant that we will be sucked into any temptation we come near. Certainly we ought to be careful—full of care—but spare me the apprehensive, antiseptic lifestyle. Jesus didn't live that way. He was accused of being a glutton and a winebibber, a friend of tax collectors and sinners. Psalm 16 states, "In His presence is fullness of joy," and this fullness appears in astonishing variety.

Too often we fall prey to slippery slope reasoning—a logical fallacy that suggests once a step is taken, it will inevitably lead to harmful ends. However, we don't avoid grocery stores that sell liquor though glimpsing the fermented brews may entice us, nor do we shun computers though they may lead us to pornography. We eat mushrooms, though some of them are poisonous. We distinguish.

Years ago, Yolanda and I joined some friends for Irish dancing. We skipped under bridges of arms, twirled at giddy speeds, and joined hands with people of many ages and races. It was far from seductive—it was fun and innocent, and we finished breathless and exhilarated. I understand it's similar to the "grand marches" of olden Adventist days.

As Christians, we live redemptively, bringing something better. What we could truly use is an acceptable term for vegetarian dancing—an active, joyful response to music that uplifts us, builds community and vibrant health, and makes us feel good about the gifts of music and movement and laughter that God gives.†

Consider the names of "vegetarian meats": Bologno. Numete. Stripples. Wham. Prosage. Prime Stakes (*stakes?*). Meatless Corned Beef. Do these lead to eating meat? No, they provide a meat *substitute.* Similarly, we can provide a redemptive *substitute* for harmful dancing—that stuff that exalts sensuality and demeans relationships.

---

*We would be a different church had we started in New Orleans instead of New England.

†Of the twenty-seven references to "dance" in the Bible, only four occur in a negative context. Sixteen references are clearly positive.

What could we call the substitute? I suppose "folk dancing" could work. Other possibilities include (a) vegeshuffling, (b) Worthington waltzing, (c) Little Debbie cakewalking, (d) Jordan River dancing, (e) seven-stepping, (f) temperance tango, (g) FriChik foxtrot, (h) Hiram Edson hop, (i) knotdancing, (j) splinkettsing, (k) grand moshing, (l) roller skating.

I'm having fun with these, but I'm also serious. For lack of a palatable term, some people are losing their religion over this. It's time to stop mourning over dancing.

"Milk" isn't always milk. "Dancing" isn't always dancing. Can we talk now? ❏

God has appointed in the church first apostles [missionaries], second prophets [preachers], third teachers, then workers of miracles, then healers, helpers, administrators, speakers in various kinds of tongues. . . . But earnestly desire the higher gifts.—1 Corinthians, chapter 12

God's Mixed-up Status Scale

Our church hierarchy is backwards. If I had my way, I'd turn our entire remuneration system upside down."

"Jaime," I laughed, "you are crazy." My friend Jaime is a radical Christian. That's radical in the good, narrow sense.

"You started me down this road," Jaime reminded me, "when you told me about rejecting the principal's job."

Back at Valley View Junior Academy in Arroyo Grande, California, I had been handling the typical teaching load of responsibilities: seven "preps" (different subjects to prepare), no plan times or grader, A.S.B. sponsor, intramurals referee, newspaper advisor, taking hot lunch orders, etc. One day my friend and principal Leon Kopitzke asked me to accompany him on a walk after school.

We were crossing the newly seeded field following our successful G.R.E.E.N. (Get Rocks Effectively Eradicated Now) campaign. Behind glistening eucalyptus trees stretched Pismo Beach and miles of sand dunes. After minutes of small talk, Leon told me that my name had come up for a possible position elsewhere as a principal. Would I be interested?

I weighed the choice before offering my response. "No, Leon," I replied, "I'm not ready to step down yet."

He barked a laugh and glanced at me. Noting that I was serious, his eyes narrowed and he nodded. "Yes, I miss being on the front lines in the classroom," he said. "I'll pass along the word: 'He's not ready to step *down*.' "

"We've got it backward," Jaime continued. "The missionaries ought to receive the highest salaries."

"But then missionaries would be tempted to be in it for the money," I countered.

"Yeah." He nodded his head sardonically. "Maybe we shouldn't pay them at all, so they'd be really pure. Purely dead."

"Your point?"

A gleam lighted Jaime's eye. "Who makes the salary structures of the world? Administrators! That's why they make the most—they decide to give themselves more. It's like the Pentagon determining what to spend on armed forces. What would happen if we didn't follow a worldly model and instead followed a biblical model? Let missionaries and preachers and teachers create the salary structure. Do you think the administrators would be on top?"

"If they created the salary structure, they would *be* administrators," I pointed out. "Anyway, administrators earn it in extra responsibilities and headaches."

"You're saying as a junior academy teacher you didn't have as many responsibilities and headaches? Dealing with dozens of squirmy students every minute? And what about those 'free summers' you spend? After cleaning up, taking classes, and preparing for next year, your last summer amounted to—what, two weeks? Then teachers have to put up with pastors who hold *workers'* meetings, as if no one else in the denomination is a worker. And people cluck their tongues when a pastor leaves the *ministry* and becomes a teacher. Give me a break."

He had me there, and he knew it. I hate it when he does that.

Jaime kept spouting. "And since missionaries cross cultural boundaries to spread the gospel, I'd include in the class of missionaries all the youth workers. Talk about communicating with a foreign culture! Anyway, I'll admit that administrators have their place," he crowed, "right above speaking in tongues."

"Whoa!" I exclaimed. "Now I know why Paul moved quickly to the 'more excellent way' of love in chapter 13. Look how we lose our love and goodwill in all these rankings. Besides, these aren't spiritual earnings, they're spiritual *gifts.*"

"You're right," Jaime admitted. "But I'd *love* to try looking at the church *gift* structure from the perspective of chapter 12 of 1 Corinthians. Hey, wouldn't it be refreshing to overhear at a church potluck a conversation that went like this: '. . . he left the conference presidency and is now pastoring a small church in Connecticut.'

" 'Well, good for him! Glad to hear he got a promotion! Maybe some day—God willing—he'll be a youth worker.' "

Crazy Jaime. ❑

Walking humbly with God allows for differing perspectives.

The Cold Truth

L
ook at my mouth make steam, Dad."

"Yeah, Dad, look at this."

My two young sons leaned forward from their seat-belted positions and exhaled. Clouds billowed from their lips.

"What about this one?" I focused a thin cirrus stream against the windshield. Then I attempted steam rings that emerged instead as great misty planets. The boys laughed. Two minutes later, Yolanda joined us to head for church.

"*Brrrrrrr,*" she shivered. "Wow, it's cold!"

"Decidedly chilly," I agreed, finding it easy to keep a stiff upper lip.

After moving from the California coast to a rental house in Maryland, we had expertly packed our one-car garage until it held everything but our car. However, we discovered that parking our old Honda Civic wagon outside on winter nights was different here. This particular morning the defroster lacked stamina, and the heater was waging the sort of drawn-out battle we'd come to expect in a cold war.

We backed out of the driveway and started up the street. Within half a block, the windshield filmed with ice. I pressed the rinser and then ran the wipers for a few moments, but neither helped—the ice must have formed quicker than usual. I wasn't much concerned. I was a veteran. I'd already pulled through three weeks of winter.

Steering off the road, I stepped out, opened the trunk, snatched up my trusty blue ice scraper, and ambled confidently to the windshield. With my first swipe, I sensed something was wrong. There was no ice. The windshield was clean.

But it was still clouded. Slowly, like a waking sloth, the cold truth crept over me. *Hey. Wait. A. Minute. The. Ice. Is. On. The. Inside.*

My breath had frozen on the inside of the car.

Climbing into the driver's seat, I began in an awed fashion scraping my breath off the windshield. My breath fell in frozen flakes and settled on my pants.

Then another thought occurred to me: *The only way to keep the windshield from icing again is to stop breathing.* Then I thought I'd better stop thinking.

Okay, Minnesotans, laugh. Chortle, North Dakotans. Whinny and wheeze, Mainiacs. Hold on to your heaving ribs, Saskatchewans. Fall down and pound the frozen tundra, Alaskans. But to this southern California boy, here was a profound experience. Here, at last, was something to tell my wide-eyed, slack-jawed grandchildren: "It was *so cold* my breath froze on the inside of the car!"*

Which brings me to the point of my story. With this experience I received a profound appreciation for cold. But what is profound to me, what is meaningful to me, may not be meaningful to you. Likewise, what is meaningful to you may not be meaningful to me.

Would you impose meaning on me? Would you inform me plainly, "Buddy, that wasn't cold"? To me it was *cold.*

Some Christians play out their spiritual existence in a sort of solipsism—believing only self exists. *Everything in my church ought to be geared for and aimed at me.* All the articles in church magazines, for instance, no matter whom they're written for, ought to appeal to me. All the music in my church service ought to target me—not anyone younger or older nor anyone more energetic or more sedate. As a result, I can come to believe, deep down, that my tastes are God's tastes.

This doesn't hold true for us in real life, of course. Imagine entering a restaurant and demanding that every item satisfy your preferences. "Sorry, you need to take that shrimp off the menu. Don't like them and never will. You should double the size of the mashed potato servings. Those saltshakers are ugly. Lose them. And you have *way* too many appetizers with cheese on them. What? Do I have to call the pasto—I mean, the manager?"

Expecting total "me" service reflects the demands of a selfish child. We ought rather to be humble and mature enough to think, *Though I don't appreciate this, it is aimed at someone with different perspectives than mine. I don't require complete satisfaction all the time.*† This may give new meaning to the word *sanctification.*

I remember a not-so-great controversy in our small church over the subject of (surprise!) music. At a board meeting, some members brought up the problem of guitars, which should not be played in the sanctuary because they are obvious relics of "secular music." Only organ music should be played, because it is "the best we can offer." Members weighed in on both sides. I pointed out that, from my background, I associated organ music mostly with professional baseball and basketball games (*Da-da-da-da da-da* "Charge!"). Not everyone appeared to appreciate this fascinating bit of personal history.

We were at a tense impasse. Then my friend Peter Nelson, who claims to like only two kinds of music ("country" and "western"), bellowed, "Well, I guess a guitar is closer to a harp than an organ!" Everyone roared with laughter. That was that. Guitars have been on the platform ever since in the San Luis Obispo Seventh-

---

*My previous best bragging line was, "It was *so smoggy* the cars on the freeway had to turn on their lights!"

†The Holy Spirit alone can bring about such a change. Pray for broader minds and softer hearts.

day Adventist Church. Oddly enough, since that time the numbers of youth and college students attending church and entering discipleship tracks have increased by 400 percent.*

We can swipe at outside influences by insisting and complaining and blaming, or we can start removing our own frozen breath to gain a fresh perspective. Frankly, we don't have to like every item on the menu. When we act as mature Christians and walk humbly with God, we encourage others to participate in church life according to their own meanings and needs, which inevitably warms us all.   ❏

Want a true peek behind the scenes at an actual General Conference session? Come on back . . .

Present Tense Behind the GC Platform

I flash my purple platform pass, mailed to me months earlier, and stroll past uniformed security people down silent white corridors tall and wide enough to hold three elephants.

My destination is as exclusive as a George W. Bush town-hall meeting. Gary Swanson, editor of *CQ* (formerly *Collegiate Quarterly*), meets and directs me to Entry B Service Corridor, to Room 176. In the two decades I have known Gary, he has always dressed neatly and spoken in terse, clipped sentences—a precise poet.

About a minute into the dome's innards, I pass a door with a sign: "Rams locker room." The Rams have been my football team since the 1960s, during the reign of Roman Gabriel and the Fearsome Foursome, when they played in the Los Angeles Coliseum. Of course, it would be inappropriate now while I'm unattended to enter this private dressing area. It's locked anyway.

As with all contemporary General Conference (GC) sessions, St. Louis's Edward Jones Dome at America's Center provides an odd setting for the 2005 proceedings. Logos of scores of advertisers stare down on us. (How would Jesus chase out these marketers?) I think of my own church-sponsored moribund Valic option as I read, "Don't fumble your retirement—contact Edward Jones." Ringed around us in large block letters appear the names of legendary spiritual giants: Merlin Ol-

---

*This reflects the church's deep commitment in all areas to reach, involve, train, and hold their young people.

sen, Dan Dierdorf, Eric Dickerson, Elroy "Crazylegs" Hirsch, Tom Mack, and David "Deacon" Jones ("Will the Deacon please come forward and pick up the quarterback?").

Outside, St. Louis bustles with bizarre bipolar energy as Fourth of July parade floats queue up alongside Sabbath worshippers. Through the long weekend, fervent, sober Adventists will mingle with tens of thousands of exuberant (and drunk) celebrants. My family enjoys playing "Pick Out the Sevey" in downtown St. Louis crowds. Generally, it's fairly easy pickings.*

I was asked to show up an hour before "0855 Platform Participants Enter and Seated," and at this time, not many people are backstage. Behind the fifteen-meter screen, two rows of folding chairs simulate the seating arrangement out front. The name of every platform participant is written in black marker on a white paper that sits atop a designated chair facing literally acres of empty seats. An invariable context inside the dome is the sense of immense space.

It's good to meet Jim Zackrison, the outgoing GC Sabbath School and Personal Ministries director, with whom I'll be sharing the podium. Jim is about seventy, a genial, laid-back fellow. His non-anxious presence dissolves some of the tension just before he informs me that this is the first GC Session Sabbath School covered by the Hope Channel, so we need to be precise in our timed assignments—dead space doesn't play well on TV. The musical prelude will begin at 8:30.

At 8:26 A.M., Gary Swanson returns from inspecting the platform. At 8:27 A.M., Don Driver, the platform organizer, receives a call on his cell phone. Gary listens in to the conversation before exclaiming indignantly, "Can you believe it?" He explains to me that someone is complaining about a dome worker who was seen vacuuming the stage. "Tell them it's a union thing," Gary suggests to Don. "We can't do anything about it." I privately wonder whether the complainer called his/her hotel to request no housekeeping service today. Moreover, as I look around at the tech people scrambling like Crazylegs himself to bring this production to life, I speculate as to why *their* work is considered kosher. Perhaps the exertion is viewed as more exotic, more "virtual"—certainly not as plebian or biblically based as pushing a vacuum cleaner.

I meet Casey Wolverton, the telegenic young adult host of Sabbath School University on the Hope Channel, who tells me I probably don't remember that we met in 1990 when I spoke outside Newcastle, Australia. He's right. In the course of conversation, Casey remarks that in his New South Wales Conference—at Avondale Adventist School, Central Coast Adventist School, and Macquarie

---

*Still wearing their badges, dressed in suits, clutching plastic 3ABN bags, walking as fast as they can through the crowds.

College, a K–12 school—only 25 percent of students are Adventist. (He adds, "Everything's a college there," to which I reply, "Here, everything's a university," and instantly reflect that, as host of one, he's probably aware of this.)

"It's changed everything," Casey says. "We're more evangelistic. More tolerant, of course. We struggle to follow up all the Bible study interests. And Adventist kids are stronger in their convictions as a result." Central Coast and Macquarie each maintain one-and-one-half full-time chaplains plus volunteers, including student missionaries. What an astounding departure from most Adventist academies in North America.

On stage, someone is hitting an immaculate high C. I hug my friend Carol Barron before she goes around front at 8:45 to belt out some hymns. I turn my cell phone off. Later, a friend will tell of sitting in a delegate's seat and phoning another delegate who was standing at the microphone to make a comment. My friend crumpled in hysterics as he witnessed the delegate fumbling frantically to kill his phone.

Cliff Goldstein arrives, a bit breathless. He has a narrow face with chiseled cheekbones and gray-flecked black hair, and he talks and moves quickly and jerkily, giving a first impression of a ruffled politician with ADHD. Perhaps he's nervous, though he admits to having felt more anxiety in Toronto five years ago. I have always liked Cliff—he's entertaining, candid, intelligent, and compassionate. We begin talking about friends and issues in the church.

It strikes me strange that though they work in the General Conference, Gary and Cliff both use the word *they* to refer to it. "They" are doing or not doing things because "they" don't get it. Not surprisingly, this is the identical rhetorical tag people *outside* the GC use when speaking of the GC. Fans of sports teams will say "*we* won" and "*they* lost." Does President Jan Paulsen use the word *they* to refer to the GC when he doesn't like what's happening?

A last-minute flurry of activity brings all platform participants together to pray for inspiration and effectiveness. Then, on cue and in proper order, we file out into the lights. From our seats on about the goal line, I can scarcely discern the audience far, far away. The only faces I recognize are those of Bill and Noelene Johnsson, who are sitting and smiling at the twenty-five, waiting for the kickoff. The sound seems muffled on stage, doubtless because the loudspeakers are turned away from us.

We remain standing to sing a rather unfamiliar hymn, but we have no hymnals, no music or words, and the dome's seven jumbo screens don't display the words. The lyrics are printed in the GC program books, translated into Russian and Zulu and Yoruba and Portuguese and Finnish and Twi and Lingala and more languages. But we left our programs backstage, so we stand and stare at the thousands of singers. Cliff uses this opportunity to revisit our conversation. Throughout the first verse, he speaks and gestures animatedly until Gary Swanson mutters from behind, "Hey, a little decorum!" I hope the Hope Channel wasn't focusing on us.

After the opening prayer, Jim introduces a video that features my Something Else Sabbath School in Lincoln, Nebraska. Expressing their appreciation for the class are a few of my friends: Mark Robison, a colleague at Union College and a Ph.D. candidate with an emphasis in Willa Cather studies; Marlyn Schwartz, a contractor and health club owner; and Al Chambers, a UPS driver who faithfully attended our class despite his not being an Adventist. They talk chiefly about prayer—the class encircling and placing our hands on Marlyn when he had cancer ("The peace I felt was indescribable."), and praying for Al's brother, who had achieved sixty days of sobriety ("That, to me, is a miracle."). Seeing Al projected on the screens in front of twenty-thousand Adventists (with more arriving by the second) somehow gives me great glee. The video also lists ideas for improving fellowship contributed by people in Sydney, Australia; Montemorelos, Mexico; St. Thomas, Virgin Islands; Anchorage, Alaska; and Austin, Texas.

As we sit together watching the video, Casey is tapping in notes on his PDA, spurring Cliff to remark that he usually preaches from his PDA, but because he has only five minutes today to speak, he's scribbled his notes elsewhere. He holds up his right hand. On his palm are five lines in blue pen. (*A southpaw.* I resist the urge to use a "palm pilot" reference.) Sitting between them, I consider that maybe I should have brought a few notes myself.

≈

Just prior to the end of the video, I walk to the podium for my part in enhancing fellowship in Sabbath Schools. After relating an anecdote about Ruth, who continued attending our class purely because I knew her name after one visit, I ask everyone in the dome to engage in "neighbor nudging," to connect with a neighbor and to leave out no one (especially the security guards) for two minutes and forty-nine seconds. During that time, they are to learn one another's names, where home is, and where they were at the age of twelve. We "agree" that the conversations stop when hands are held high. "Ready?" I ask rhetorically. "Go."

The dome hums like a hive. People pivot in their seats to converse or seek out someone sitting alone thirty rows over in another section. I talk with Jim, and after two minutes and forty-nine seconds or so, I walk to the podium and raise my hand and the hive—amazingly—hushes.

"If we can do this with twenty thousand, you can do this in your Sabbath School. Let's make certain no one in any class is left out, that all realize they are valued every week."

Jim steps up with the second part of our presentation—intercessory prayer. He states, "Now turn to the person you just met and ask what's one thing you could pray about for that person. This is how we achieve depth of fellowship quickly in Sabbath School. Let's pray for each other now."

Jim and I pray together. All around, people are praying for one another. It's working. After a suitable time, Jim approaches the podium, ends with a corporate prayer, and summarizes how these two activities can be a part of every Sabbath School.

We are finished. I feel relief, exhilaration, and gratefulness. Getting twenty thousand to cooperate is, after all, more than a perfunctory kick for the extra point.

Three petite women in colorful native dress from Korea, Japan, and Taiwan appear on stage in front of us. Instantly, the floor swarms with flash and video cameras. I lean out around Taiwan, hoping for a mention in Asian photo albums. ("Here are the three lovely ladies. I don't know who is the smiling bearded fellow.")

Casey introduces the Sabbath School University video, presenting him as a moderator along with four bright, ethnically diverse Australian young adults offering responses to a question about the week's lesson. While the production quality is good, I yearn for more dialectical drama. Perhaps they could take opposing sides of a question. ("*Did* Jesus come soon? What does 'soon' mean?") They would model how to engage tough questions and disagree agreeably, which would be an enormous step forward for many Sabbath Schools.

Cliff gets up to speak. "I've been an Adventist," he glances at his right palm, "for about twenty-five years." He goes on to describe how our salvation is sure only through the gracious sacrifice of Christ, how if we depend on any internal righteousness, we are surely lost.

When he returns to his seat, I say, "Good job."

Cliff leans toward me. "I want to give them the *gospel,*" he says. "I don't often get a chance to talk to this many people."

Next, the thirteen division presidents file in. They stand at attention while Jim introduces the quarter's lesson and the brief talks each president will provide.

"That worked out well," I murmur to Cliff. "Thirteen presidents and thirteen weeks in the quarter."

He laughs. "Yeah."

Gary says in a stage whisper, "You can leave the platform if you want to." He tries to sound casual, but I think he wants a bit more decorum and a bit less us. I look around at the scene. *No way am I leaving. This is too good.*

Dozens of photographers and videographers jockey for position in front of the stage. Flashes punctuate the air like a pulsing lightning storm. "A media scrum," Casey observes.

We can see only their thirteen backs silhouetted by the stage lights. Apart from the paucity of gender and age differences, their racial spectrum—so many heights and hues—our marvelous diversity from my God's hand and voice, moves me, and

I feel my throat constrict. As I do at each GC Session, I've caught a fresh vision of the world church.

Casey tells me about tuning in to a St. Louis "Christian radio" station this morning and hearing an interview with Walter Rea. The interviewer was extremely hostile toward Adventists, selecting passages from *Counsels on Diet and Foods* before concluding, "This, ladies and gentlemen, is a false prophet!"

I ask, "How did Walter Rea sound?"

"Old," he says.

One of the division presidents is at the podium speaking smoothly and confidently. From behind, however, we can see his right leg vibrating like a fresh-plucked lute. I think, *That is courage.*

Gary confers briefly with Jim at the side of the podium, after which Gary sits behind me.

"Chris, they're running short," he says in my ear. "Would you be willing to go up to talk for a couple minutes?"

My mind races as a wave of energy consumes me.

"Sure," I say. Gary sits back. The world recedes. *What will I say to probably twenty-five-thousand people for two minutes?* I determine to talk about Sabbath School as a time for training people every week to be disciples of Jesus—to live out prayer, money, time, study, and social ministries. This is the familiar theme of our local Sabbath School. Gary is talking to me again.

"We won't need you," he says.

After Jim sums up, all five of us—Jim, Gary, Cliff, Casey, and I—leave the platform. A primed full orchestra sits to our right, and the Oakwood College Aeolians stand on risers to our left. A moving line of people, including some women, streams by us to take our spots and start the worship service.

Once behind the screen, Jim exults, "We made it with thirty seconds to spare!"

"Well," I said, "that was fun."

Past tense.   ❏

Not everything is as it first seems, is it?

Five Reasons I'm Not an Adventist

1. I'm not an Adventist because my parents are Adventists. They weren't/ aren't, so I don't qualify as a Dadventist.

2. I'm not an Adventist because Adventists live longer. Those longevity studies are cool, but I'm really not much interested in hitting 106. I'm not even interested in achieving everlasting life if life continues as it is. Duration, by itself, is not supremely attractive to me. By contrast, eternal life is about quality—a friendship with God that brings peace, joy, freedom, and love. That's why eternal life begins now. The kingdom of heaven is now.

3. I'm not an Adventist because I think Adventist churches and schools are perfect. They aren't, and this side of the Second Coming, they won't be.

4. I'm not an Adventist because I disagree with everything that is "non-Adventist." I believe all truth is God's truth no matter where it's found. Adventists can learn much of eternal value from others. (This has a great deal to do with walking humbly.) Adventism will never corner the truth market.

5. I'm not an Adventist because I want to go to heaven. (Take a deep breath . . .) Heaven is a fabulous freshman orientation for the new earth, but just landing in heaven is not my goal. My goal is to form enduring friendships with God and His creation based on selfless love.   ❏

And Five Reasons I Am

1. I fell in love with God through Adventism's picture. What a remarkable rendering of the Father in particular. Then there's Jesus. And the indwelling Spirit. I'm still in love.

2. Adventist beliefs make sense to me—and I'm a highly skeptical person.* The package Adventism presents is the best I've found, and I've looked all around.

3. I like swimming in the godly, deep, balanced countercurrent of an Adventist lifestyle. As explained in "Yes, I Don't 'Abstain,' " the Adventist life is one of redemptive protest. We swim continually toward something better.

4. Central to Adventists is the saving grace of Jesus. Despite the claims of eccentric offshoots and bogus attacks from critics, yes, grace is directly in the center of our existence. We live by grace, we move by grace, we are by grace. "In him we live and move and have our being" (Acts, chapter 17). The self-made person is a lie, a grotesque mockery.

Every breath that fills our lungs is grace. Every inchworm that hangs from a leaf is grace. Every exhausting motor vehicle that growls past is grace. Every delectably distinguishing taste bud is grace. Every syllable vibrating through versatile vocal cords is grace. Every speck under every sun within every one of a trillion galaxies is grace. It's all grace.

---

*I am so skeptical that I'm feeling skeptical about being highly skeptical.

5. Union College. I watch them enter jaded and truculent, insouciant and naïve, quixotic and predictable—students who slip into cramped desks and listen to my words. Each year they amaze me as they grow in godly ways. Confronting life, they get knocked to their knees and become adaptable, nimble, responsive, resilient. I hear the trenchant Holy Spirit in their keen questions. They take me back to that place I used to be—the searching, nonconformist, English major basketball player, who is now, of all things, an Adventist.   ❏

What is God's plan for your life? (It's probably GDTOSALBMBOI.)

Beyond WWJD

Past the Resurrection Eggs and Bible Beanies. Around "The Joy of the Lord" stationery stickers. Under framed pictures of grapes and angels, teddy bears and floating Christs. Through the looming forest of children's products that sprouts VeggieTales headquarters and a five-foot asparagus, Bible Blurt! and Spine Chillers Mysteries ("Parents: A Christian Alternative"). Next to the name tags with obviously Christian fish swimming in the background and the five-hundred-piece boxes of soft Communion bread ("uniform size wrapped in plastic bag guaranteed fresh"), before the "Jesus Is Lord" pencils, Footprints bookmarks, Testamints, and Heaven's Best Chocolates ("A Sweet Reminder of God's Holy Word"), I see it.

The WWJD section. WWJD T-shirts. WWJD four-color posters ("Go and do likewise!"). WWJD cards by Argus. WWJD bumper stickers.

I'm in the local "Christian bookstore," and I'm looking for a book. The WWJD phenomenon has spurred on "Christian marketers" much as the Chicken Soup stock flavored other markets. WWJD began in Charles Sheldon's classic and inspiring multimillion bestseller *In His Steps*, in which Henry Maxwell, Rachel Winslow, and others begin to live by the motto "What would Jesus do?" This is an ennobling question, an elevating consideration. With one caution.

God doesn't want Jesus clones. If we were to do what Jesus did, we would never pursue a formal education, never travel overseas, never get married, never wear glasses. We would walk virtually everywhere we go.* We would wear sandals and robes. We would never use a microwave oven, an electric can opener, a phone, a radio, a wristwatch. Moreover, if we adhere strictly to biblical accounts, we wouldn't blink, cough, laugh, clip our fingernails, or comb our hair.

---

*Unless we rode a revved-up donkey.

Instead of asking "What would Jesus do?" we ought to ask, "What would Jesus have me do?" (WWJHMD). God desires us to be distinct individuals. When I'm walking closest to my Savior, I ask, "God, what would You have me do?" and wait quietly for an impression.

Or what about the GHAPFYL* approach? Whenever I hear GHAPFYL, I get nervous. It's meant to communicate security, I know, but if by "plan" we mean "blueprint," our lives can be marked by frustration and fear. Suppose I make one bad decision and bollix the blueprint—the walls of my life may come crashing down. Suppose I'm not sure *exactly* what God wants. Suppose my "chosen one" is living in Accra, Ghana? *Oh, no!* This blueprint model has God declaring, "You can have anything in the store—as long as it's the Bible Beanies." At times, many choices are completely within God's will for us.

We ponder particularly about the colossal questions of career and spouse. As a father, I believe I have some understanding of God's desires for His children. My plan for my sons was not that they choose to be an accountant or marry Susie Freestone,† but that their lives would be noble, caring, honest, deep, fun, and humble. Beyond that, I want them to use one of God's great gifts—the human brain—to make decisions.

God's plan is less like a blueprint than a marriage commitment. When a marriage ceremony takes place, we don't hear these vows: "Do you promise to take out the trash three times a week and to twisty-tie the tops? Do you promise to speak sweetly to your in-laws on the phone, to visit them at least twice a year, and not to bring up *you-know-what*? Do you promise to fill the car with gas before the needle kisses E? Do you promise to do the dishes, even the ones with two-day-old Special K casserole welded like a freakishly strong amalgam?"

No, when you marry you commit yourself to a person, not a plan.

That's how it is with God. He asks *us* to be His bride. What a concept! God commits Himself to *us*, not to a plan. God's "plan" for me knows a thousand possible paths, and He promises, "I will be with you on each of them. As I promised, I will never leave you."

Really, would you have it any other way? Would you want your spouse to plot out your life to the smallest particular? Would you desire any parent to do that for a child? Instead, God proposes, "I already know the plans I have for you. I will help you, not hurt you. I will give you a future and a hope" (Jeremiah, chapter 29).

Two plans—help and hope. Vowed in love. What more could the Bridegroom give?

Freedom is sacred to God. He would rather have us free than have us saved.

---

*God has a plan for your life.
†She's a peach.

Otherwise, He would force us to be saved. We can't comprehend the immensity of freedom and the resulting horrors God endures. All the world's joy and suffering are byproducts of freedom. God will never take it away.

Instead of WWJD, I'd like to see GDTOSALBMBOI.* A prime earmark of any cult is that its members forfeit their individuality. Christianity is different. "For *freedom*," Paul pointed out, "Christ has set us free" (Galatians, chapter 5). Our remarkable diversity makes us a sturdy, supple, more compelling body.

The WWJD campaign screams with irony. Would Jesus manage this high-gloss, bumper-sticker marketing blitz? Too often we find our rhetoric filled with shallow optimism and easy piety. We can live beyond sloganeering, wrestling with real issues that invest our minds, emotions, and creative energies.

Anyway, it's what Jesus would do. ❑

God made man because He loves stories.—Elie Wiesel

"Tell Me Your Story"

It's a sure bet in the church service. During the children's story, everyone in the sanctuary perks up. The children listen (those that have been weaned) while the story lasts, but the *instant* The Moral appears, they retreat to scooting sideways, whispering, shushing, and waving with glazed eyes. True, young children think concretely and cannot decipher abstract connections. However, a story captivates children of every age. "Our lives are stories," contends William R. White, "and in a sense, any good story is about us."

When I first met with Mark, Dan, and Ric for our Four Amigos support group, we began by telling our life stories. Using paper/rock/scissors,† we determined who would tell his story for up to one hour—wherever we wished to start, whatever we chose to say, however we wanted to end. Through sharing our stories, we grew to know and appreciate each other. Moreover, each time I tell my story, emphases and flavors change—I learn something new about myself.

We live in a story-shaped world. Our Bible is a fertile, redolent anthology of tales, and Jesus the Messiah is its most prolific Storyteller.

In his book *The Call of Stories: Teaching and the Moral Imagination*, Harvard professor Robert Coles reveals the power of stories to heal. As a psychiatrist, he

---

*God desires that our service and love be marked by our individuality.
†A modern-day Urim and Thummim.

learned from a mentor how to use stories to unearth who people are. He remembers, "Dr. Ludwig wanted me to worry about messages omitted, yarns gone untold, details brushed aside altogether, in the rush to come to a conclusion." Coles refers to one patient who "kept himself aloof, his story unspoken, while he tested, with his questions, my willingness to surrender enough of myself (my story) to show reasonable good will toward him."

Often I hear of opportunities to "reach millions with the gospel" through radio, television, pamphlets, or other venues of "mass evangelism." While these can be valuable opening wedges, we should realize that exposing people to our words is not reaching them. Sponsoring Rose Parade floats and dropping copies of *Steps to Christ* on doorsteps doesn't reach anybody—yet. We reach people only through dialogue—by listening and sharing. Otherwise, we are arrogantly assuming we know them and their personal needs.

Today the new motivating slogan for the Adventist Church is "Go tell the world." A better one, it seems to me, would be "Go dialogue with the world." Telling is too one-sided; I don't appreciate people who tell but don't listen. Our world is already awash with words. Sharing quantum mechanics with a kindergartener isn't reaching her.

Once I asked a student, Becky Lane, to interview and videotape twenty-five random people on the streets of Lincoln, asking, "What do you think of Seventh-day Adventists?" The results were revealing. In a city with six Adventist churches, an Adventist union conference headquarters, an Adventist college, an Adventist high school, two Adventist elementary schools, an Adventist child care center, an Adventist publishing house for people who are blind, an Adventist community services center, Adventist community ball fields and public swimming pool, seventeen of the twenty-five people answered, "I don't know anything about them." The rest of the answers:

"One time I had to get out of their house because it was their Sabbath."

"Sometimes they come door-to-door with *Watchtower*."

"I liked them. They actually wanted to hear what I want to say."

"They helped my mother in one of their hospitals."

"Someone's religion doesn't really make a lot of difference to me when it comes down to who they are personally."

"I wouldn't know them because I'm Catholic."

"It's a beautiful church and campus, but that doesn't reflect on the people necessarily."

"Everyone has their own beliefs. There are a lot of Seventh-day Adventists around, but I can't say I really know any."

Dialogue is the evangelistic model of Jesus—with Nicodemus, the woman at the well, the man born blind, the demoniacs, the thief on the cross, with every disciple. In each case, He first (somehow) knew their stories; He dialogued with them; and at last, recognizing their individual struggles, He revealed the Light. His coming to our planet demonstrates the absolute necessity of personal interaction.

The following story makes plain the importance of knowing our audience deeply. Once a primitive village was given a television set and a generator. For weeks, all of the children and adults gathered around the set, watching program after program. After three months, however, the set was turned off and never watched again. A visitor to the village asked, "Why do you no longer watch the television?"

The chief said, "We have decided to listen to the storytellers."

"Doesn't the television know more stories?" asked the visitor.

"Yes," the chief replied, "but the storyteller knows me."

We can relish the profound nature of story, metaphor, and creativity. As poet William Carlos Williams asserted, "Their story, yours, mine—it's what we all carry with us on this trip we take, and we owe it to each other to respect our stories and learn from them."

Before we share His story, we can humbly encourage people to tell us theirs. ❑

Suspected that you've messed up too much? Ravaged by "if only" regrets?

Redemption

They had covered eighty miles. From Nazareth, it had taken five days. For most of the miles, Mary walked; the burro jounced too heavily when she rode. Occasionally she mounted it to relieve the pressure in her swollen feet, until the jarring made her moan to stop. It was odd to see a woman in her ninth month of pregnancy making such a journey.

The trip exacted its toll. Mary's labor began as they entered Bethlehem. Desperate, Joseph begged for a spare room—anything—for his suffering young wife, but all that was left was a cave where the animals were kept.

They took it. Joseph tied up the burro amid the greasy mud and soupy manure, and in one stall he spread new hay over the crusted hay. Then Mary gripped his hand fiercely and called out. No, there wasn't time to fetch a midwife. Trembling, Joseph ran for a flask of hot water.

Now the miles of inhaling dust were over. The frantic searching was past. The agonized cries were ended. Mary gazed at her newborn Boy, who lay in a feeding trough cut from a stone shelf. Around them, rank animal smells mingled with the odor of old oats and barley. Joseph brought Him to where she lay, and she unwrapped the strips of linen cloth that bound Him and rubbed salt and oil on the tiny squirming body. Binding Him again, she held Him close and kissed Him, then handed Him to Joseph, who gently kissed Him and laid Him in the trough. Then Joseph sat down on the hay next to Mary. "What's wrong?" he asked.

She smiled faintly, that he should know her so well after so short a time. "I thank God for you, and for my Son," she said.

"And . . .?"

She bit her lower lip. "If only we had traveled faster. We might have gotten a decent room. We might have had time for the midwife . . ."

"We had to rest. You might have given birth on the way," he replied.

She sighed. "I wanted everything to be perfect."

"He's alive and healthy."

"But *here?* With the animals?" Her voice dripped with remorse. "Joseph, *do you know whose Son this is?*"

Joseph held her eyes a long moment. "Yes," he said finally. "I know who He is." Joseph reached over and plucked hay from her hair. "And I know who we are also. We are doing our best."

Mary turned her face away. "Oh, Joseph," she whispered. "What can He possibly do with such a beginning?" ❏

They can drive you crazy. But when the world grows dim and desolate and you look around for a twig to grasp—there they are.

Thank You, God, for Knotheads

Hi, Mrs. Turner," I said. "Would you like me to nail up the soffit on the east side of your house?"

The Turners lived west of the Blakes in a house built in the 1940s, and their soffit* drooped three feet. With Mrs. Turner in her eighties and Mr. Turner an invalid, I figured they might appreciate my help.

They did. After planting my aluminum ladder under the Turners' eave, I hoisted a box of four-inch nails and a hammer. Pressing the sheet up, I drove a nail flush. To my amazement, the board bounced like a springboard. Three more nails eased into the old wood above the soffit with identical results. The wood was mush. I tried other places. Nothing solid remained to hold a nail. Then I spotted it. A knot.

---

*The wooden sheet on the underside of an overhanging roof.

I'd watched knots bend my nails before. Nailers typically avoid knots; the remnant of an original limb is too dense, too resilient. Lacking other options, however, I aimed one nail toward the knot. It held. I looked for every knot I could find and pierced each, pinning the soffit securely. The job was finished within fifteen minutes, yet I've thought about the experience ever since.

Some people are like wooden knots. Actually, they're *knotheads*. Knotheads are the chewing gum in the parking lot of life. They're the eggshells in your omelet, the driver with the stuck right-turn signal, the screaming baby behind you, the snarling dog on the path ahead. They're as popular as a paper cut, as subtle as an ingrown toenail.

They're in your church.

Knotheaded church members by nature resist change. For them, whatever the past's problems, it appears rosier than the murky future. They may be black-or-white guardians. They quote the *Testimonies* and Paul Harvey, buck current trends, bark up the same tree, back into a corner. They're intractable. Inflexible. Stubborn.

Thank God for knotheads.

Now, whenever I think of knotheads, I think of Jesus and His words,* of Paul's obstinacy, of times of trouble and the infamous time of trouble—because above all, the time of Jacob's trouble is about being a stubborn knothead, about doing nothing but clinging to our God and braying, "I *will not* let you go."† And whenever those times come, whether we're a humble goat herder or vice president of operations of the striped goats division, life drives us to our knees, or past our knees to our faces, leaving us clutching for something palpable and godly and pithy.

I knew Geraldine Nagel as a seventy-something friend who wouldn't budge on a letter of doctrine. With a voice like a rusty hinge, she'd trumpet, "Righteousness by faith alone!" Gerry's convictions about carpet color in the fellowship hall ran as staunchly as her bedrock Adventist beliefs. Though softhearted, she could be as prickly as a sea urchin with an attitude.

Shortly after our family moved away, a car accident killed Gerry.‡ Her funeral astounded some members. Over the phone, my friend Peter told me about it.

"The church was *packed*. And there were as many non-Adventists as Adventists! I've never seen so many non-Adventists in our church. She must have been in ten community service groups." Apparently, Gerry had been as knotheaded about serving others as she was about her doctrines.

---

*See Luke, chapter 21, verse 33.

†See Genesis, chapter 32.

‡I didn't write the ubiquitous phrase "tragic car accident" because all deadly car accidents are tragic.

I've had encounters with other knotheads. When my father lay dying, the ravenous cancer having strangled his kidneys, my knotheaded sisters and mother resolutely bathed his excreting skin with a sponge.

When false rumor swirled about me in a rancid fog, a knotheaded colleague called me directly and asked, "Hey, what's up with this?"

When our second son took all night to be born, a knotheaded friend stayed all night on a couch in our home with our firstborn.

We need to admit it. In the future when the espresso stands crumble, when cyberspace implodes, when (not if) the stock market crashes, our feel-good, go-with-the-flow "Christian" friends will stick like cotton candy in a hurricane.

But we know from the Crucifixion that Christ's body can hold a nail.

Especially in church, knotheads can be aggravating obstacles. Yet when the world completely loses its solid center and we can't count on anyone, the knotheads will be constant and true—*there* for us—stubborn to the end.

God, help me at the right time, in the right way, to be a knothead. ❑

"Now, don't you let them be corrupted, you hear?"

Apples Out of the Barrel

"Jan" was a leader in the school where I taught. Bright, pretty, fun, and spiritual, she brought a wholesome vitality to each school activity. When the week of prayer was held, Jan was the first to stand for Jesus. At the Christmas program, Jan sang with virtuosity. During intramural basketball season, she was one of few girls who participated, and she did so with *élan*. After Jan left for boarding academy, I watched her progress. She was a leader there, too.

Then Jan attended a Seventh-day Adventist college, and in her first year, Jan lost her faith. From what I heard later, some of Jan's misconceptions were dismantled in one of her Bible classes, and, apparently, she didn't reconstruct anything of lasting worth. She took her emptiness and her questions to her agnostic boyfriend, who shared her feelings, his habitation, and eventually their children.

When I first heard Jan's story, I felt angry and hurt. I also secretly wondered if I had failed her. Should I have done anything differently? What's expected of a good teacher? How should an educator approach a subject? As a result of grappling with these thoughts, I reached a conclusion. *The best teachers do not teach subjects. They teach people.* For these teachers, when the year ends, no matter how many themes or theologies or theorems they've "covered," the subject isn't finished. Only when a life ends is the subject finished, the assignment completed.

Of course, this approach to teaching is fraught with frustration. It means we must hand over our teaching material to the television for three hours a night, or send our subject to a home where self-esteem is shredded and self-discipline scorned. It means our efforts will be nullified to some degree each day and in succeeding years, as in Jan's case.

It's safer to teach textbooks. It's easier to teach facts. It's less frustrating, even, to teach the truth. When we teach people, we take some responsibility for who they are, for what they become. With this in mind, I felt that I might have failed to prepare Jan adequately for her future, and I decided to make certain (as far as possible) that no more of my students would repeat her experience.

≈

My main thrust in adequately preparing students took place in teaching academy Bible. The ninth- and tenth-grade Bible class operated on a points basis; I had gone through the textbook and assigned points to certain projects. Among the required projects was the following four-part assignment, which turned out the best.

1. Each student is required to attend the main worship service of another religion or denomination. Students must attend in pairs, and only one pair may attend each church. Below is a list of possible area churches.* You may choose to attend one of these or another of your own choosing. (50 points)

Assembly of God	Jehovah's Witnesses
Baptist	Jewish synagogue
Baha'i	Lutheran
Southern Baptist	Mennonite
Brethren	Nazarene
Catholic	Nondenominational
Christian Science	Orthodox
Church of Christ	Pentecostal
Church of God	Presbyterian
Church of Jesus Christ	Roman Catholic
of Latter-day Saints	Salvation Army
Episcopal	Unitarian Universalist
Grace	United Church of Christ
Interdenominational	United Methodist

*Taken from the telephone book's yellow pages. Addresses and phone numbers were supplied.

If a student couldn't find a partner, I volunteered to go along. I never regretted taking this opportunity. In one instance, we worshiped with a college-age Four-square Gospel congregation in a rented Odd Fellows Hall, and I experienced the most spiritually moving song service I've ever heard.

> 2. After attending the service, each student must deliver an oral report to the class describing the experience. (50 points possible)

During this report, I questioned each student closely. "How was it different from Seventh-day Adventist services? What were the people like? How did you feel while you were there? What did you like? What didn't you like?"

Sherri gave her report after visiting a Pentecostal church. She had expected it to be friendly, but she relayed her surprise that not one person had shaken her hand.

"What?" I exclaimed. "Not one person shook your hand?"

"No," replied Sherri, giggling, "but I was hugged about a hundred times!"

I asked follow-up questions directed toward the entire class. Do you like this aspect of the service better than ours? Is this aspect sacred? What would happen if we tried this in our church? Who would be offended? Why? Would it be worth making the change anyway?

The ensuing discussions were invariably lively and enlightening. Often, students defended the traditional Seventh-day Adventist liturgy.

> 3. Invite a speaker from the worshiping body to speak to our class-room. (**Optional:** 50 points) Note: The speaker must show up in our classroom for you to receive credit!

I told the students specific times on certain days when we could receive guests, and the students had to make all the arrangements. In fact, I made it clear that while a guest speaker was in our classroom, I wouldn't say one word.* My deafening silence meant the students were on their own.

An incident I won't soon forget occurred when a Latter-day Saint began relating his views on the state of the dead. My students peered over their shoulders at me with lifted eyebrows. I smiled back benignly. Then *every one of them* reached for his or her Bible. It was my proudest moment. For the rest of the period, the sound of riffling pages filled the air. Turning to the texts quoted, the students challenged the implied context or pointed out contradictory passages while the speaker grinned and waffled or backpedaled and pulled out a verse that had the students scratching their heads.

---

*I did take copious notes.

After the guest speaker left, the class and I held stimulating discussions. An atmosphere of deep interest and openness prevailed. Often, I used some of the more puzzling problems as a basis for future study or an optional project.

4. Write a report summarizing what you learned from this experience. Include in your summary:
   a. what you expected to find, and what you actually found
   b. some questions you have thought about as a result of your visit
   c. some answers you discovered
   d. how you can apply what you've learned to practical living
(50 points possible)

This helped me probe into any lurking or residual doubts and provided closure and a commitment to grow. Without exception, each student expressed appreciation for having gone through the experience. Moreover, in the year-end evaluations (when students grade *me*), more than half of them chose the "Visit Other Churches" assignment as the most valuable experience of the year.

The only impugning comment I received on the assignment took place when I picked up John to go to a church service. John's grandfather walked us to my car and, turning to me with a half smile, said, "Now don't you let him be corrupted, you hear?"

"Ed," I replied, "the apples surest to be corrupted are the ones that never get out of the barrel."

Adults may find challenging questions threatening. But young people like Jan *will* ask questions at some time—that is certain. It's up to us to decide whether we'll be around to answer them.   ❑

We mentally kicked ourselves. Then we carried our bruised brains into the house.

Appointment With Disappointment

It began as a peaceful Friday. No snarling, rabid dogs. No bleary-eyed, careening drivers. None of the usual menaces had threatened me on my early-morning jog. What's more, I had arrived home in uncharacteristic style—upright and nearly coherent.

For my morning worship, I had read from Acts in *The Living Bible*. My breakfast had been hot and hearty. When I left for work, my young sons had consented to kiss me. A splendid start.

From then on it had been a breeze. Until 3:18 P.M., when my office telephone rang.

"Remember that house that I said I liked?" Yolanda began. "The blue one on Via La Barranca?"

"Yes, I—"

"It's for *sale!* I can't believe it! Georgia just called me. She thinks it's a great price for that house. I'll meet you there with the kids at four o'clock."

And so, at the appointed hour, the Blake clan converged on the blue house at Via La Barranca. We toured it with a smiling realtor. The house was attractive. It had put on its best face and scent.* Yolanda was interested.

As the Sabbath approached, we learned there would be an open house on Sunday. We decided to talk business with the realtor then. On Sabbath, we put it out of our minds completely.

Saturday night it was time to talk business. With each other.

"It's even nicer than I thought!" Yolanda raved. "The track lighting in the living room, the colors are *perfect*—"

"We can't afford it."

"The carpets and drapes look new, the boys' rooms are a good size—"

"We can't afford it."

"The backyard is kept up, the garage is large, the kitchen is open—"

"We can't afford it."

"Why *not?*" she wailed.

Now, before we continue, you should know something about my wife, whom I love dearly. If I want to buy a book for $8.95, the following dialogue usually ensues.

"We can't afford it."

"Why *not?*" I wail.

"Because today's the twenty-seventh. We have twelve dollars and thirty-nine cents to last us till the first of the month. Do you want to spend more than half of it on a book? What about the kids?"

"What about our savings account?" I counter. After all, it's a *good* book.

"Nothing doing, and I mean that literally," she says. "Your last yen for Philip Yancey took care of that."

"We could take out a loan . . ."

"*No.* We can't afford it."

You get the picture, I trust. She can be a real penurious person, even for a worthy cause. So imagine my surprise when she blurted, "Why *not?*"

---

*The classic ploy of fresh bread baking in the oven.

"Why *not?*" I repeated. "Because it's *way* out of our price range. Our monthly house payments would nearly double! That's why not."

"We can do it."

I got a grip on myself. Drew a deep breath. Looked deeply into her lovely brown eyes. Smiled ironically. Fluttered my eyelashes. And uttered one crushing, pulverizing word.

"How?"

She paused, momentarily stunned. "I'll cut back."

"Where can you do that?" I exclaimed. "You've already cut the sugar out of the cookies."

"I'll find ways."

"What about that newly used car we were going to buy?"

"I don't need a car."

"What about that small travel trailer so we can get away?"

"We wouldn't need to get away."

"What about that sound movie camera* to take pictures of the kids?"

"I hear enough sound as it is."

I sensed an opening. "What about that Apple IIc[†] *I've* wanted?"

"We'll pay on installment. I'll even help you input."

Maybe it wasn't too far out after all. I did hate to disappoint her.

"All right," I relented. "I can see you're serious about this. We'll go to the open house tomorrow."

The next day we parked in front of the blue house on Via La Barranca the minute the open house was to begin. The realtor was there, still smiling. Yolanda began by asking about some specific terms on the house.

"Oh," the realtor said, "we sold the house yesterday."

I watched Yolanda stare in disbelief.

"Yes," the realtor continued, "a young couple came by on Friday night and made an offer on Saturday. Their offer was accepted."

We had lost it over the Sabbath.

It was a dismal drive home. We mentally kicked ourselves for not putting in an offer late Friday afternoon, and then we carried our bruised brains and battered emotions into our old house. An hour elapsed before we could speak to each other about our disappointment. In truth, my disappointment was largely generated by seeing Yolanda's disappointment, but it was real nonetheless. At last we drew close and talked.

---

*This was 1984. Really cutting-edge, high-techno Orwellian stuff here.

[†](See above.)

"You know, Yol," I said, "if we can't get this, then God has something better for us. As long as we put Him first, He'll never let us down. It's always worked out that way. It always will."*

"I know," she sighed. "You're right." Then she patted my arm and smiled. "That's a good thing to remember, isn't it?"

"Yes, it is," I agreed, nodding sagely.

"Especially the next time," she added, her eyes sparkling.

My voice trembled slightly. "The *next* time?"

"The next time," she said, "you feel like buying another book." ❑

It was decision time at the Anthillton Inn.

Ralph's Answer

Ralph was an earnest ant. He'd been invited to the annual Ants Conference for a third consecutive year, but was still undecided. His "committed to being uncommitted" slogan brought far fewer chuckles and sympathetic nods than before. The time for decision had come.

The antechamber of the plush Anthillton Inn was jammed with colonies and committees representing every ant subspecies in existence. Ants had traveled from as far away as Antarctica to convene here to discuss and petition their views. Hundreds of ants of all sizes, hues, and dispositions scurried madly about. Various factions lobbied or held semi-closed sessions. Swollen honey ants (provided by the Inn) clung to the ceiling, and wherever one looked, aphids abounded.

Ralph witnessed the spectacle with increasing interest. An hour before the opening anthem, groups were already stating their platforms and encouraging an audience. Ralph knew this afforded one final opportunity to make an intelligent, thoughtful selection. During the assembly there would be no time to reconsider. Whom could he endorse?

The different delegations spread out before him like plates at a picnic. He headed first to his right, toward a grand gathering of queen ants, where an aged, wingless matriarch was holding forth in a nasal monotone. "In actuality, you see," she proclaimed, "there exists nothing beyond ants. Ants have always been, and will always be. It's simply a matter of breeding—and culture, of course. I should know;

---

*Our next house *was* better. It was down the block from Via La Barranca—about twenty-eight hundred miles.

my ancestors have been evolving for many decades. Why, I had a great-great-aunt who . . ."

Ralph was threading his way out of the gallery by then. Exalting the past or living in it didn't appeal to him. The matriarch's theory prevailed among "learned circles," but Ralph felt certain there remained something more—something he couldn't explain.

Near the center of the chamber, he spotted a group of bright-red fire ants. Their spokesant appeared to be staging quite a performance. Ralph hurried along with a throng of others to hear.

"Excelsior, my friends! There's nothing ants can't do if we put our minds and bodies to it! Build higher, grow bigger, go faster—but don't limit yourselves! Look, look at our progress! The antiquated rules and precepts of the past aren't relevant anymore!" The speaker stomped three of his feet for emphasis. *"Times have changed!"*

Amidst enthusiastic applause, Ralph wandered off again, shaking his head. Clearly, a solid, enduring foundation was necessary. The rapidly declining state of antkind and its "unlimited" society provided prime evidence for that. If ants were subject only to the whims of other ants, what of lasting worth could be maintained?

". . . are things we should preserve." Ralph stumbled into an ongoing discussion. He recognized the participants as harvester ants, known for their steady, basic, thrifty natures. A sudden rush of confidence swept Ralph's thorax. Surely *these* ants would be grounded in truth! Harvester ants stood acutely aware of the problems confronting ants today, and they had proposed prudent solutions during the past two conventions. One middle-aged male, his young family at his side, began to speak.

"Let's be realistic," he said. "It's obvious we live in troubled times. Society, as we have known it, is disintegrating. What can we do? Brethren, I say preserve and store up your ant goods while you have them, stay together, prepare for the worst, and we will survive."

On that note, a few of the listeners dispersed, and Ralph trudged after them. "There must be *something* we can do," someone muttered.

Ralph looked up and noticed a huge army ant, blind and totally without fear, stationed near the entrance. No one had had the nerve not to invite at least one representative from that relentless division. Besides (it was thought), an army ant would keep out or silence any antagonizers. Ralph shuddered slightly and the bristles on his forelegs tingled. Then he raced across the floor as fast as his six legs could carry him.

After much of the usual jostling and climbing over others, Ralph arrived at the other end of the chamber. Here he found a booth set up by a union of worker ants from Antioch. All were busy making placards and passing out statements, volunteering and registering at such a frantic pace that Ralph soon grew weary from watching.

Presently, a female with a large abdomen ascended the platform to address the body in a shrill, fevered pitch, her antennae bobbing wildly with each syllable. "There is only one antidote—work! That's why ants are here, and that's the only way ants are going to get anywhere. Put some purpose to your life! Believe me, you'll be amazed how your problems disappear!" She paused and popped an antacid into her mouth. "Anyway," she added, chewing vigorously, "in the end, it will all be worth it."

Ralph eyed one quivering antenna until it trembled to a stop. He went away thinking perhaps he could do something. He knew he ought to contribute more. Suppose work did work?

As the time of the assembly drew near, Ralph decided to sample one last opinion. A crowd of Amazon ants attracted his attention. One young male sporting an outsized jaw was pressing his point with fervor.

"Can we hold back the floodwaters after the rain? No. We are but lowly ants. We are not equipped to do truly meaningful work. And fellow believers, you must agree that there is *more* to life than work." At that, all nodded sagely. "If there is work to be done," he continued, looking over the crowd, "then let those ants for whom work is important do it. We have faith that other ants will work. But we will grow beyond the work! We must be vigilant, we shall be valiant, in not working."

Now Ralph was really confused. He shuffled off directly into the teeming mass of rushing, worrying, scurrying delegates and tried to untangle his thoughts, reflecting upon what he had heard. Phrases from each group tumbled and whirled in his head: "My ancestors have been evolving . . ." "antiquated rules aren't relevant . . ." "store up your ant goods . . ." "silence any antagonizers . . ." "only one antidote . . ." "we shall be valiant . . ."

What were they saying?

Then he realized. *Ants!* Each group had its attention focused on ants. Queen ants, fire ants, harvester ants, army ants, worker ants, Amazon ants—all were looking to ants for the way out, for the best path, for the truth. They could see no further than themselves. And not just these groups: *Every* delegation did this—all except one.

Ralph scanned the room quickly. He found them at last, standing apart from the hubbub, conversing joyfully. Their platform was known, their views were clear, their stand was firm—but they were few, and easily out-shouted.

Ralph knew they didn't elevate themselves. Rather, they strove for selfless service in an attitude of submission. Advocating balance and temperance in all areas, they based their beliefs on words from an ancient Book; yet the aged Book supplied meaning and direction to life for today.

These ants also were concerned about the condition of antkind, but they seldom dwelt upon food or furnishings or annoyances. Instead, they talked of testaments and testimonies; of grace and gratitude; of love, hope, and faith; and of One greater than themselves who had totally embodied these traits. They professed to follow this One.

Ralph could easily tell that these ants were more than talk. They never hoarded or parceled out their "goods." They exuded their belief, and patient love flowed from them as from an underground spring, pure and unceasing. They spoke of work and faith, too, but of a blending, a cooperation, not a separation—of a faith that works with love to glorify the One. For all things and accomplishments, they gave credit to One only. They lived for One as One lived for them.

Their focus was not on ants, Ralph thought, and they didn't rely upon ants for their answers. But in surrendering self-reliance to One wiser and more powerful, they claimed an ant could be cleansed of any antipathies.

Ralph sifted and weighed and questioned and contrasted, and finally, with every doubt dissolved and his spirit renewed, a surge of energy and peace filled his being. It seemed as though a great burden had been lifted from him. He had made his choice for depend ants.   ❑

Humble, daily beginnings can sprout significant outcomes. God has given each of us vital positions, more important than we normally judge.

How to Change the World

God has a challenge for you. He says, "I want you—yes, you with your eyeballs racing over these words—to change the world." You might think He's kidding, but He's not. Not only that, He's already demonstrated how to do it, because Jesus landed on this spinning blue ball clutching the same assignment in His tiny fists: "Change the world!" How did He meet the challenge?

Can you imagine the public relations campaign Jesus could orchestrate? How many kingdoms could He conquer through His charisma? Picture Him opening His own rabbinical university system to train students. Or would He invent the printing press or a solar-powered energy source? Instead, Jesus gathered a few thin-skinned, thickheaded men and simply and powerfully shared Himself. That's it, basically.

We should be aware that we *will* change the world. We can't exist without influence. My every thought, word, and action affects my environment. One of the most telling indicators of this appears in what Jesus did immediately after His resurrection. He rolled His head covering and placed it neatly in a corner! (I believe that would be one of the last things I would think of doing after *my* resurrection.) But the folded cloth, this seemingly insignificant act of housekeeping, became one more compelling piece of evidence that thieves didn't steal His body. Everything matters.

What we do in our free time determines who we are. Jesus said, "The person who is faithful in little things can be trusted with the bigger things." In other words, if we can't be trusted in our dinky spheres here, could we be trusted with the universe? We can render to God no better service than being trustworthy in the daily moments of life. In *Mere Christianity*, C. S. Lewis commented, "Good and evil both increase at compound interest. That is why the little decisions you and I make every day are of such infinite importance. The smallest good act today is the capture of a strategic point from which, a few months later, you may be able to go on to victories you never dreamed of."

Humility is a supremely attractive quality. In *Blue Like Jazz*, Donald Miller describes how he and five other friends, the only Christians that he knew of at Reed College, decided to build a confessional booth for students at the "most secular school" in the country—but with one catch, as his friend Tony explained:

> "We are not actually going to accept confessions." We all looked at [Tony] in confusion. He continued, "We are going to confess to them. We are going to confess that, as followers of Jesus, we have not been very loving; we have been bitter, and for that we are sorry. We will apologize for the Crusades, we will apologize for televangelists, we will apologize for neglecting the poor and the lonely, we will ask them to forgive us, and we will tell them that in our selfishness, we have misrepresented Jesus on this campus. We will tell people who come into the booth that Jesus loves them."
>
> All of us sat there in silence because it was obvious that something beautiful and true had hit the table with a thud.

Donald really didn't want to go through with it, but he did. The first person who showed up at the booth was Jake, who was unexpectedly moved by the encounter.

> [Jake's] eyes were watering again. "This is cool what you guys are doing," he repeated. "I am going to tell my friends about this."
>
> "I don't know whether to thank you for that or not," I laughed. "I have to sit here and confess all my crap."

He looked at me very seriously. "It's worth it," he said. He shook my hand, and when he left the booth there was somebody else ready to get in. It went like that for a couple of hours. I talked to about thirty people, and Tony took confessions on a picnic table outside the booth. Many people wanted a hug when we were done. All of the people who visited the booth were grateful and gracious. I was being changed through the process. I went in with doubts and came out believing so strongly in Jesus I was ready to die and be with Him. I think that night was the beginning of change for a lot of us.

The truly humble person is the truly happy person. She is not troubled as to whether she is getting all that she deserves. When I read the opening pages of *The Desire of Ages,* I caught a new vision of *glory:* "It will be seen that the glory shining in the face of Jesus is the glory of self-sacrificing love."

Later in the book, Ellen White contended, "There are many who believe and profess to claim the Lord's promise; they talk *about* Christ or *about* the Holy Spirit, yet receive no benefit. They do not surrender the soul to be guided and controlled by the divine agencies. We cannot use the Holy Spirit. The Spirit is to use us. . . . Only to those who wait humbly upon God, who watch for His guidance and grace, is the Spirit given."

At Pentecost, the humility of gathered believers enabled them—just as we are enabled—to be used by God. Thus the world is changed.

To walk humbly with God calls for endurance. To illustrate, Brian McLaren tells the parable of the race.*

As the race is about to begin, believers crowd the starting line in expectation. When the gun sounds and the race begins, they take a couple steps across the line and then abruptly stop. "I have crossed the starting line!" one man exults. A woman shouts over and over "I am a race runner!" as she stands and exchanges high-fives with others. Several believers form a circle and pray, thanking God for the privilege of crossing the starting line. One by one, each racer treats the starting line as if it were the finish line. In doing so, they completely miss the point. The point is humbly *running the race* with peace, freedom, and stamina. Our joy is in the journey.

Jesus says, "Because wickedness is multiplied, most men's love will grow cold. But he who endures to the end will be saved" (Matthew, chapter 24).

The Sabbath afternoon following two days in which the president of the United States was acquitted and the president of the Seventh-day Adventist Church

---

*From *Adventures in Missing the Point,* with Tony Campolo.

resigned, I asked my family how the two events had affected them. The consensus was not a whole lot. They said they had expected the first, and they were saddened by the second, but their lives weren't seriously altered, and their belief system hadn't changed.

Suddenly, I was struck with an epiphany. I said, "Well, being a president *is* an important job. It's almost as important as being a mother or a father." We were quiet for a while, reflecting on the import of the statement.* If something happens to a parent or a child, it matters more to us than all the headlines in the century. God has given all of us incredibly important positions here on earth, more important than we normally judge.

When we speak of greatness, we tend to use terms denoting largeness—enormity, vastness, magnitude—but Jesus came down, emptying Himself, to establish an upside-down kingdom. He appeared as an embryo in the womb of a teenager. He concentrated His ministry on a small group of followers. He told stories about children and mustard seeds and leaven. He spoke to people one-on-one. His early church met in small groups in their homes. Anyone who has focused the sun's light through a magnifying glass knows why He worked this way. The heat is greatest when the circle is smallest.

Not long before returning to heaven, Jesus asked us to remember that greatness lies in humble things. His salvation is represented in a piece of bread and a cup. ❏

Who holds our heart? Who fills our thoughts? Of whom do we love to converse?

Let's Talk About . . .

In *Memoirs of a Lunatic,* the great Russian author and Christian convert Leo Tolstoy[†] recounted this story:

> I well remember the second time madness seized me. It was when Auntie was telling us about Christ. She told her story and got up to leave the room. But we held her back.
>
> "Tell us more about Jesus Christ!" we said.
>
> "I must go," she replied.
>
> "No, tell us more, please," Mitinka insisted, and she repeated all that she had said before. She told us how they crucified Him, how they beat

---

*Other roles, such as those of a sibling or close friend, are similarly significant.
†Who was also a spiritual mentor of Mohandas Gandhi.

and martyred Him, and how He went on praying and did not blame them.

"Auntie, why did they torture Him?"

"They were wicked."

"But wasn't He God?"

"Be still—it is nine o'clock; don't you hear the clock striking?"

"Why did they beat Him? He had forgiven them. Then why did they hit Him? Did it hurt Him? Auntie, did it hurt?"

"Be quiet, I say, I am going to the dining room to have tea now."

"But perhaps it never happened, perhaps He was not beaten by them."

"I am going!"

"No, Auntie, don't go. . . ." And again my madness took possession of me; I sobbed and sobbed, and began knocking my head against the wall.

The picture of little Leo slamming his head against the wall has stuck with me. At times I have felt a similar urge when I've been exposed to responses and broadcasts of amazing gracelessness. Like a small ring bearer at a wedding, we appear fidgety and bored by all the hoopla: "Yes, I've heard about Jesus and all that. [Yawn] So . . . what?" Is God's sacrifice that easy to leave behind as we rush out to our tea times and tee times?

If it was your earthly father who had been betrayed by a traitor, beaten and bone-whipped senseless, tried and found innocent, then spiked to a stake and left to die, and if he did it all to take your place so that *you could live,* do you think you would be saying glibly, "Yes, I've heard about my father"? Would you not brim with tears each time you thought of him? Could you shrug it off if someone spoke poorly of him, or would you speak up indignantly in his defense? Could you forget about him—ever?

Perhaps we've been inoculated with just enough Jesus to become immune. In one of his remarkable tales from Lake Wobegon, Garrison Keillor describes an older relative who cried whenever he prayed publicly as he got to the part about Jesus dying for us. "Everyone else seemed to have gotten over it," Keillor deadpans.

I remember when I first encountered Yeshua, the Rabbi from Nazareth, small-town Carpenter, fearless Denunciator of oppression, Healer of loathsome disease, Friend of sinners. I couldn't get enough of Him. Any possible opening to bring Him into the conversation, I snatched it. About a year after my baptism, when I was attending something called vespers, my friend Warren Hamrick picked up his guitar and started singing a tune I'd never heard: "Let's talk about Jesus, the King of kings is He . . ." I nearly wept for joy. That song was living bread to my hungry soul; it sopped up all the thickening soup of my life.

About that time, I came across the chapter "The Test of Discipleship" in El-len White's *Steps to Christ*, detailing the only way we can *know* that we are saved. She exclaimed, "Who has the heart? With whom are our thoughts? Of whom do we love to converse? Who has our warmest affections and our best energies? If we are Christ's, our thoughts are with Him, and our sweetest thoughts are of Him."

Talking about Jesus may require intentional planning. While I worked at the Review and Herald Publishing Association, I found I wasn't thinking about Jesus enough, so every Wednesday I set up a "Jesus table" in the cafeteria, with a posted question about Jesus. "Where would Jesus work if He worked here?"* "Did Jesus laugh?"† "What would Jesus drive?"‡ "How would Jesus vote?"§ Employees ate and discussed or just stopped by to add their nuggets of insight. Laughter and probing questions often filled the air. Do you think you could set up a discussion question each week if it helped keep your mind focused on Jesus?

Possible Jesus topics can include what Jesus felt,** types of stories about Jesus,†† and the faces of Jesus.‡‡ When Jesus said His Father was like this (see John, chapter 14), what did He mean? How does His picture conflict with typical pictures of God? What about the lovely beast of Revelation—the Lamb?

These days I find it increasingly difficult to talk about Jesus. There are so many "good" topics to take His place, particularly on Sabbath. So many comfortable discussions. But so you know, if you ever get to talking about Jesus when I'm around, you'll have a willing audience, a rapt listener, an eager conversational partner.

Just don't flit past the subject. That tends to give me a headache, if you know what I mean.   ❑

---

*In plant services, as a carpenter.

†Yes. Especially after His resurrection, Jesus became downright frisky, playing hide-and-seek and practical jokes. ("Try throwing your net on the *other* side of the boat!") He appeared to be relieved, and He should have been. Likely, no one mentioned His laughter because it was too typical—like washing His hands or clipping His fingernails.

‡Not sure. (Not a Hummer?)

§Next question!

**I found twenty-nine different feelings, including angry, tempted, tired, troubled, frustrated, ridiculed, alone, depressed, protective, renewed, shocked, disappointed, popular, and accepted.

††Including nativity, calling, recognition, witness, encounter, conflict, pronouncement, miracle, and passion stories.

‡‡Dueling Wit, surprise Artist, compassionate Healer, angry Remonstrator, submissive Hero, playful Seeker, conquering Hero, One of us.

Clothe yourselves, all of you, with humility toward one another, for "God opposes the proud, but gives grace to the humble."—1 Peter, chapter 5

Walking Humbly

Naturally, pride is the first sin, the worst sin. Arrogance separates us from God and from all creation. Nothing on earth is so universally hated.

Yet many Christians have not grasped one reason for Christ's sacrifice—to make us humble and thus teachable. The essence of humility is a genuine recognition of reality. Those who remain haughty and exclusive become unfit for the new earth. In fact, they haven't accepted the Messiah's sacrifice.

Walking humbly with God requires asking for forgiveness in clear, ringing tones. As a corporate body, at times the Adventist Church has transgressed God's will. The following prayer is a petition for integrity.

Merciful God, forgive us.

Forgive us for ignoring, downplaying, and airbrushing our flaws and deficiencies when we should be transparently honest.

Forgive us for talking to ourselves, becoming absorbed in Adventist triumphalism, while a dying world wanders off into oblivion.

Forgive us for our morbid craving for controversy, for the resulting stupid, senseless disputes, and for those lives we have wrecked in the process.

Forgive us for not understanding that it is not what goes into the mouth that defiles a person, but what comes out of the mouth.

Forgive us for ever placing the word "but" after the words, "You are saved through Jesus Christ."

Forgive us for shrinking away from emotionalism until we have truly diminished the role of the Holy Spirit.

Forgive us for doing more to prohibit smoking and drinking in our schools than to prohibit meanness.

Forgive us for saying we renounce the world and then acting like a panting puppy when the world gives us some attention.

Forgive us for talking about You in place of experiencing You, for preferring the menu to the meal.

Forgive us for receiving mystery and imagination and wonder only to suction out the life until what remains are dates, how-to formulas, and slogans.

Forgive us for believing that the Adventist Church possesses all Truth so we don't need to learn from others—thus making ourselves inflexible, brittle, and narrow-minded.

Forgive us for egregiously mistreating women and minorities.

Forgive us for making Sabbath mornings the most racially segregated hours of the week.

Forgive us for our paralyzing emphases on program and performance until our Sabbath Schools and church services are as flat as road kill at rush hour.

Forgive us for contending that You value most the praise of words and music on Sabbath, when instead You value most the praise of selfless, loving acts during the week.

Forgive us for using institutional rigidness to crush hopeful creativity and helpful dissent.

Forgive us for placating church bullies while our weaker brethren—the youth and young adults—leave, squashed and disillusioned and angry, never to return.

Forgive us for treating singles and public school students like second-class members.

Forgive us for officially encouraging individuality of thought but in actual practice rewarding unquestioning conformity.

Forgive us for confusing indoctrination with education, mistaking what to think for how to think.

Forgive us for suggesting that all movement to music is evil when in fact some movement can build community, health, and innocent joy.

Forgive us for turning countless people away from You through willful insistence on peripheral matters of personal taste.

Forgive us for not showing our children that following You is the most creative, sensible, fearless, freeing, fun adventure in the world.

Forgive us for keeping close track of the people coming in but not of the people going out.

Forgive us for succumbing to negativity and cynicism instead of living with defiant optimism.

Forgive us for not praying and loving more.

Inhabit us so we will swim with You against the current.

Help us start afresh, to do justly, love mercy, and walk humbly, forever and ever.

We ask this in Jesus' name.

Amen. ❏

If this book inspired you, you'll want to read these:

Searching for a God to Love
Chris Blake

Control issues. Unloving, judgmental people. Boredom. It had little to do with God, but it all got mixed up together. You have questions. You have doubts. You've been hurt. You ache for something more than rhetoric, preaching, and simplistic reasoning.

Great.

You qualify to take the journey this book defines. *Searching for a God to Love* will surprise you. It isn't what you expect. But maybe that's what God is all about.

This is a sharing book for those closest to you who have drifted from God or simply have never found a God they could love.

Paperback, 256 pages.   0-8163-1719-4   US$11.99

Searching for the God of Grace
Stuart Tyner

There's a glorious treasure right under our noses, but we can't see it. *Searching for the God of Grace* reveals the treasure placed before us that we cannot yet see. In this book, Stuart Tyner explores God's perfect gift as revealed in the plan of salvation, the pages of history, and the principles of God's character. Tyner's destination is the happiness that God wants you to have and the priceless and shining gift of your place in His eternity.

Paperback, 320 pages.   0-8163-2152-3   US$17.99

Order from your ABC by calling **1-800-765-6955**, or get online and shop our virtual store at **http://www.AdventistBookCenter.com.**
- Read a chapter from your favorite book
- Order online
- Sign up for e-mail notices on new products

Prices subject to change without notice.